LEAN
Manufacturing Implementation

A Complete Execution Manual
for Any Size Manufacturer

BY DENNIS P. HOBBS, CPIM

THE EDUCATIONAL SOCIETY
FOR RESOURCE MANAGEMENT

Copyright ©2004 by J. Ross Publishing, Inc.

ISBN 1-932159-14-2

Printed and bound in the U.S.A. Printed on acid-free paper
10 9 8 7 6 5 4 3

Library of Congress Cataloging-in-Publication Data

Hobbs, Dennis P., 1947–
   Lean manufacturing implementation : a complete execution manual for
any size manufacturer / by Dennis P. Hobbs
      p. cm.
   ISBN 1-932159-14-2 (alk. paper)
   1. Production management—Handbooks, manuals, etc.   2. Costs,
Industrial—Handbooks, manuals, etc.   I. Title.
1936–
   TS155.H575 2003
   658.5—dc22

                                                          2003013930

Phone: (561) 869-3900
Fax: (561) 892-0700
Web: www.jrosspub.com

TABLE OF CONTENTS

**Part II: The Methodologies for Transforming
Your Facility to Lean Manufacturing**

PREFACE

Usually with much enthusiasm and fanfare, companies launch their projects to implement Lean manufacturing in the factory. A project leader is appointed and a team of strong individual contributors is drafted to participate in the Lean project. Shortly after start-up, the current-state nonvalue-added analysis and a vision of a future are soon developed. Once developed, though, it is not uncommon for the project team to begin to struggle with just how to implement its future-state vision and where to begin.

There is no shortage of good ideas, and all team members will have an opinion. The good ideas become projects themselves and often return mixed results. More often than not, the original enthusiasm wanes and companies become frustrated as their Lean project stalls. Unfortunately, the promised benefits of a Lean factory implementation may evade the project team, sometimes with career-changing consequences!

This is too bad. Lean manufacturing is too important a methodology to give up on because of frustration. The reasons for this frustration are understandable, however. It is usually not due to the competence or the enthusiasm of the project leader or the manufacturing personnel charged with the job of implementing Lean in the factory. Hard-working, dedicated manufacturing professionals are always first in line to champion a better way.

It is certainly not because of the glowing success stories and reports from consultants who implement Lean methodologies every day as part of their consultancy. There is plenty of consulting expertise available, and consultants will be more than happy to contract with you for projects to help implement your Lean initiative. While there are good reasons for contracting with external consulting groups to lead or assist with your Lean implementation project, doing so should be considered an alternative strategy.

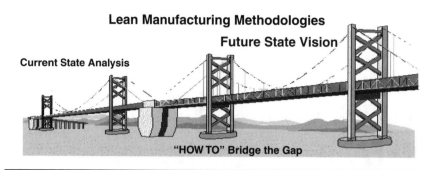

From the Current-State to the Future-State Vision

Most manufacturing companies have excellent project managers who are capable of leading projects to implement Lean manufacturing methodologies and find it difficult to justify hiring consultants to do what they know they can do themselves. Many other companies that sorely need to implement the Lean manufacturing methodologies simply do not have the funds available to contract with a Lean consulting group for an implementation project. The truth is that a factory conversion to Lean manufacturing can be accomplished using a company's internal resources.

It is from this point that most manufacturers start their factory transformation to Lean manufacturing, and it is no small task! It is a wide gap from the current Material Requirements Planning (MRP) shop floor execution systems to a Lean manufacturing methodology. It is not difficult to understand why it is easy for manufacturers to become frustrated when faced with the challenge of changing their current operating system.

What is lacking is a step-by-step, "how-to" methodology or recipe book that explains to internal project managers exactly how to accomplish their Lean factory transformation project. They need guidance to choose from the dozens of good ideas and sort through the opinions being offered. Project managers need a set of "Lean manufacturing methodologies" to describe a series of consistent, repeatable procedures and techniques that can be applied to move manufacturers from their current-state analysis through to their desired future-state vision.

I have written this book to provide the manufacturer with a sequential, step-by-step methodology that can be used to systematically transform a manufacturing facility from its traditional batch-based, computer-driven manufacturing systems to a balanced, one-piece-flow, Lean manufacturing system. It is a methodology I have used over the last decade in transforming manufacturers to Lean.

In the past, these methodologies were often referred to as "flow-processing" techniques. The term *flow* is used to describe a manufacturing process where product is produced at an even rate, like liquid flowing through a pipeline. Over the years, as the term "Lean" manufacturing became more and more popular, the interpretation and definition of what Lean manufacturing was also became more and more confusing. These proven techniques offer manufacturing professionals an objective and repeatable methodology that can be consistently applied to any product and series of manufacturing processes to lead them to achieve their Lean manufacturing objectives.

There is no single source for these techniques. Rather, they are the compilation and the result of the evolution of long-existing techniques. The methodologies described in this book have their roots in the early days of Henry Ford and Frederick Taylor and reflect their efforts in work documentation and assembly line balancing. These techniques were later enhanced by post–World War II Japanese car manufacturers, who perfected the kanban material-handling systems. In the 1980s, these methodologies were revisited and reintroduced to Western manufacturers using terms such as flow processing, JIT, kanban, Toyota Production System, continuous flow manufacturing, agile, and others.

Lean manufacturing has the capability to produce product using the least amount of nonvalue-adding activities that add time and subsequently cost to the manufacturing process. The methodologies described in this book include mathematical formulas that balance work being performed to optimize the manufacturing resources necessary to achieve customer demand while helping to model the ideal physical layout of the manufacturing shop floor. Also described are the mathematical application, use, and design of modern material kanban systems. Because these modeling processes are mathematically based, they are both consistent and repeatable — regardless of the products manufactured or the processes used to manufacture them. They provide an objective set of tools for designing manufacturing processes with the minimum wait, move, and queue time normally embedded in launched and routed shop-order-based systems.

To derive the line layout and material-handling configuration solutions, information regarding the products, demand volumes, processes, and work content must be collected and analyzed. Collection of this information can represent a significant task for the manufacturer, particularly if this information does not currently exist. When the collection of information is complete, the mathematical modeling process can be completed, with the recommended results applied to actual shop floor layout configurations.

This information collection process is very powerful and often challenges the status quo. While demand volume, process descriptions, work tasks, and standard times can all be debated during the information-gathering process, in the end, the data collected simply become numerators and denominators in a mathematical formula. The information collected is extremely objective in nature. Because of this objectivity, individual opinions and prejudices are difficult to interject into the process. When completed, the optimum answers are the output of a mathematical formula. Little room remains for private agendas or defending personal management systems.

While the methodologies described in this book are straightforward to understand and implement, their application may challenge the entire organization to rethink its relationship with manufacturing. In most cases, a reconfiguration of the shop floor is typically required. Implementation of these new manufacturing systems will generally challenge the existing operating culture, requiring the manufacturer to scrutinize existing policies and procedures. This self-examination is often a revealing experience.

The effort required to make the transition to Lean manufacturing should not be underestimated. Changing the company manufacturing system requires a commitment from top management down through the organization to the shop floor. Anything short of this strong commitment to the conversion will result in compromise of the methodology when difficult decisions have to be made. Compromise can shortchange receiving the maximum benefits of a Lean implementation.

Potentially changing the current environment can be a painful and frightening experience for many managers, particularly those who have been in place for many years and have had the time to develop personal systems for managing recurring shop floor problems. The impending new application of the existing data set can mean *change*! Often, personal careers have been built around the maintenance of existing systems. Loyal allegiance to historical methodology and the comfort level ingrained in users can result in reluctance or outright resistance to change. Because the methodologies of Lean manufacturing are based on the reapplication of existing data, this fierce loyalty is often misplaced.

Reluctance to accept Lean manufacturing principles is often rooted in the operation and maintenance of an MRP system. MRP systems create action recommendations in the form of production orders authorizing work to be done in manufacturing and purchase orders authorizing the purchase of materials. These orders are issued to the purchasing or manufacturing department. The purchasing department subsequently deals with the creation and maintenance of purchase orders. For manufacturing, a shop floor control (SFC) or a production activity control system is used to monitor and manage the orders created by the MRP system.

SFC systems are common in mature MRP manufacturing facilities. For every order generated by the MRP system for launch into manufacturing, the SFC system requires that a routing file (router) be attached. The router is then used to track the progress of the order through manufacturing. It also informs manufacturing as to the correct sequence of manufacture, department by department. In return, manufacturing must report the status of the order. It must record the quantity of material produced, the amount of labor used to complete the work, the materials used, and any resultant scrap quantities.

The amount of work required to use and maintain the routing file accurately can translate into a large time commitment for staffing planners, schedulers, and expediters. Moreover, the industrial engineering resources needed to create and maintain the routings must be in place. Based on the structure of the routing file, the number of transactions necessary to document the work and material used can be quite significant.

Once an SFC system is turned on, several organizational components soon come to depend on its output. Cost accounting uses the standard hour reporting features for its labor-reporting system in an attempt to determine product costs. Engineering uses the labor reporting for the establishment of standard hours. Material management uses the tracking status to determine on-hand or scheduled receipts by department for the next MRP iteration. Schedules are established, present and future capacity requirements are derived, and performance measurements are created based on the output. Production management depends on the output of SFC information to justify future staffing requirements.

While the MRP process that generates orders for purchasing is still required for the Lean manufacturing model, the output generated in the form of manufacturing orders for the operation of a one-piece Lean line is not. Since orders are not necessary, then routings are also unnecessary. If routings are not required, all the ancillary systems that rely on the shop order and routing routines for their input will also no longer be required.

The Lean manufacturing methodologies do not rely on the output of the MRP system for the execution of a manufacturing plan. This missing dependency on associated support systems for information often presents the majority of barriers when implementing Lean manufacturing systems. Employees from the shop floor operator to manufacturing management are usually quick to embrace Lean methodologies. Support organizations with systems designed around the operation and maintenance of MRP are usually the most difficult to transform.

The Lean manufacturing model is the optimum way to operate any manufacturing facility. Manufacturers that remain dependent on their existing planning models to improve response time, reduce working capital costs, and improve quality risk yielding market share to those competitors that have made the transition to Lean. It is true that internal challenges can be difficult to manage while making the successful transformation. However, the effort is well worth it for your company.

Regardless of what improvement initiatives are undertaken, adherence to the fundamental principles is required. Deviation from or modification of the basic tenets denigrates the final results. This holds true for Lean systems the same as it does for MRP, accounting, engineering, or any other system.

Perhaps the most daunting of challenges is the incorporation of the fundamental cultural change necessary to make the new system work. The degree of difficulty is directly proportional to the degree to which the traditional manufacturing system is entrenched. Because long-term managers typically develop individual systems to solve their departmental problems in the absence of a standardized, company-wide solution, they often develop a comfort level within the organization and have little incentive to embrace new systems that may challenge their personal systems and methodologies.

As Lean methodologies confront these systems, resistance to change is imminent. Therefore, transforming a manufacturing facility to the Lean methodologies often requires a delicate balancing act between forced implementation and negotiation. To keep the project moving forward, compromise may sometimes be required.

Unfortunately, compromise will reduce the benefits of the Lean implementation. The key is to manage compromise so the change agent or project manager lives to fight another day. Change will not happen easily and may occur at a rate slower than desired. Perseverance, tenacity, and patience are valuable attributes for the champion of Lean implementation.

Knowing that legacy methodologies will provide resistance, it is wise to rely on the methodologies presented in this book. These mathematical solutions always reveal the best answer. The best answer is a goal to be achieved. Subsequent continuous process improvement projects are a matter of moving the organization, department, or systems toward the best answer. Be prepared to repeat this process several times. Process improvement is an iterative process!

As you read this book, you will notice an absence of success stories, personal war stories, anecdotal benefits, and project manager testimonials. This is intentional. I have left these for others to document. Plenty of such stories are available for those who want to see what others have done with Lean manufacturing in their facilities. While there is value in reading about the success of others when looking to motivate an organization to change, I hope the reason you are reading this book is that you are beyond the need to marvel at the triumphs of others and are now looking to write your own Lean manufacturing success story in your facility.

If you are past the point of needing to be dazzled by the promised benefits of Lean manufacturing and are ready to get down to the work of transforming your facility, this book is written to provide you with that step-by-step sequential "how-to" methodology you have been looking for.

It is my experience that there is really nothing new under the sun. This is true even with manufacturing methodologies. The methodologies presented in this book are the ones I have used with great success over the last decade working as a manufacturing consultant leading companies to convert their factories to Lean. Robust methodologies ebb and flow in popularity over time. There may even be other manufacturing methodologies unknown to me that can deliver similar results to the manufacturer. I know the ones in this book work!

Even though books have been published on the subject of Lean manufacturing and professional organizations such as APICS provide numerous opportunities to learn about Lean manufacturing, actual step-by-step techniques for converting factories to Lean seem to be limited to the secrets held by manufacturing consultants. Certainly, this book documents the Lean manufacturing methodologies I have learned as a consultant.

During Lean implementations, I have frequently heard manufacturers comment that these techniques seem to be just common sense or they can remember the techniques as the way they used to do manufacturing years ago. They are correct when they make these observations. Even though I have been in manufacturing for over 30 years, I cannot recall operating systems that did not include the computerized planning systems and procedures in use today. While the number of active practitioners is diminishing, manufacturers who were active in the 1970s can recall the days before the arrival of their computerized planning systems.

It is the same for subsequent generations of manufacturing practitioners. They simply have no memory of any way to manufacture product other than with today's computerized planning systems. Modern operating systems have taught us more about maintaining and operating the systems than about how to manufacture products. The Lean manufacturing methodologies require rethinking about how products are manufactured beyond the limitations imposed by modern planning systems. I think this is healthy and is a catalyst for many significant process improvement initiatives.

The Lean manufacturing methodologies are not "rocket science" techniques. What is interesting is that while these methodologies are not difficult, they are also not intuitive for most MRP practitioners. That is because most manufacturing professionals today are second- and third-generation MRP users and have known nothing but computer-based planning systems. Most of these manufacturing professionals can scarcely imagine operating their facilities without the output from a planning system. There will always be fear and skepticism when presented with alternative methodologies for operating their manufacturing facilities. Be sensitive to the fear these professionals will experience when introduced to these methodologies. Everyone processes information at a different speed, and the light bulb comes on faster for some than others. Except in rare instances, the light bulb eventually comes on for everybody. Be patient.

There is nothing absolute in any methodology for every project and every company. Each company has a unique operating culture and a different appetite for change. There is no way to predict every issue that could occur with every Lean implementation project, but I am confident that if the project elements of each milestone documented in this book are completed in the sequence presented, and you combine them with your excellent project management skills, you will experience great success with your Lean manufacturing implementation project.

ACKNOWLEDGMENTS

No person operates in a vacuum. I have been the beneficiary of the wisdom of many people over the years. It was no less true during the creation of this book. My former partner, Edd Freeman, patiently kept my feet on the ground whenever I began to stray from reality. My son, Brian, spent many hours editing my manuscript, making countless suggestions for improvement. My wife of 36 years, Dianne, single-handedly kept our life together regardless of where my head was at any point in time. Thank you all for your support and assistance.

Careers are developed over long periods of time. My successful long-term career in this field is the result of an accumulation of both knowledge and experience. I would like to acknowledge the opportunity and experience gained during my four-year association with JCIT International in Englewood, Colorado. Some of the materials that appear in my book are based on concepts of Demand Flow Technology created by JCIT International and appear in this book with JCIT's permission.

Early training and work-a-day experiences were learned through my association with the Vendo Company and Marion Laboratories in Kansas City, Missouri. Much of this experience is reflected in this book. Practical application of my knowledge and experience has been tested under fire from the dozens of manufacturing companies where I was invited as a consultant to help with the improvement of their manufacturing operations. Learning has always been a symbiotic relationship. I have learned much from each of these opportunities, and I thank all of them for this education.

Dennis P. Hobbs

THE AUTHOR

Dennis P. Hobbs, CPIM, has over 30 years of line and staff experience in production planning, inventory control, and materials and operations management in both the pharmaceutical and electromechanical manufacturing industries. A graduate of the University of Missouri with a BBA, he has led the implementation of two MRP systems that later achieved Class A status. He has also developed, implemented, and operated an industry-recognized Supplier Certification program for the pharmaceutical industry. As the Director of Program Development, he has designed and delivered training programs, seminars, conferences, and workshops for FDA GMP validation technologies.

Over the last decade, serving as Vice President and Senior Consultant, Mr. Hobbs has concentrated on the implementation and education of Lean manufacturing systems. During that time, as a professional instructor, he has trained over 2500 manufacturing professionals in the Lean manufacturing techniques.

Currently the President of Mfg Matters, LLC, a leading boutique consulting firm that specializes in the training and implementation of the Lean manufacturing methodologies, Mr. Hobbs helps manufacturers across a wide variety of industries convert their current operating systems from the traditional order launch/expedite system to a Lean manufacturing system. He has implemented the Lean manufacturing methodologies in numerous companies of different size, product category, and industry type. Many of these companies are members of the Fortune 100. Author of numerous articles and a sought-after speaker, Mr.

Hobbs has presented at the APICS annual conferences and local chapter meetings. He has also introduced the Lean manufacturing methods in China, India, New Zealand, Australia, and throughout Southeast Asia.

You can contact Mr. Hobbs at dennis.hobbs@mfgmatters.com or visit his website at www.mfgmatters.com.

ABOUT APICS

APICS — The Educational Society for Resource Management is a not-for-profit international educational organization recognized as the global leader and premier provider of resource management education and information. APICS is respected throughout the world for its education and professional certification programs. With more than 60,000 individual and corporate members in 20,000 companies worldwide, APICS is dedicated to providing education to improve an organization's bottom line. No matter what your title or need, by tapping into the APICS community you will find the education necessary for success.

APICS is recognized globally as:

- The source of knowledge and expertise for manufacturing and service industries across the entire supply chain
- The leading provider of high-quality, cutting-edge educational programs that advance organizational success in a changing, competitive marketplace
- A successful developer of two internationally recognized certification programs, Certified in Production and Inventory Management (CPIM) and Certified in Integrated Resource Management (CIRM)
- A source of solutions, support, and networking for manufacturing and service professionals

For more information about APICS programs, services, or membership, visit www.apics.org or contact APICS Customer Support at (800) 444-2742 or (703) 354-8851.

*Free value-added materials available from
the Download Resource Center at www.jrosspub.com*

At J. Ross Publishing we are committed to providing today's professional with practical, hands-on tools that enhance the learning experience and give readers an opportunity to apply what they have learned. That is why we offer free ancillary materials available for download on this book and all participating Web Added Value™ publications. These online resources may include interactive versions of material that appears in the book or supplemental templates, worksheets, models, plans, case studies, proposals, spreadsheets and assessment tools, among other things. Whenever you see the WAV™ symbol in any of our publications, it means bonus materials accompany the book and are available from the Web Added Value Download Resource Center at www.jrosspub.com.

Downloads available for *Lean Manufacturing Implementation* consist of worksheets, charts, templates, checklists, and a glossary of Lean manufacturing terms.

INTRODUCTION

One thing is for sure. Manufacturing has no shortage of buzzwords, catchphrases, acronyms, homilies, platitudes, advice, or New Age dogma. The terminology can be overwhelming! There's JIT, TQM, TOC, TQC, CFM, ERP, MRP and MRPII, Agile, and Lean! Recently, terms such as APS, ASP, CRM, MES, SCM, e-commerce, e-business, e-fulfillment, e-marketplace, e-procurement, e-manufacturing, WMS, ALM, C2b, ETO, PLM, EAM, and electronic have been added to the alphabet soup.

There is so much technology out there that we often feel we have failed in our duty to compare and contrast each to justify our decision to pursue one revolutionary technology versus another. We feel guilty that we have not had the opportunity to fully understand or be avid practitioners of each and every one of these wonderful technologies. We may even avoid peer discussions for fear of exposing our lack of detailed knowledge of each subject. It's just too hard to keep up!

It's easy to become intimidated by all this heady technology! It shouldn't be that way. We are all members of the manufacturing alliance. When the day is done, manufacturing professionals all seek the same thing — gaining a larger share of our market using manufacturing as a market differential. Terminology simply describes the choice of methodology used to achieve that goal.

Why is the percentage of market share such an important measurement? It measures how much of one company's products is chosen over the competitor's. Consider the benefits of owning a 100% market share where all competitors have been eliminated from the marketplace. Total market share allows profit to be established by selling price. Using the model Selling Price = Cost + Profit, the manufacturer with 100% market share can establish its own selling price, with profit limited only by sales volume. Because setting selling price is such an appealing scenario, all manufacturers should strive to capture total market share, with maximum profit as the ultimate goal — the ultimate capitalistic model!

Fortunately for consumers, this very same capitalistic model allows many manufacturers to participate in the same market. As a result, few manufacturers accomplish the nirvana of owning 100% market share and must share it with competitors. In a competitive environment, with a choice of suppliers, the customer establishes the selling price. The model is now Profit = Selling Price – Cost. Therefore, the manufacturer's profit is externally dictated by what the customer is willing to pay. The manufacturer is left with only the management of cost as a way to achieve the desired profit.

Given that competitors in the same market offer essentially the same product technology to a shared customer pool that dictates selling price, how do manufacturers differentiate themselves from their competitors in the quest for market share? What can they do to convince customers to buy their product and not the others? How can they claim "Buy me, I'm better" to their customers?

One way is to constantly redesign the product to make it newer, improved, shinier, faster, louder, bigger, and sexier than the competition. Unfortunately, these elements of differentiation are the domain of sales, marketing, and design engineering. Manufacturers have little input into these glitzier elements of product development.

Manufacturing's potential contribution to product differentiation, then, is usually limited to manufacturing cost, with its impact on profitability. Because a desired profit margin is a stated corporate goal, manufacturing's ability to affect a reduction of profit to offset higher product cost is usually not an option. This leaves manufacturing with the responsibility to manage product cost. The components of product cost are materials, labor, and overhead. Other market differentiators controlled by manufacturing are delivery time and quality.

Faced with this challenge, it's no wonder so much time is spent in pursuit of the ultimate manufacturing system. Driven by this need to contribute to their companies' success coupled with frustration caused by the limitations inherent in current methodologies, manufacturers continue to seek the Holy Grail of manufacturing. It is this search for the ultimate system that leads to the plethora of terms and buzzwords. Which methodology is the magic bullet that will provide the solution for faster response time, reduced inventories, parts-per-million levels of quality, and reduced overhead costs? Beyond optimizing performance to these measurements, what more can manufacturing do to help the company differentiate itself and increase its market share?

Proactive companies are not discouraged by these challenges. Being able to compete with the lowest cost and highest quality with the speediest delivery is a hard-to-beat combination for capturing market share from competitors. The ability to meet or exceed customers' expectation provides a significant differentiation over competitors unable to meet those same expectations. The ability to consistently deliver these differentiators should be a core competency of any manufacturing company to allow the sales organization to beat any competitor where delivery, price, and quantity are expected by the customer.

Competitors certainly are not standing still waiting to follow the leader. They continually seek ways to establish their own product differentiators. As a way to address these competitive challenges, many manufacturers have begun to question the current systems and methodologies in use today. Many have achieved the optimum performance for their existing manufacturing systems, only to discover that it is still not enough.

Today's operating system tools are designed to maximize the efficiency and utilization of labor while at the same time minimizing purchased materials. Proficient users agree that these tools do an excellent job of achieving their intended purpose but often find they must make trade-offs with other variables that contribute to their company's competitiveness. In addition, the tools themselves often become something to be managed. The systems often become a case of the tail wagging the dog as the limitations imposed by the system tools dictate policy on the shop floor.

As an alternative to simply trying to wring additional enhancements from the existing system tools one more time, many manufacturing companies have begun to look to the Lean manufacturing methodologies as way to achieve these competitive advantages. Lean manufacturing is an entirely different operating system. Lean methodologies applied to manufacturing are a series of techniques where work time required to produce a product is built sequentially, one unit at a time, at a formulated rate, without wait time, queue time, or other delays. The goal of Lean manufacturing is to establish and design a manufacturing line capable of producing multiple products using only the amount of time required to actually build the product. Wait time, queue time, and other delays are considered waste and are greatly minimized or eliminated in Lean manufacturing.

PRODUCING PRODUCTS ONE AT A TIME VERSUS ROUTING IN BATCHES

Products can be produced in one of two different ways. They can be manufactured using a one-piece Lean methodology or in batch quantities routed through traditional work centers or departments. Batch manufacturing methods group similar work types and machines together, creating departments or work centers. These departments and work centers are usually located in geographically separate areas of the facility, and work is moved from department to department until the product is completed. Batch manufacturing allows machines and people to appear more productive when large quantities of a product are built.

While departmentalization simplifies organizational control by facilitating the collection of performance, routing, and inventory data, lot sizing is based upon what would make machines or labor more productive and not necessarily what the market requires. This sole focus on the productivity of machines and people has pitted manufacturing departments against marketing departments throughout industry when it comes to decisions about the best utilization of those resources. The benefits of batch processing are offset by the problems created for manufacturing when responding to actual customer demand when trying to build a dynamic mix of products and volumes.

In addition, this grouping of work and machines usually provides little consideration for the equal distribution of capacity. This unequal distribution of capacity can create imbalances between manufacturing processes. These imbalances are often manifested in pools of excess inventory residing between imbalanced departments.

One-piece Lean manufacturing is a proven technique that allows work to be performed without bottlenecks or delays. In the Lean environment, these activities do not add value to the product and are considered a waste. One-piece Lean processing causes the reasons for delays, bottlenecks, and stoppages to be eliminated. The Lean manufacturing methodologies eliminate these wasteful activities by linking and balancing equal amounts of work steps together, enabling products to be consumed directly into the next step, one piece at a time until completed.

The sum of the work time minus the added queue and wait time required to progress through the manufacturing processes is always shorter than the time required to route products through a factory in batches. Visualize the flowing of product in its actual work time as if it flowed through a tube with no interruptions. This ability to produce product approaching its actual work content time is the source of significant benefits realized by Lean manufacturers.

Lean manufacturing lines are arranged in a facility layout so that all the processes necessary to produce a product are located adjacent to one another. Only resources necessary to meet demand are located on the Lean line. Grouping of similar labor and machine resources into departments is no longer necessary. Without the imbalance of capacity between departments, pools of work in process cannot accumulate, causing inventories to be greatly reduced.

Physically locating manufacturing processes close together allows the completed output of one process to be directly consumed into the next, dramatically reducing inventories and cycle times. This physical linkage allows the standard work tasks to be accomplished in a sequential and progressive manner at each workstation until the product is 100% completed. Wait and queue time normally associated with batches routed through the different manufacturing departments is greatly reduced or eliminated.

THE TWO-BIN MATERIAL KANBAN STRATEGY

Two resources are needed to produce any product: its labor content and its parts. While simple, this truism is fairly profound as a statement of the way products are manufactured. Thinking of products simply as labor and parts is a significant departure from the way modern planning systems approach the manufacture of product. The required labor components are designed into Lean manufacturing lines as manufacturers balance and link their manufacturing processes together. Once completed, the Lean line requires a strategy for presenting materials needed to produce the products of the Lean line. In a Lean environment, materials required to build product are placed on the line using a kanban technique. A kanban system utilizes a series of signals to indicate when parts are needed to maintain production.

The kanban methodology is a material presentation method designed to simplify material handling and inventory management. Instead of materials being placed in "kits" or allocated to a shop order and launched into manufacturing based on a production schedule, materials are instead replenished with a kanban or "signal."

Kanban systems require fewer inventory transactions and reduce the amount of system maintenance activities normally required to keep up with the real-time environment of the shop floor. Materials from suppliers are transacted into stores or directly into an in-process location. Material is then relieved from "in process" using a *backflush* transaction. The backflush transaction reduces the available on-hand inventory in the "in-process" location by deducting the purchased material content of a product's bill of material.

In a kanban system, a relationship that identifies where materials are used and where they are refilled must be established. These relationships are known as a *pull sequence*. A series of sequences linked together describing all restocking points is called a *pull chain*. When material has been consumed through the building of a product, a "kanban" signal is created. The empty kanban "signals" the need to refill or replace the materials used. This signal can be a card or the empty container itself.

A goal of any kanban system is to keep inventory moving through the manufacturing process at a rapid pace. This velocity improves the turn rate usage of the inventory investment and reduces the working capital requirements of the business. As a delivery frequency is established for each pull sequence for each part or component, the amount of inventory investment will be in direct proportion to the frequency of its replenishment. The longer the replenishment times, the greater the inventory investment. Kanban systems establish an optimum strategy for balancing inventory investment and material-handling costs.

A kanban system that places materials directly on the Lean line at the workstation where parts are consumed directly into the product offers several advantages to the Lean manufacturer. All material in manufacturing is available for use on any product. Because components are not assigned to a specific shop order and are already on the line, any product demanded by the customer can be manufactured immediately, in its work content time down the Lean line.

With a kanban system, parts do not need to be "deallocated' from one shop order and reallocated to another. The nonvalue-added "robbing Peter to pay Paul" time is greatly diminished on a Lean line. The capability for all material in the manufacturing inventory pool to be available for any requirement gives the Lean manufacturer a great deal of flexibility in rapidly meeting customer needs. Kanban systems provide the flexibility necessary to ensure a rapid response time to the customer.

LEAN MANAGEMENT OF DEMAND

When establishing a differentiation from their competitors, manufacturers are motivated to convert their factories to Lean for a variety of reasons. It may be the shortened response time that can be offered to the customer with the new Lean line design. It may be the improvements in inventory and corresponding working capital reduction that allows improved competitive pricing. Or it might be the enhanced quality created with parts-per-million levels of quality or the improved productivity, better floor space utilization, reductions in scrap and rework, increased employee participation, and simplified administrative routines available with the implementation of the Lean manufacturing methodologies.

It is not uncommon for one benefit to appeal to a manufacturer more than another. Priority and urgency of the Lean benefits are usually determined in response to the specific pain being felt by the manufacturer. In the rush to relief, little thought is usually given to the whole series of improvements manufacturers receive as a result of converting their factories to Lean. The unanticipated benefits always come as a pleasant surprise to the Lean manufacturer.

One of those benefits that Lean manufacturers enjoy is the ability to produce a wide variety of their products on any given day without the need to forecast their demand. The ability to do this provides the manufacturer maximum flexibility in meeting customer demand. Customers are not as loyal to their suppliers as they used to be. Today's customers have an expectation of a much shorter order fulfillment time than they did just a few years ago, and it seems to be getting shorter and shorter by the day. In addition, there is always a new competitor that has better quality, faster delivery, or a lower price.

The configuration of the manufacturing processes into a Lean line combined with a kanban material strategy provides the manufacturer with a powerful tool to meet customer demand. This capability allows the Lean manufacturer to produce product in the work content time. The Lean line just needs a sequencing routine to know which product to produce on the line next. For customers that demand rapid delivery time, this is a major differentiator from the competitor.

This capability also has benefits to the manufacturer beyond rapid response and happier customers. The shorter the manufacturing lead time and the quicker the response to a customer order, the less the need to carry finished goods or work-in-process inventory. Typically there is work-in-process inventory equivalent to the total number of days of factory lead time. If the response time through the factory is reduced, there will be a corresponding reduction in the amount of work in process and finished goods inventory. Inventory reductions in these two key areas can be significant.

MORE TERMINOLOGY?

There is specific terminology for the Lean manufacturing methodologies. Each evolution of technology introduces a new vocabulary. This has certainly been the case with Lean manufacturing. There has to be a name for the techniques and methodologies used to describe line design and kanban processes. However, Lean manufacturers are not hung up on semantics or vocabulary. Lean manufacturing professionals want results. The terms used to achieve those results are really unimportant. Their goal is to provide the differentiator for their company by producing products with the fastest response time, lowest cost, and highest quality. They want to give their sales force all the ammunition they can to eliminate the competition. They want to own their market!

Lean manufacturers have even found their facilities easier to manage on a day-to-day basis. However, easier does not mean that manufacturers can abdicate their responsibilities to operate their Lean factories as a system. Lean manufacturers continue to get better as response time is reduced. Lean manufacturers thrive on the benefits of kaizen and the other continuous improvement tools.

Anecdotal examples of the benefits of Lean manufacturing emanate from numerous Lean factories today. Ample documentation of these benefits is also available in industry press. For conscientious manufacturers continually seeking to improve their manufacturing processes, the lure of those benefits is hard to resist. In recent years, many manufacturers have embraced these Lean manufacturing initiatives.

For other manufacturers, the benefits of implementing Lean manufacturing in their facilities versus the risks, timing, and resources required for a transformation to Lean are still being debated. For still other manufacturers, maintaining the status quo or improving upon existing manufacturing models remains the plan for the future.

After more than a decade of conversions by all types of industries to Lean manufacturing, the benefits being realized by these manufacturers are indisputable. Companies still deciding whether or not a new approach is necessary may be in jeopardy of relinquishing whatever market share they hold today. Comfort, loyalty, and reliance on the old models of production to meet the increasing needs of the Internet-age customer will separate the marginal companies from the leaders in their industries.

Many companies have come to the conclusion that tweaking the existing operating model another time just will not give them that leap forward they need to capture more market share and improve their operating profit. Once a decision has been made to convert to a Lean manufacturing methodology and enthusiasm builds, with a mood for change in the air, where to begin usually looms as the next biggest question.

Change of this magnitude is not without cost. What will the costs be to transform the factory to Lean? Is inventory investment required? How receptive to change is the workforce? What training is necessary? How soon will the company see a return on investment? How does a company change all those years of comfort with and loyalty to the tried-and-true methods? How are the organizations within the company going to be impacted? How will jobs change? What will the new culture look like? How will the MRP/ERP system be altered? Without previous experience in company transformations, these questions are difficult to answer.

As manufacturers seek a way to achieve the lofty goals of improved customer response time, reduced cost, and improved manufacturing performance, they frequently look to computer-based systems to provide guidance and solutions for implementing their new Lean initiatives. Good honest skepticism for unrealistic promises made about the ease of implementation and a fast and easy return on the computer-based solution is both healthy and good!

As a stand-alone solution, buying and installing new software is not the answer. Software is only a tool to operate a good system. MRP systems are often blamed for operating failures to justify repurchase and reinstallation projects every few years as a solution to fixing the "system." It does not make sense to

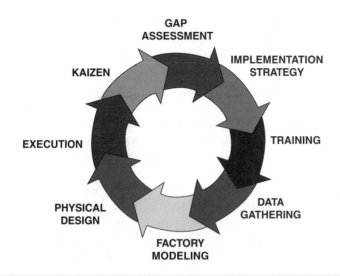

Figure 1 A Disciplined Approach

buy software, install it, and proclaim to the world that you are now Lean. Doing so could cause chaos inside a company and possibly reverberate outside the four walls to customers and suppliers.

The best place to begin improvement is in your own factory. Not only is this where the money is, but cleaning up your own backyard should always be the first thing to tackle. Begin by understanding the products and manufacturing processes, their demand, and the real goals of response time, quality, and minimum working capital investment versus efficiency and utilization. Create a "critical mass" of employees who will champion the transformation in your company. The Lean implementation will force you to do this, and the exercise often reveals surprising introspection about your company.

The process of implementing Lean manufacturing in your company should be a methodical and disciplined approach (Figure 1). While the transformation process should proceed quickly, the pace of implementation must allow the organization and culture time to adapt to the changes being made. Taking too much time will evaporate the high energy and enthusiasm. If it is too fast, and the organization cannot absorb the changes.

There is also no reason to throw out your current legacy planning system to run your new Lean factory using some new expensive computer program. The optimum solution for manufacturing is to use traditional MRP/ERP for long-range planning in combination with the techniques and methodologies of Lean manufacturing for the execution of those plans.

Customer expectations continue to rise. Customization, shorter response time, reduced inventories, and the trend toward the manufacture of products in smaller lot size quantities will continue as customers continue to demand specialized products. The Lean manufacturing methodologies provide the manufacturer incredible flexibility by building a lot size of one. The Lean methodologies reduce waste in the manufacturing processes by managing product to progress sequentially through manufacturing with a minimum of nonvalue-added wait and queue time. Products can be introduced to manufacturing based on actual customer demand, eliminating manufacturing resources wasted on forecasted demand.

In addition, with access to the Internet, both suppliers and customers are expanding the incredible amount of sourcing information available today. This puts increasing amounts of pressure on all suppliers and manufacturers to match or exceed the best in their markets. Suppliers and manufacturers are increasingly held to world-class quality standards and must deliver world-class customer service.

PART I:
THE BENEFITS OF
IMPLEMENTING A LEAN
MANUFACTURING SYSTEM

1

HISTORY AND MODERN APPLICATIONS OF LEAN MANUFACTURING

The old saying that "there is nothing new under the sun" certainly is true as it pertains to manufacturing technologies. However, the level of sophistication and application of these technologies have continued to evolve over the years. Examples are Lean manufacturing and MRP/ERP batch manufacturing systems. Neither is a new or radical concept, and each concept has existed independently for decades.

These tried-and-true technologies have been available to manufacturers for many years. During that time, both have been misunderstood, incorrectly applied, or frequently overlooked as a solution for improving a manufacturing company's performance. The goal of any manufacturing system is to produce the highest quality products in the shortest lead time possible with the least amount of resource investment delivered to the customer at the lowest possible cost. It has been argued that the goals of these two approaches to manufacturing even conflict with one another. Using elements of both methodologies provides a manufacturer a set of common-sense tools that can be used to optimize its manufacturing process as a competitive tool for the company.

The goal of this book is not to be a history book. Plenty has already been written in much greater detail about the evolution of manufacturing. However, a short review of how manufacturing has evolved over the last century to arrive where it is today can provide some perspective on how the Lean manufacturing methodologies compare to other modern manufacturing systems

When the industrial revolution began in the 1860s, one of the first challenges for manufacturing was how to manage a machine with its enormous product output. Machine output far outpaced that of a person performing the same task. These early machines were concentrated in industries that involved weaving cloth. Products that required the shaping or cutting of metals were still extremely labor intensive. The major issue of management within these industries was still the productivity of the workers.

Around 1885, these management issues were first addressed when Frederick Winslow Taylor began publishing his work. Taylor proposed that all work should be broken down into individual tasks, with a supporting view that these tasks could be shortened or eliminated. His early studies focused on individual motivation as much as the work that was being performed. Taylor began proving his theories in multiple industrial applications that focused on finding the "one best way." The application of this scientific method coupled with the time study techniques introduced by Frank Gilbreth eventually led to maximum efficiency in industrial work.*

Additional credibility was given for these theories when Henry Ford began building large manufacturing facilities for his new motorcars. The Henry Ford model of assembly line production caused a manufacturing transformation from individual craft production to mass production. This helped to create a market-place based on economies of scale and scope. Later, giant organizations designed around functional specialization and minute divisions of labor grew out of the need to meet the requirements of the new economies of scale. Spreading fixed expenses, especially investments in plant and equipment and the organization of production lines, over larger volumes of output produced economies of scale. This dynamic reduced unit costs.**

Ford also made contributions to mass production and consumption in the realm of process engineering. The hallmark of this system was standardization. This meant the standardization of components, manufacturing processes, and a simple, easy-to-manufacture standard product. Standardization required nearly perfect interchangeability of parts. To achieve this, Ford exploited the advances being made in machine tools and gauging systems. These innovations facilitated the sequential building of products made on a moving, continuous assembly line.**

By the 1930s, Ford's standardized product, with his direct planning and control systems, was made obsolete by innovations in marketing and organization at General Motors. Just as Ford made history of the horse and buggy, so

---

* *The Fundamentals of Flow Manufacturing*, JD Edwards White Paper, November 1999.
** Fred Thompson, *Fordism, Post-Fordism and the Flexible System of Production*, Willamette University, Salem, Oregon.

too did GM's Alfred P. Sloan make history of the Model T. By 1927, the Chevrolet had a water pump cooling system, an oil gauge on the dash, a reliable ignition system, a foot accelerator, and a gas tank in the rear for safety and convenience. In addition, the new Chevrolets came in colors! The era of Ford's dominance based on standardization was over.*

Albert P. Sloan is also credited with setting the standard for modern management organizations. He is best known for the multiproduct organization structure in which each major operating division serves as a distinct product market. When Sloan took over GM in the early 1920s, it was a loose confederation of car and car parts companies. Sloan repositioned the car companies to create a five-model product range from Chevrolet to Cadillac. Under this system, each division kept its own books and its manager was evaluated in terms of a return-on-assets target.

The challenge in manufacturing during the 1930s shifted to product variety. While manufacturing through the 1930s and 1940s was still driven by large-quantity production runs, the huge production runs enjoyed by the 17 years of the Model T were no longer possible. Consumers were more and more the drivers of change in a product life cycle. As the 1950s began, demand for specialized products started to take hold. Not only were products more specialized, but they also had limited life cycles.

Up until this time, manufacturers had focused primarily on labor productivity to achieve a competitive advantage. Innovations in technology became the new productivity tools that allowed many manufacturers to remain competitive. This technology and productivity was a key differentiator between one manufacturer and another. This period marked the advent of technological changes in machine tool cutting points, synthetic abrasives, and multiple rotary cutting points, particularly in lathes and milling machines. These machine tool innovations and the Sloan return-on-investment performance measurements were custom made for each other.

Batch manufacturing methods had arrived! In batch manufacturing, production run quantities are based on what makes a machine productive and not necessarily on what the market requires. This focus on economies of scale batch production continues to pit manufacturing departments against marketing departments throughout all industry. This conflict is still evident in manufacturing companies today. Batch manufacturing had allowed machines to become productive when large quantities of a product were built. Conversely, batch processing created problems for manufacturing when trying to build a dissimilar mix of products. What is the optimum amount? How much is too much?

---

* Fred Thompson, *Fordism, Post-Fordism and the Flexible System of Production*, Willamette University, Salem, Oregon.

During the 1950s, the commercial availability of computers began to have a profound effect on business information processing. Until the advent of the computer, the functions of logistics, inventory management, and production planning constituted a chronic, intractable problem for any discrete manufacturer engaged in multiple-stage production of products from raw material to finished product. Precomputer inventory control techniques available at the time were simply imperfect, but represented the best that could be done under the circumstances.

Around the early 1960s, as computing power began to be more cost effective, early pioneers began the development and installation of the early computer-based MRP systems. Some of these earliest pioneers included Joseph Orlicky, George Plossl, and Oliver W. Wight. From the original handful, the number of systems grew to 150 installed systems by 1971!* Since that time and with the help of the American Production and Inventory Control Society (APICS), the number of MRP installations approaches the total number of manufacturing companies. Today, the MRP system is the primary tool used for production planning, inventory control, shop floor control, costing, and capacity planning by the modern manufacturer.

While an MRP system is a valuable weapon in the manufacturing arsenal, practitioners continue to grapple with the still conflicting objectives of batch manufacturing and optimizing inventories. Confronted with the conflicting policies, it is often the MRP system itself that takes the blame for disappointing results. Unless filtered as a system parameter, the MRP solution will solve for the smallest inventory and shortest manufacturing lead time. If followed precisely, MRP recommendations will yield the expected results. Modifications, and work rules put in place to optimize efficiency and utilization of individual work centers, generally degrade the output of the MRP system. Compromise is the culprit of a diminished MRP system.

During the 1950s and 1960s in the Far East, particularly Japan, a different manufacturing model was being formulated. Leading this charge was the Toyota Motor Company. Toyota contended that the standard thinking of Cost + Profit = Sales Price was incorrect. It believed that Profit = Sales Price – Costs. From this premise, Toyota began to create a manufacturing system that would concentrate on the management of costs. Cost became translated as waste, and wastes of all varieties were targeted for elimination. The large bureaucratic overhead required to manage planning systems became suspect.

Key areas targeted were work-in-process inventory and safety stock. While many companies in the United States and Europe were attempting to calculate the optimum batch sizes for production, Toyota worked toward the goal of being

---

* Joseph Orlicky, *Material Requirements Planning*, McGraw-Hill, New York, 1975, p. ix.

able to build a mix of products in a one-piece flow. Having the capability to build a mix of products in a one-piece flow (mixed-product Lean line) satisfied many key objectives for Toyota, raising productivity and reducing costs and inventory while simultaneously creating rapid customer response.*

Through the 1960s and into the 1970s, these two models of manufacturing developed down separate paths. One sought better ways to manage batch production by making ongoing improvements to the MRP planning model, while the other concentrated on finding and fine-tuning ways to allow a one-piece flow of a mix of products. Soon, the benefits achieved by these two disparate strategies made themselves apparent.

Into the 1980s, many product markets in the United States and Europe started to come under pressure from foreign manufacturers. Products were being brought to market with higher quality and lower price. The days of planned obsolescence were over. Consumers came to expect higher quality and lower prices as a requisite for purchase. Western manufacturers began to lose market share. Some manufacturers faded away while others began to look diligently for better ways to compete. Many abandoned the old batch manufacturing models in favor of the more responsive method of Lean manufacturing in pursuit of the goals of faster response, fewer inventories, higher quality, and reduced costs.

THE POPULARITY OF MRP SYSTEMS
AND THEIR IMPACT ON ORGANIZATIONS

The operating system of choice for most manufacturers remains the MRP system. Since the early 1970s, when many companies began to investigate the benefits of computer-based inventory management systems, the number of MRP installations has grown exponentially. Today, a manufacturing company operating without a computer-based planning/inventory control system is an anomaly.

The growth in popularity of the MRP system as a solution for the pains experienced by professional material managers, production planners, and manufacturing managers happened to coincide with the maturation of computer technology. In the early days of computer technology development, if there was ever the question of a "solution looking for a problem," manufacturing professionals stood ready to oblige. Or perhaps it was the manufacturing professionals who were desperately seeking solutions that found their answers in the new computer technology. In the final analysis, it may always be a "chicken or egg" question.

Regardless of who discovered whom, manufacturers found much to like in the new computer technology. Now, with computers that were capable of han-

---

* *The Fundamentals of Flow Manufacturing*, JD Edwards White Paper, November 1999.

dling volumes of information at lightning speeds, manufacturers no longer found themselves constrained by the inventory management tools available at that time. The mainstays of conventional inventory management became subject to reappraisal as to their validity, relevance, and applicability to managing inventories. The discovery that better success could be had not by simply refining old existing tools but by exploring radically different approaches to solving age-old problems was truly a revelation.

PRECOMPUTER INVENTORY MANAGEMENT TOOLS*

- Stock replenishment system
- Square root approach to economic order quantity
- Aggregate inventory management techniques
- Reorder point techniques
- Analysis and categorization of inventory by function
- ABC inventory classification

With the time phasing of requirements now visible to the planner, not only were the "what" and "how much" known, but also the "when." This was a major breakthrough in managing inventories and working capital dollars. It allowed planners to delay committing their companies' material resources much closer to their planned consumption in production than ever before.

For the MRP system to perform its planning routine, the following inputs of information are needed:

- An accurate indented bill of material (BOM) for each product
- Accurate inventory records for every item number
- A forecast of future demand
- A statement of actual customer orders
- A statement of open purchase orders

Successful operation of the MRP system requires significant effort to establish and maintain the data necessary to affect the planning and inventory control processes. Indeed, all the required information resides in separate databases within the MRP system itself. For an MRP system to be effective, the accuracy of these databases must be paramount. A common saying about the effectiveness of the output of MRP has been and still is "garbage in–garbage out!"

For every part number planned, using the information listed above, the following netting formula is calculated by the MRP system:

* Joseph Orlicky, *Material Requirements Planning*, McGraw-Hill, New York, 1975, p. 5.

Gross Requirements – (On Hand + Scheduled Receipts) = Net Requirements

where gross requirements = forecast + open customer orders, on hand = inventory balance, and scheduled receipts = orders to be received from the supplier or production.

If the part being planned is a purchased item, the net requirement becomes a purchase order. If the part number is a manufactured item, it becomes a shop order and eventually part of a production schedule.

To establish the correct due date of these net requirements, an indented BOM is required. The indented BOM is one of the key databases for the operation of an MRP system. The BOM not only lists the parts and quantities required to build a product, but also captures the lead time offset information required for time-phasing calculations necessary to establish start and due dates for MRP-generated orders. It does this by recording the lead time of each process as it passes sequentially through manufacturing. This BOM offset feature electronically communicates to the MRP system how the product is manufactured.

The indented BOM has also had an interesting impact on how manufacturing facilities are organized. When inspecting an indented BOM, the organization of the factory is often reflected in the levels of the BOM. Common functions or processes are usually grouped together in separate departments that mimic the BOM. The levels typically model the sequential build of the product through the manufacturing facility.

This presents an interesting question: Did the functional grouping of processes into their current departmental structure exist before the advent of the planning system, or did the introduction of the indented BOM dictate the departmental designation? Another "chicken or egg" question? What were the criteria used for establishing existing department structures today?

Regardless of criteria, the implementation of the MRP system forced these organizational decisions to be made. Coupled with the organization functionality designed after the GM Sloan model where individual managers are made responsible for the return on investment of their respective departments, the installation of the MRP system had much to do with establishing the structure of current-day organization charts. It feels quite logical and natural to assign responsibility for required data elements necessary to operate the MRP system to functional organizations within the company (e.g., BOMs to design engineering, forecasting to sales and marketing, and planning and inventory management to materials management).

It has been over 30 years since the early MRP systems were first implemented. It would be safe to say that most manufacturing companies today are now completely structured around the maintenance and operation of their MRP systems. Those first generations of MRP pioneers in companies have either retired or are close to doing so. Subsequent generations and current practitioners have little awareness of and give little thought to life before the MRP environment. They cannot imagine operating their manufacturing lines without the MRP system.

RETHINKING THE MRP MODEL — "THE SYSTEM WON'T LET ME DO IT!"

MRP systems have continued to evolve into extremely robust tools. Today, MRP practitioners are better trained and more experienced, relying on the lessons learned by generations of planning system pioneers who have come before them. Materials planning/inventory control professionals are now recognized as an important discipline with their own body of knowledge, right along with accounting, engineering, and quality control. There is great comfort with the MRP model.

Even beyond the materials/inventory planning organization, the front-line recipient of the benefits of the MRP system, the entire company usually has come to be quite comfortable with the MRP model. In fact, entire departments, from the shop floor to the back office, have been organized around supporting and operating the MRP system. Organizational hierarchy has been built around the MRP system. Individual careers have been established based on their support of the MRP system. Much like the 800-pound gorilla, the MRP system has a life of its own.

While so much attention was being paid to cultivating the necessary changes needed to implement and operate the MRP model over the last 30 years, changes in the marketplace continued to occur, sometimes without notice. Unfortunately, these changes often quietly sneak up on the manufacturer, making crisis management the order of the day.

The loss of market share suffered by many industries during the MRP growth phase because of global competition has been well documented. The acceptance of "planned obsolescence" (products produced with maximum efficiency and utilization at convenience) has shifted to "quality, variety, and low cost" as a minimum consumer expectation. Where American manufacturers had always enjoyed market leadership before, entry into the marketplace by global competitors began to transform their industry groups into commodities. Commodity products have many competitors with few feature differentiators and are price sensitive with less customer loyalty. History has recorded the fate of numerous companies unsuccessful in meeting these competitive challenges.

MRP practitioners continue to work hard and diligently to meet these challenges. It is a testament to those manufacturers that endure and thrive in the face of these tough competitive challenges. But it never gets easier. The challenges are greater and greater. The customers are less and less loyal. Competitors get better and better. They respond faster, have better quality, and sell at a lower price! Even as market leadership is achieved, the competition is always close behind.

Improving response time is one of the first areas where competitors gain a foothold. Followed by price reduction and improvements in quality, market share begins to erode. A first line of defense is usually to increase inventories. Forecasts of future sales are made. Finished goods inventories are built, consuming valuable capital and plant capacity. When customers frustrate manufacturing efforts to predict the final configuration and the quantity and timing of their demand, finished goods inventories swell. To avoid rising finished goods inventory levels, the decision is often made to keep inventory at the work-in-process level, completing the final configuration closer to the receipt of the customer order. The reasoning is that by having partially completed inventory on hand, response to last-minute customer configuration and demand will be faster.

Soon, work-in-process inventory balloons. Demands for working capital increase proportionately. Even though they are working harder and harder to meet the competition, manufacturers find that their systems are strained to meet their increased need for both flexibility and speed. Panic sets in, and upgrades to the MRP system are recommended. Even after the installation of newer, faster, better revisions of MRP, manufacturers often are disappointed to discover that the new version is simply a new permutation of the same old model.

Having been through this cycle more than once, manufacturers have begun to question if their planning *system* is really the problem or if the MRP methodology itself is still the best answer. They start to question the rigidity of the planning system. They feel constrained by lot sizes that do not match the ever-changing customer demand. They feel trapped by the reliance on a forecast of sales far into the future for the commitment of manufacturing and purchasing resources. They are tired of the lack of flexibility and the shop floor upheaval caused when responding to last-minute customer demand. They are frustrated by the constant expediting and the "robbing of Peter to pay Paul" parts allocation methodology. Countless parts shortages still plague the production lines even though there are endless inventory transactions and system reporting.

While flexibility is restricted by the MRP system, materials planners also find they must maintain consideration for the rest of the organization. The meeting of department and corporate goals has been designed around the operation and maintenance of the MRP system. Lot sizes have been developed to optimize the efficiency and utilization of shop floor manufacturing resources, and inventory levels are set to satisfy sales and marketing quotas. Purchasing has arranged supplier minimum order quantities to receive quantity discounts, and cost accounting has directives for labor collection information. In addition, the materials vice-president has a turn rate goal based on minimum inventory levels.

It is difficult to decide which of these priorities to respond to. Is the priority based on who shouts the loudest today? Will the priority of today be different tomorrow? Will the requirements of manufacturing be sacrificed for the needs of finance, or will efficiency be sacrificed for inventory goals? Is MRP a system for managing manufacturing or a system for managing corporate hierarchy and goals? Is the manufacturing dog wagging the tail of organizational needs, or are organizational needs wagging the dog of manufacturing? Who should be disappointed; who should be favored? Where should loyalty reside?

A series of conflicting objectives arises amid cries of "The system won't let me do it!" Are there any alternatives?

THE SEARCH FOR THE HOLY GRAIL OF MANUFACTURING

For some, the search begins for the better system. For others, the search continues!

One thing is certain: When the search begins, there will be no shortage of solutions available to the manufacturing professional. Buzzwords, catchphrases, acronyms, homilies, platitudes, advice, and New Age dogma abound. It is up to the manufacturing professional to sort through all the jargon and select the best set of tools for the company.

When all is said and done, regardless of terminology, manufacturing professionals are all seeking the same thing — a way to shorten response time, reduce inventory, improve quality, and maintain productivity goals, while improving profits and increasing market share for their companies.

Manufacturers continue to seek the Holy Grail!

THE LEAN MANUFACTURING MODEL

This search by manufacturers for solutions to the rigid rules mandated by their MRP systems has led many to the techniques of Lean manufacturing. Lean manufacturing methodologies are not new technologies for the millennium, but are, in fact, a compilation of many of the techniques manufacturers have used in the past and are familiar with. The difference is the consolidation of these techniques into one set of powerful methodologies and their application. Achieving Lean goals using one-piece Lean manufacturing methods is essentially a line-balancing methodology used in conjunction with a series of kanban material-handling techniques. Mathematical models are created and iterated until the optimum utilization of manufacturing resources is identified.

Specifically, the Lean manufacturing methodologies are a series of techniques that allow product to be produced one unit at a time, at a formulated rate, while eliminating nonvalue-adding wait time, queue time, or other delays. Product is pulled through the line, in response to actual demand as opposed to being pushed through by the launch of orders based on the output of a planning system. Thought of in terms of a pipeline, discrete product can be made to move through the manufacturing processes without stopping. If product can move without stopping, it can be thought of much like liquid through a pipeline. This metaphor of moving product through a pipe is the source for the term *flow*.

If only the actual touch work time required to produce a product through its various manufacturing processes were summed, that time is almost always shorter than the time required to route batches of products through a factory one department at a time (Figure 1.1). Typically, the sum of the times required to route product through manufacturing becomes the customer-quoted lead time. Often, this customer-quoted lead time becomes a self-fulfilling prophecy to the detriment of achieving customer satisfaction. The Lean manufacturing methodologies consider all the other times associated with moving "lot-sized" orders through manufacturing as "nonvalue-added" time. Lean seeks to eliminate this nonvalue-added time.

The goal of Lean manufacturing, then, is to establish and design a manufacturing line capable of producing multiple products, one at a time, using only the amount of time required to actually build the product. The techniques of Lean manufacturing seek to reduce the nonvalue-adding wait, scheduling, and queue times to zero. The resulting, often significant, reduction in manufacturing lead time is the basis for all the associated benefits of Lean manufacturing.

A Lean manufacturing line requires that a rate of flow through the pipeline be established. The rate at which work progresses through the factory is called a *flow rate* or *Takt*. The "flow" of a product is achieved by causing all of its work tasks to be grouped and balanced to a calculated formulated Takt time. Takt time establishes a relationship between volume and the time available to produce that volume.

$$\text{Takt} = \frac{\text{Work Minutes per Shift} \times \text{\# of Shifts per Day}}{\text{Throughput Volume per Day}}$$

Takt time, in most cases, is expressed in minutes or percentage of a minute.

Regardless of the total time necessary to produce a product, its total time is divided into elements of work equal to its Takt time. A single unit of work (a Takt time's worth) is performed by a person and/or a machine. The partially

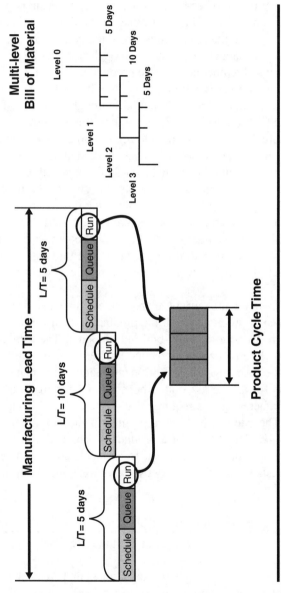

Figure 1.1 Touch Work Time versus Manufacturing Lead Time

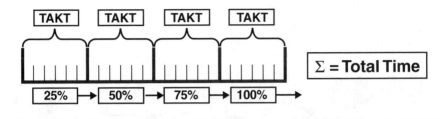

Figure 1.2   Sequential Work in Takt Time Increments

completed unit is then passed to the next resource down the line, where another "Takt" worth of work tasks is performed. The unit of work progresses sequentially through all the manufacturing processes until all of the required work has been completed (Figure 1.2).

Lean manufacturers can choose to change the output of the line to closer match the mix and volume of customer requirements. With a line designed to produce products using a formulated Takt time, the Lean manufacturer has the ability to regulate the "rate" and, therefore, the output of the line. This rate must be determined every day based on *that* day's customer requirements.

In the example in Figure 1.2, work is completed in four equal Takt times. If each Takt time were staffed with an operator, the throughput volume used for the Takt calculation would be produced each day. If, however, staffing were reduced to three operators, then only three-fourths of the throughput would be achieved, as one operator has to complete two Takt times to complete one unit. Effectively, every fourth Takt time would be missed. By intentionally causing Takt times to be missed or gained, the rate of production can is adjusted with a simple staffing decision of the number of labor resources assigned to the line that day.

This ability to change output rate every day, driven by changes in customer order requirements, is a powerful tool for managing both work-in-process and finished goods inventories. With this capability, a manufacturer is no longer forced to commit its manufacturing resources to a schedule driven by a questionable forecast of future demand.

As in the Sloan model, grouping similar types of work and machines together creates traditional departments and work centers. This grouping of work and machines assists with organizational control and facilitates the collection of performance, routing, and inventory-reporting data. In most cases, the similar work and machines are then geographically located in one area of the facility. In most cases, this grouping of work or machines allows little consideration for the equal distribution of capacity. This unequal distribution of capacity can create imbalances between manufacturing processes. These imbalances are often manifested in pools of excess inventory (Figure 1.3).

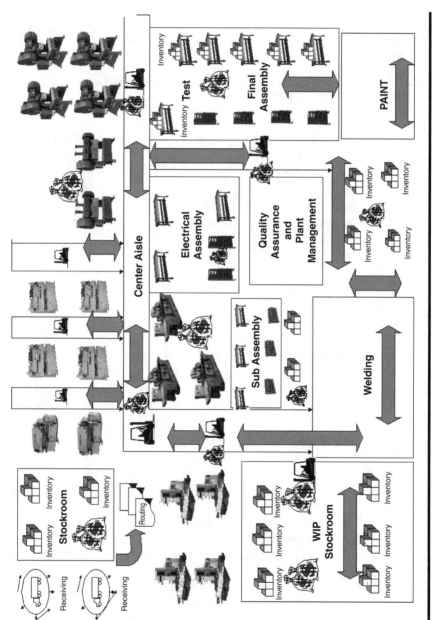

Figure 1.3   Grouping Similar Work and Machines into Departments

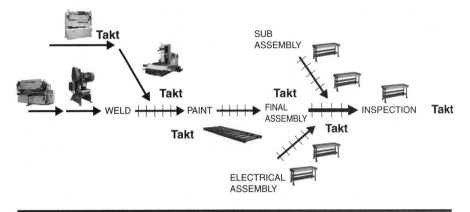

Figure 1.4 The Lean Manufacturing Model

A Lean line overcomes this imbalance problem. Lean lines are progressive assembly lines established with a facility layout that allow standard work tasks to be accomplished in a sequential and progressive manner. Where possible, all the processes necessary to produce a product are physically *linked* together. The physical arrangement of the resources is important as it allows work tasks to be distributed, accumulated, and balanced evenly throughout the entire manufacturing cycle (Figure 1.4).

Balancing to Takt and physically linking manufacturing processes together so the completed output of one process can be directly consumed by another dramatically reduces inventories and cycle times. Because manufacturing processes are simply divided into equal elements of work, the grouping of similar labor and machines into "departments" is no longer necessary. Only the resources required to produce the required throughput are located on the line.

When no longer constrained by the rules of imbalanced departments, pools of work in process do not accumulate. Because the manufacturing processes have been balanced and linked together in sequence, products can be produced in the time approaching their work content time only, ratcheting one at a time through all processes and off the end of the line every Takt time. The usual wait and queue times necessary for the normal routing of products through the different manufacturing departments in batches are eliminated.

Many manufacturers produce products by families. These families define which products will be run on which production line. This family designation often dictates the dedication of manufacturing resources to specific products and production lines. In most cases, these families have not been defined by manufacturing. Family definitions are usually reserved for the sales, marketing, or financial groups, with little regard given to the actual manufacturing requirements of the product.

Lean manufacturers also produce products using a family definition. However, family member selections for multiproduct Lean lines are based first on the commonality of their processing paths or their *process flow diagram*. Further selections are based on similar work element times and the commonality of work steps and materials used. Lean manufacturing lines are optimally designed to produce a "family" of similar products that all share common manufacturing processes and materials. By grouping products in this manner, all family members advance through their required resources one unit at a time on the same line, sharing the same shop floor square footage.

The capability to produce multiple products on the same line has many benefits for the Lean manufacturer. A multiproduct line allows the production of a multitude of products using the same shop floor footprint. This can be important to the Lean manufacturer to delay or avoid the costs of bricks-and-mortar expansion. Also, it is not unusual for different products to have different demand patterns and sales cycles. If product lines have been dedicated to fewer product types, their alternating demand patterns can lead to the "hiring/firing" of employees in an attempt to match production capacity to customer requirements. Lean lines like to run a variety of products on a single line. The more products run on a single line, the less the impact of alternating demand on valuable manufacturing resources.

The length of lead time through a factory also has a direct and predictable impact on the amount of in-process inventory that exists. Manufacturing response time in a Lean factory is measured by determining the critical time required through the process relationships required to build the product. The less the lead time, the less work-in-process inventory needed to support it.

Lead time through the factory can be so significantly reduced that shop floor tracking and expediting can be reduced or eliminated. The Lean response time is always shorter than the time it takes to route products in batches through manufacturing using the multilevel BOM.

THE KANBAN METHODOLOGY

There are two primary resources needed to produce any product: labor and material. Lean manufacturers balance and link their manufacturing processes together, staffing those resources to customer requirements to produce products. The component materials required to build those products are placed at the point of usage on the Lean line utilizing a technique called *kanban*. The kanban system utilizes a series of signals to indicate when parts are needed to replenish production.

Kanban methodology is a material presentation method designed to simplify material handling and inventory management. Instead of materials being staged in "kits" and issued to production to follow the routing, materials are physically placed at the point of usage on the line and replenished only when a "kanban" or "signal" is generated by their consumption into the product.

Kanban systems require fewer inventory transactions and reduce the amount of system maintenance activities normally needed to keep up with the real-time environment of the shop floor. Materials received from suppliers are transacted into stores or directly into an in-process location. Material is then relieved from "in process" using a *backflush* transaction. The backflush transaction reduces the on-hand inventory in the "in-process" location by deducting the material recorded in the product's BOM. At the same time, one completed unit is added to the finished goods inventory.

The backflush transaction occurs after all work to build the product is finished and all required materials are consumed into the end item. Reducing the number of material input and output transactions causes the on-hand inventory to be highly accurate. Unless mandated by regulation, many Lean manufacturers have greatly reduced or eliminated cycle counting and physical inventories.

A kanban system that places material directly onto the line at the point it is consumed into the product offers a real competitive advantage to the Lean manufacturer. Because all the material needed for manufacturing is located on the line and not allocated to a specific production order, it is available for consumption on any product that happens to move down the line. All materials become available for all products. With a kanban system, parts do not need to be "deallocated" from one shop order and reallocated to another when necessary to respond to changes in priority. Because parts are not assigned to specific shop orders and simply reside on the line, response to changes in customer order priority is limited only by the work content time of the product.

The kanban system establishes a relationship that identifies where materials are used, and where they are refilled must be established. These relationships are known as *pull paths, pull codes,* or *pull sequences.* When kanban material has been consumed by the building of product, a signal is created. The empty kanban "signals" the need to refill or replace the material used. This signal can be a card or the empty container itself.

A refilling point for material used on the production line will be located within a short distance from the line. The designated pull sequence identifies the "used at" (consumption point) and "refilled from" (replenishment point) locations. This information is provided to facilitate the material handler responsible

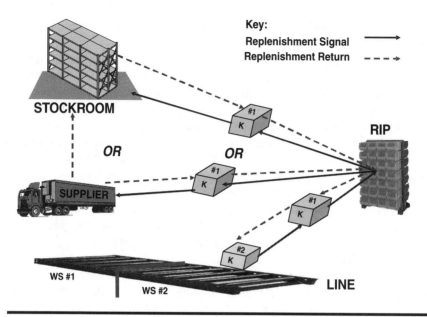

Figure 1.5   Kanban Pull Chain

for performing the actual replenishment. Empty kanban containers are then refilled from a designated replenishment point location. In turn, replenishment point kanbans are then refilled either from stores or directly from a supplier. If suppliers are certified for reliability and dependability, materials can be delivered directly to the replenishment point location, bypassing the stockroom. Suppliers, as members of the supply chain, can be notified by receiving these signals electronically (via the Internet) based on real-time shop floor usage (Figure 1.5).

This pull sequence routine is the direct link to and provides the required platform from the shop floor to the supplier when using an electronic kanban communication beyond the four walls of manufacturing.

A goal of a kanban system is to keep inventory moving through the manufacturing process at a rapid pace. This velocity is intended to improve the turn rate usage of the inventory investment and to reduce the working capital requirements of the business. The key to this rapid turning of inventory is the frequency of replenishment of the kanban signals. Empty kanbans are refilled based on the predetermined *delivery frequency*.

A delivery frequency must, therefore, be established for each pull sequence for each part number in the kanban system. The delivery frequency establishes a relationship between the amount of inventory investment and the amount of material-handling activity. The amount of inventory investment is in proportion to how often material is replenished. The longer the replenishment times, the greater the inventory investment. Conversely, more frequent replenishment means smaller inventory.

More frequent replenishment also means more material-handling time. While it is tempting to think only of the benefits of reduced inventories, kanban systems must ultimately establish the optimum strategy that balances inventory investment with material-handling costs. Usually, this is an iterative process until optimum balance between the two is achieved.

Another type of kanban system is used to signal the next unit of production on the line itself. An *in-process kanban* (IPK) is used to signal the next unit in sequence. Kanban signaling generates the communication that indicates to the shop floor when to begin work on a specific product. Products are planned into the Lean line one unit at a time in a specific sequence to ensure a balanced "flow" of work through the factory.

SEQUENCING PRODUCTION ONE PIECE AT A TIME ON THE LEAN LINE

Scheduling production in a Lean factory is significantly simplified once the factory layout and kanban signaling drive the flow of work through the factory. Production planning on the Lean line occurs at the beginning (operation #1) of the line at the finished goods level. Subassemblies are produced on feeder processes with production signaled using the IPK methodology. With the IPK method, there is no need to schedule batch subassembly production. The output from these feeder processes is consumed directly into the downstream processes, and subsequent production in the feeder is initiated using the IPK kanban as a signal for replenishment.

Because products are manufactured one unit at a time, they can be sequenced to move down the Lean line in the same order the customer requirement was received. The planner has only to determine the order of manufacture. The operator in the first workstation of the Lean line, upon receiving an empty IPK signal, simply begins production of the next unit in the same order the planner has chosen — a first-in–first-out methodology.

In special cases such as configure-to-order custom products, a sales order configuration document sequenced with the product may be required. This configuration traveler accompanies the product as it advances down the Lean line. The traveler indicates to the operator which parts from the workstation are to be used to build the special configuration.

THE BENEFITS OF EMBRACING LEAN TECHNIQUES FOR MANUFACTURING

While discussion and debate over differing manufacturing methodologies could go on endlessly, one thing is certain. Significant benefits must result from any change in operating systems. Every manufacturing company is different from the next. Each has its own reason for considering such an important change. At any given time, each manufacturer is uniquely positioned in its marketplace, with one benefit appealing to its needs more than another. Certainly, one or more of the benefits of the Lean methodologies must be a result of the implementation project. There must be a return on the investment of time and resources required to make the change.

Because the benefits of converting to the Lean manufacturing methodologies are dovetailed together, it is impossible to separate one goal from another. When implemented, many manufacturers are pleasantly surprised to discover that other unplanned benefits are suddenly available to them. Just implementing the Lean manufacturing methodologies causes a series of behaviors to occur that deliver benefits to the manufacturer. Listed below are reasons manufacturers pursue Lean manufacturing.

Improved Response Time to Customer Demand

No matter the product, more and more competitors seem to be entering the marketplace every year. Each of these competitors has some attribute that differentiates itself from its competitors. Customers have numerous choices when it comes to buying their products. Combined with the choices available to the consumer and the expectation of shorter order fulfillment lead times, customers have become more fickle in their purchasing decisions and less loyal to their old long-standing business relationships.

Products with similar features and price offered by multiple manufacturers begin to approach commodity status. Once designated or perceived by the customer as a commodity, product differentiation becomes more and more critical. If the manufacturer cannot differentiate its product with improved technology, quality, or price, other criteria must be developed as a way to attract and satisfy those customers. If a customer perceives no difference between products, but expects rapid delivery of configured products, the manufacturer with the ability to respond to this demand faster than the competitor will earn the business. For many manufacturers, this rapid-response delivery capability provides the differentiation needed to maintain and gain market share from its competitor.

Lean factories that produce product in its actual work content time achieve a significantly shorter manufacturing lead time. The shorter the manufacturing lead time, the faster the response to a customer order. Shorter manufacturing lead time usually allows a reduction in the amount of finished goods and/or work-in-process inventories typically carried as an offset to quickly respond to customer demand. If response to demand is shorter than the current customer-quoted lead time (CQLT), there is little need to maintain forecasted product in a finished goods warehouse. This is a key market differentiator for the Lean manufacturer. The ability to deliver product faster in a commodity-type market ultimately means an increase in market share from those customers to whom fastest response time is the primary purchase decision criterion.

Reduced Inventories

Because response time can be reduced on a Lean line, the reasons for maintaining large amounts of work in process are also eliminated. The amount of the reduction is usually in direct proportion to the CQLT. CQLTs are established based on the minimum time required to route product through the manufacturing processes. Regardless of the capability of the manufacturing facility to deliver product faster than the quoted lead time, it often becomes a self-fulfilling prophecy. Producing product in less than the CQLT becomes an anomaly requiring heroic effort on the part of planners, production managers, and purchasing personnel.

In some cases, the CQLT may be artificially inflated to allow maximum productively to be gained by grouping work through departments. The CQLT sets the inventory policy for the company. While inadvertent, the establishment of CQLT has a significant impact on inventory policy. If quoted lead time is unacceptable to customers, both work in process and finished goods inventories are frequently maintained to compensate for the gap between CQLT and manufacturing response time.

Over time, many different variations of inventory strategies have evolved to accommodate the time gap between CQLT and actual manufacturing response time. Building to a partial level of completion through the common levels of the BOM and finishing assembly with additional configurable materials based on the receipt of actual customer demand is a common strategy. Purchase of this component inventory is based on the forecasted projection of the final configuration the customer would order. As with any forecast, if the customer fails to purchase the projected configuration, excess, slow-moving parts or obsolete parts result. Regardless of the chosen technique, it always includes some sort of inventory investment.

Historical approaches have always concentrated on improving these work-in-process models. It wasn't until manufacturers began to realize the enormous cost associated with these models that they began to investigate and understand the benefits that could be achieved with the Lean methodologies.

As lead time reductions are accomplished, matching inventory reductions are also accomplished. In addition, the balancing achieved throughout the factory also drives work-in-process requirements down. As work-in-process levels come down and confidence in line capabilities grows, subsequent reductions in finished goods inventory levels also occur.

Reduced Working Capital Requirements

The point in time from when purchased material enters the manufacturing process until it is converted into a completed product is the manufacturing lead time. Customers expect their orders to be shipped within lead time. When manufacturing lead time is greater than the customer's expected lead time, customer satisfaction may suffer. To satisfy customer orders, manufacturers may purchase materials from suppliers well in advance of actual demand. When manufacturing lead time is greater than the customer's expectation for delivery, manufacturers have different solutions to consider:

- Simply tell the customer to wait your manufacturing lead time for delivery. If there is no competition and your company is the only supplier, this may be a valid solution.
- Build work-in-process inventory of assemblies or subassemblies to be completed closer to the receipt of the actual customer order. These items can be produced in shorter lead time.
- Ship products produced in advance from a finished goods inventory. This is a common solution that works well if products are generic and order patterns are predictable. If the product(s) customers are willing to buy are custom configured or designed to order, predicting finished goods inventory can be an expensive solution.

Inventory levels are usually determined by forecasting the quantities of work in process or finished goods inventory to be maintained to assure the ideal customer response solution. Since no customer is likely to wait both the supplier lead time plus manufacturing lead time, even supplier delivery lead time will dictate quantities of purchased materials necessary to be kept on hand in stores inventory. Regardless of the customer satisfaction solution chosen, every manufacturer must determine the appropriate amount of inventory to be maintained to achieve maximum customer satisfaction. The trade-off between customer on-time delivery goals and ideal inventory levels is often argued and subject to much debate.

Inventory levels can become unacceptably large and require proportionately greater inventory investment! The sum of these inventories can have significant working capital implications. Inventories require space on the shop floor, in warehouses, and in distribution centers; the space required is not free and adds overhead to the cost of doing business. Inventory has significant financial implications! Working capital requirements can be calculated by summing raw materials plus work in process plus finished goods inventory plus accounts receivable while subtracting money owed for the material purchases (accounts payable).

The Lean manufacturing line can reduce the working capital investment required to operate a business just by reducing response time. In addition to the direct benefit of a shorter lead time response to customers, improving the time through manufacturing also yields a reduction in working capital requirements, as less money is committed to financing buffer inventory.

Cash becomes invested in purchased inventory in the following ways:

- If suppliers expect to be paid in 30 days (net 30), paid purchased materials will reside in the stockroom 30 days before work begins in manufacturing.
- If manufacturing conversion takes four weeks, money is committed another four weeks to support work in process.
- If finished goods inventory levels are three to four weeks, cash is committed for an additional three to four weeks.
- If invoices are not always paid immediately after products have been shipped to satisfy customer demand, cash is committed even longer.

With this typical inventory investment example, money has been committed for at least 12 to 13 weeks, resulting in an inventory turn of four. A working capital requirement of 25 cents of every dollar shipped in revenue is necessary to support this level of committed purchased inventories.

When significant improvement in response time through manufacturing occurs and manufacturing lead time is shortened, the reduction in inventories required to support manufacturing can begin. This inventory reduction liberates cash that can be put to use for a multitude of other purposes. This newly found cash asset can either be invested or brought to the bottom line. The inventory reduction is not just a one-time improvement. Because inventories can be managed at significantly lower levels, the elimination of additional overhead and inventory carrying costs represents $\pm20\%$ of the value of the inventory.

Simplicity and Visual Control

A key benefit for the Lean manufacturer is the ability to perform "MBWA," management by walking around. By walking through a Lean facility, it is very easy to see what is happening on the shop floor. The one-piece-at-a-time product flow indicates the status of products as they move through manufacturing.

Everybody working on the Lean line knows what to do and when to do it. Supervision can often be decreased simply because of the Lean line layout.

Organization and discipline are important elements of the Lean working environment, and a Lean implementation supports the simultaneous implementation of the 5S principles. All material locations are clearly marked and maintained. Only the necessary tools, fixtures, gauges, and other resources are located at the workstations. Clutter and sloppiness are not tolerated on the Lean line. Because the Lean line is designed to follow the process flow of a product, reliance on the output of a shop floor control system to determine the location or progress of an order is greatly reduced or completely unnecessary.

Sequencing boards at the beginning of the line and some of the feeder processes clearly communicate the product mix to be built that day. At the end of the line, a linearity measurement is posted along with the production rate indicating how the line is performing that day. The kanban system indicates how fast material is turning and highlights potential shortages. At the end of the day, the IPKs and workstations reveal if the line was under- or overstaffed.

In the Lean factory, products are manufactured sequentially, accumulating work as they move progressively from workstation to workstation. The unit of measure being transferred between workstations is always one. Accumulation of semi-finished product between workstations is limited to the number of total workstations on the line. Piles of work-in-process inventory between departments cannot build up as there is no space to allow its accumulation. On most Lean lines, a variety of product configurations are being built at any point in time on the line.

Producing product on the Lean line does not require or advocate "chaining" an operator to a workstation or machine. To throttle the line up or down in response to daily customer requirements, people resources are intentionally added to or removed from the line. When the mixed-product Lean line does need to operate with less than a full complement of people, operators are required to move or "flex" from workstation to workstation to achieve the planned daily rate. Highly flexible and cross-trained operators are a key source of productivity in Lean manufacturing.

Because work has been balanced, operators are not required to rush through their work, but instead are encouraged to take the appropriate time to ensure that the units transferred to the next downstream workstation meet quality standards. Workmanship quality is greatly enhanced by allowing the time necessary to perform quality inspection work for every product at each workstation.

An intrinsic value for operators working on a Lean line is job satisfaction. Because of the requirement to flex with the flow of the product, operators receive an extensive amount of training in a variety of jobs. Operators are encouraged to participate in kaizen (continuous process improvement) activities, and their input and expertise in producing the product are actively sought. Improvements to the manufacturing process often result from their daily feedback to production management. The operators in a Lean factory are usually highly motivated and in many cases can be self-managed.

Productivity Improvement

The actual quantity of units produced by a team of people compared to the standard amount of time needed to produce those units is generally accepted as the measurement of a factory's productivity. While productivity improvement itself is not typically a stated goal of the Lean manufacturer, the methodologies of Lean manufacturing inherently cause process improvement to occur. Formal strategies, like kaizen, focus on the incremental reductions of wait time, queue time, and other nonvalue-adding activities. By eliminating wasteful time elements embedded in manufacturing processes, manufacturing operators are able to spend more of the working day producing products. Productivity improvement is an ancillary benefit of Lean manufacturing.

Operational Benefits

Using linked processes and the IPK system, the need for subassembly production planning can be virtually eliminated. Over time, multilevel BOMs can be dramatically compressed or flattened. Designed output variances can be managed by simply adding to or subtracting from the line's staffing level to match the required daily rate. The Lean manufacturer tends to drive production planning with a make-to-order production schedule. Actual customer orders drive the labor resources required in the production process each day.

As the Lean line matures, even cost accounting methods have an opportunity to be simplified as a result of the implementation of the Lean manufacturing methods. Because lead time through a Lean facility is consistent, repeatable, and not sensitive to volume changes, simpler activity-based costing methodologies can be implemented. Labor costs become elements included in overhead and applied proportionally to each product. Additional variable overhead costs may also be created to account for extraordinary conversion costs driven by the use of special machines or resources.

LEAN MANUFACTURING CHALLENGES TO THE MRP PARADIGM

Although Lean manufacturing and MRP systems seek to achieve the optimum utilization of resources, the approach each takes to achieve that goal is certainly different. Both methodologies rely on the same basic information set to make their resource allocation decisions. However, the techniques of Lean manufacturing force the manufacturer to re-evaluate its existing policies and procedures. This close self-examination challenges the manufacturer to rethink its performance measurements and definition of success.

Potentially changing the status quo can be a painful and scary experience. The impending new application of the existing data set can mean *change*! Often, personal careers have been built around the design and maintenance of existing systems. Loyal allegiance to historical methodology and the comfort level ingrained in users can result in reluctance or outright resistance to change.

The Lean manufacturing model is a superior model for operating the manufacturing facility. Manufacturers steadfastly loyal to their existing planning models while attempting to improve response time, reduce working capital costs, and improve quality risk yielding market share to those competitors that have made the transition to Lean manufacturing systems. Because the methodologies of Lean manufacturing use a simple reapplication of existing data, hard-core loyalty to the status quo is undeserved. Why, then, are manufacturers reluctant to rethink their approach to meeting the competitive challenges? Do not look to competitors for the answer.

The reason is usually the allegiance given to the existing planning system. Recall the MRP netting formula:

Gross Requirements – (On Hand + Scheduled Receipts) = Net Requirements

MRP is an order-based system. A calculation is performed at both the master schedule and MRP level. The Master Production Schedule (MPS)/MRP system then determines start dates, due dates, and quantities by the time phasing of requirements based on the lead times documented in the BOM. This process is commonly called an *explosion*. The net requirement created by the explosion process is recorded as an "order" in the system.

Based on the information in the item master, material can be either purchased from a supplier or manufactured in-house. The net requirements output of MRP is then separated into orders that must be purchased and orders that must be manufactured. "Make or buy" designations are usually the result of an extensive decision-making process. Typically, the order is presented to a planner in the form of a "recommended action." This is done on a part-by-part basis.

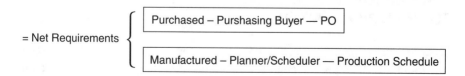

Purchased items are the responsibility of a buyer and manufactured items are the responsibility of a planner. The planner or buyer can then respond to the recommended action by (1) doing nothing; (2) changing the order by moving the due date in or out, increasing or decreasing the quantity; or (3) simply canceling the requirement.

This MRP activity is performed for each end-item product and for the parts residing in its BOM. The MRP explosion (time-phasing requirements × quantities on the BOM) is done on a predetermined time basis. There are two methods for doing this explosion process: (1) regenerative and (2) net change. Regardless of the method chosen, MRP recommended actions are created, so both planners and buyers must respond in one of the three ways to the suggested recommendations.

MRP systems also provide mechanisms for dealing with the orders once they have been issued to purchasing or to manufacturing. The purchasing department subsequently deals with the creation and maintenance of purchase orders. For manufacturing, a shop floor control (SFC) or a production activity control system is used to monitor and manage the manufacturing or "shop" orders created by the MRP system.

SFC systems are common in mature MRP manufacturing facilities. For every order generated by the MRP system for launch into manufacturing, the SFC system requires that a routing file be attached. The routing is then used to track the progress of the order through manufacturing. It also informs manufacturing as to the correct sequence of manufacture, department by department. In return, manufacturing must report the status of the order. It must record the quantity of material produced, the amount of labor used to complete the work, materials used, and scrap.

The amount of work required to use and maintain the routing file accurately can mean a large commitment to staff, including planners, schedulers, and expediters. Also, the industrial engineering resources needed to create and maintain the routings must be in place. Based on the structure of the routing file, the number of transactions necessary can be significant.

Once the SFC system has been turned on, several organization components soon come to depend on its output. Cost accounting uses the standard hour reporting features for its labor-reporting system. Engineering uses the labor reporting for the establishment of standard hours. Material management uses the tracking status to determine on-hand or scheduled receipts by department for the next explosion iteration. Schedules are established, present and future capacity requirements are derived, and performance measurements are created based on the output. Production management depends on the output of SFC information to develop future staffing requirements.

While that part of the MRP process that generates orders for purchasing is still required for Lean manufacturing, the output generated in the form of manufacturing orders for the operation of a Lean line is not. If manufacturing shop orders are not necessary, routings are not necessary. If routings are not required, all the ancillary systems that rely on the shop order and routing routines for their input become unsupported.

Lean manufacturing's nonreliance on the output of the MRP system for execution of a plan and the lack of dependency on the associated support systems create the majority of barriers for manufacturers when implementing their Lean manufacturing systems. The methodologies of Lean manufacturing are straightforward. Employees from the shop floor operator to manufacturing management are usually quick to embrace the technology. However, support organizations with their systems designed around maintaining the shop floor control see little benefit for themselves and are often the most difficult to convert. They may even see the implementation of the Lean methodologies as a threat to their organization.

THE CONTINUING EVOLUTION TO LEAN MANUFACTURING

Traditional MRP manufacturing methodology requires having sufficient raw material, work-in-process, and finished goods inventories in stock when an order is received. Planning and scheduling are forecast driven to deal with manufacturing lead times that exceed customer expectations for delivery. These forecast-driven schedules usually translate into large batch lots of products being routed through the manufacturing departments. Large batch sizes lead to increasing quantities of inventories across all categories as manufacturing resources get committed to forecast-driven demand in advance of actual demand.

Customer demands are increasing every day, and traditional manufacturing is always seeking better ways to answer these demands. During the last decade, many Fortune 100 companies embraced the Lean manufacturing strategies to help meet the demands of the new e-business economy. Increasing corporate mandates for increased profitability and lower working capital have management staffs constantly searching for ways to reduce manufacturing lead times, increase capacity, decrease cost, eliminate waste, and reduce working capital requirements.

Lean manufacturing today is a proven technique. Linking and balancing work steps to enable products to flow one at a time causes significant improvements to be made in the manufacturing process. Although products may vary in volume, type, and mix, the techniques always remain the same. Using a basic set of methodologies, Lean manufacturing lines can be created along with an optimum replenishment of material.

Over the years, manufacturers have been asked to understand and evaluate many new technologies. Among the latest are the Lean techniques. Because of the abundance of buzzwords, the plethora of terminology often causes more misunderstanding than the technology itself. This has been true with MRP/ERP and Lean. The two have often been represented as conflicting technologies when, if fact, they are complementary.

The MRP and Lean models are not mutually exclusive of one another! In fact, each has strengths that enhance the other. Working together in concert, MRP and Lean can make a formidable team. The key is exploiting the individual strengths of each system. The benefits to be gained from the marriage of these two technologies are more evident today than ever before.

The shared relationship between MRP and Lean is the basis for collaboration using the Lean manufacturing methodologies. Even for the Lean manufacturer, there is still no better methodology for projecting future requirements than the MRP techniques. Lean techniques, on the other hand, are the best for the allocation of machine, labor, and material resources and shop floor execution of demand requirements. MRP excels in planning requirements while Lean is a superior execution system.

ENTER THE INTERNET AND E-COMMERCE TECHNOLOGIES

During the last few years, new opportunities have emerged with the Internet and other e-commerce technologies. With their beginnings a radical premise, e-commerce technologies have emerged as the future of business-to-business transactions. E-commerce offers everything available to be purchased, from sophisticated components to low-tech commodity items, through the Internet, effecting efficiencies in processes, time, and costs. With many different business models still available to explore, the electronic revolution is upon the manufacturer. Whether characterized as an evolution or a revolution, the movement to business-to-business transactions through the Internet is here to stay. It is not going away.

It was only a couple of years ago that the whole notion of e-commerce began to take hold. The ability to connect businesses via the Internet and enable them to buy and sell goods and services among each other is an exciting concept. Real-time communication, elimination of the middleman, instant order processing, tightened inventories, and other efficiencies offer a company the opportunity to transform obsolete procedures and reduce costs.

Manufacturers have to consider the possibilities that exist with a global, on-line network of industry-specific marketplaces and application providers, where commerce is streamlined, automated, and nearly instantaneous, with access to vital data and essential services a few keystrokes away.

Certainly this e-commerce scenario is very tempting to the manufacturer looking to reduce costs. While quick to understand the potential benefits, there is a still a good deal of the usual confusion, speculation, hesitation, and misinformation surrounding the wholesale adoption of the e-commerce models. Many companies have quickly and successfully embraced the technologies and are enjoying the resulting benefits. Still others are wondering what it is, how it works, who is going to run it, why they should invest in it, and how it will ultimately affect their bottom line.

How does a manufacturer still grappling with the improvements needed to meet the corporate mandates for improved customer service and reduced working capital now add the challenges of the Internet and e-commerce to its already overflowing plate?

Because a high-speed Internet connection can transmit information at the speed of light, there must be a system in place to assure that information is as correct as possible. Lean methodologies are a platform to make these e-commerce transactions accurate and meaningful for the manufacturer. The Lean manufacturer will have balanced and linked manufacturing processes capable of producing products one at a time in their true manufacturing lead time. In addition, material kanban systems will generate material replenishment signals directly to the supplier based on real consumption rather than forecast. Electronic kanban transactions only require an extended pull sequence communicating electronically, outside the four walls of manufacturing, the demand from the customer through manufacturing back to the supplier (Figure 1.6).

Without this platform in place, what would the basis for transactions be? Would it be the MRP action item report transmitted at the speed of light only to be retransmitted with the next iteration of MRP? How many cycles of changed dates and quantities transmitted at the speed of light would it take for a supplier to pronounce the end of its participation in any e-commerce experiment?

Manufacturers should exercise caution and not get caught up in the buzzwords surrounding these technologies. Concentrate on the fundamental information transfer and methodologies that will best serve the goals of your company. Establish systems (both operational and electronic) that support these methodologies. Investigate and understand the Lean technologies and how your company can benefit from them. Learn how legacy MRP systems are still viable in this new environment and how MRP can work in concert with the Lean methods.

With the implementation of any system, electronic or otherwise, choose the one that best addresses company needs and provides sufficient return on invest-

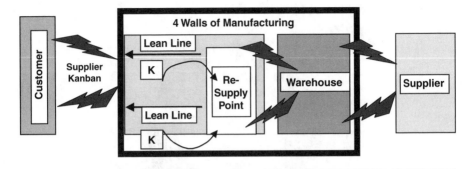

Figure 1.6 Extending Beyond the Four Walls of Manufacturing

ment for the effort. The successful new system will definitely alter the operating culture. Many times, the technology will be the easiest component of any implementation. Changing the culture is often the most difficult challenge.

WHY GO THROUGH THE PAIN OF CHANGE?

After a decade of conversions by all types of industries to Lean manufacturing, the benefits being realized by these companies are indisputable. For companies still deciding whether or not a new approach to manufacturing is necessary, the fact is, those companies may be in jeopardy of relinquishing whatever market share they hold today. Comfort, loyalty, and reliance on the old models of production to meet the increasing needs of the Internet-age customer will separate the marginal companies from the stars of their industry.

Change of this magnitude is not without cost. What are the costs to redesign my factory? What will my inventory investment be? How receptive to change is my workforce? How much training is necessary? How soon can I start to see the benefits? Without previous experience in company transformations, these questions are fearful and difficult to answer.

Once a decision to convert manufacturing to the Lean methodologies has been made, where to begin usually looms as the biggest question. Where does a company begin to change those years of comfort and loyalty to the tried-and-true methods? How are the organizations within the company going to be impacted? How will jobs change? What will the new culture look like? Will the MRP system be modified?

The answer is not installing some new software. Software is a tool. It does not make sense to buy software, install it, and proclaim to the world that you are now a Lean manufacturer. This would not only cause chaos inside your

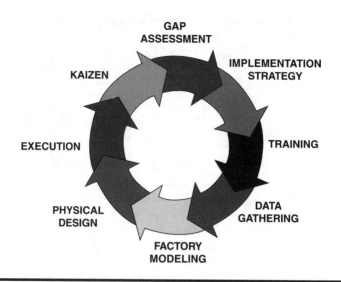

Figure 1.7 A Disciplined Approach

company, but that chaos would be magnified beyond the four walls of your company to your customers and suppliers.

The best place to start is in your own factory, first because this is where the money is and second because cleaning up your own backyard is always the first thing to do. Begin by understanding your products and manufacturing processes, their demand, and the real goals of response time, quality, and minimum working capital investment versus efficiency and utilization. Create a "critical mass" of employees who will champion the transformation in your company. The Lean implementation project will guide you to do this. This exercise can often reveal surprising introspection about your company.

The process of implementing Lean manufacturing in your company should be a methodical and disciplined approach (Figure 1.7). While the transformation process should proceed quickly, the pace of implementation must allow the organization and culture time to adapt to the changes being made. If it takes too much time, the high energy and enthusiasm will evaporate. If it is too fast, the organization cannot absorb the changes.

Optimization and modeling of resources offer a competitive advantage from the shop floor to the customer. These tools of the Lean manufacturing methodologies are mathematically based and will model the optimum manufacturing facility. Lean manufacturing can significantly trim lead time, often from weeks to days and from days to hours. Once manufacturing lead time is less than CQLT, the corporate mandate for productive and cost-effective manufacturing operations will be realized.

Change can be uncomfortable, but our competitors are unsympathetic to our pain. They are unwilling to wait for us to achieve our goals or to stand by as their market share erodes. As conscientious manufacturers determined to do everything possible to help make our companies as competitive as possible, the benefits of operating our factories as Lean facilities cannot be overlooked.

2

PERFORMING A STRATEGIC BUSINESS ANALYSIS

Any company that understands the benefits available to it by converting its manufacturing facility to Lean must also understand the fundamental changes Lean initiatives require of its core business processes. Achieving success through implementation of Lean manufacturing methodologies in manufacturing ultimately fosters changes throughout the entire company. Because of the company-wide impact, implementation of Lean manufacturing methodologies should never be started as a short-term project with a beginning and end date. A Lean implementation causes a company to always be in transition, undergoing continuous improvement.

The methodologies used to make the Lean transformation in a facility are straightforward and simple to understand, and Lean manufacturing implementation will improve the metrics of a company almost immediately after line start-up. The methodologies consist of basic mathematical equations that calculate ideal solutions for modeling the manufacturing shop floor and suggest optimum inventory levels. Once the initial implementation goals have been achieved, these changes should become the catalyst for continuous process improvements within a company. Oftentimes, these ideal solutions conflict with existing system recommendations, company policies, and departmental procedures.

Implementation of these methodologies is not merely an academic exercise. Considering the domino effect that can occur throughout the company, changing manufacturing operating systems should not be entered into lightly. The successful operation of the Lean manufacturing methodologies requires cultural change throughout the organization to occur. It is risky to go off to a seminar, return home, and begin a Lean implementation in the factory. Good managers must exercise their best decision-making skills before committing to the scope of change needed to implement the Lean manufacturing methodologies. Investing the time and energy to develop a strategic business analysis (SBA) is a good first step toward making the decision to move forward with Lean in your facility.

The purpose of performing an SBA is to quantify the potential financial benefits of a conversion to the Lean manufacturing methodologies. In addition to benefits, the SBA should also identify the potential organizational and cultural challenges that may be necessary. The SBA must identify and project the return on investment in real dollars to the Lean manufacturer. To justify the cost, any improvement initiative must provide a significant financial return on the investment of time, people, and capital that must be expended to make the transformation.

The Lean manufacturing methodologies project must be justified the same as any other project risk/reward investment decision is justified. The projected return must exceed the costs for the investment of work time by the team members participating in the implementation plus any costs that might be used for outside consulting services. Benefits should also offset the cost of anticipated factory rearrangement and training and the potential costs of new racks, fixtures, bins, and labels required for installation of a kanban system. A thorough review of the potential impact on the organization must be studied. Gaining maximum benefit from any system can only be realized with the implementation of all of its components. Compromise reduces potential benefits. The level of improvement achieved is in direct proportion to the amount of compromise made.

If the return on investment cannot be quantified in dollars, justification for an implementation must then rely on intangibles. Some of these intangible benefits include the value of providing quicker response times than the competition, which aids in increasing market share, the reduction of workmanship quality issues, and the potential reduction in the number of operating shifts, management time, and the overhead costs resulting from productivity gains. Among the most important are the value of "management by walking around," ease of production supervision, facilitation of self-directed work teams, elimination of reliance on complex legacy systems, fewer electronic transactions, implementation of 5S, a platform for continuous process improvement (kaizen), improved employee morale, increased quality of life, and higher job satisfaction.

Every company must determine on its own if the costs justify the effort required to complete an implementation. Working with the Lean champion, the internal project leader who completes the SBA must make his or her best effort to quantify these benefits so the manufacturer can make an informed comparison of benefits it can expect to realize with the anticipated cost of the conversion to Lean.

While the Lean champion and project leader may be enthusiastic to complete a Lean implementation in their facility, the temptation to overstate potential benefits simply to justify the project should be avoided. If the SBA is used only as a lever to start a long-anticipated project or fulfill some other agenda, and the results ultimately do not meet expectations, the project may be considered a failure. The estimates of benefits outlined in the SBA will always be used as the baseline for the final performance evaluation of the implementation. When projected benefits exceed what an implementation can realistically deliver, the SBA becomes the scorecard for success or failure. In most companies, the consequences of a failed project include rejection of that project ever being attempted again.

Artificial inflation of benefits is a disservice to the company and can damage the career of the project manager and Lean champion. It is better to conservatively estimate benefits and overperform rather than overestimate benefits and underperform. The good news is that implementations of the Lean manufacturing methodologies typically yield benefits that easily exceed company expectations, so the need to inflate benefits is unnecessary.

Strict adherence to Lean manufacturing methodologies will deliver the greatest benefits. However, typical implementations are characterized by compromise. Often, a contentious mandated compromise might negatively impact projected benefits. When the project is completed, manufacturers tend to forget about requested compromises made in the heat of battle. It is the responsibility of the project manager and Lean champion to explain, educate, reconcile differences, and document the impact of any compromises to the projected benefits stated in the SBA.

The resource requirements necessary to complete the SBA vary. Based on the size of the facility, the SBA requires the efforts of one or two people, over a duration of several days. The SBA activity should not be rushed and consists of gathering both quantitative and qualitative information about the company. This information is gathered through interviews with persons who have the best knowledge on the subject for which benefits will be estimated. In addition to the quantitative information gathered for the SBA, other more subjective information should also be gathered about manufacturing and the organization in general. For instance, what are the current political issues in the organization, ongoing power struggles, level of dedication to projects, readiness and willingness to make changes, and who is *really* in charge?

The best efforts of the project manager and the Lean sponsor are required to achieve optimum results from any implementation; they will always be held responsible for the success or failure of an implementation. The SBA should be approached with extreme thoroughness and due diligence. It is extremely important to learn the motivation, dedication, and commitment to completing the project.

Often, the desire to change is championed by one or more enthusiastic persons in the organization. Regardless of their position in the company, successful implementation requires the input and coordination of the entire company. If the organization itself is not prepared to make the changes necessary, the implementation goals can be difficult to achieve. Resistance to change will likely manifest itself in subversion, withholding of information, lack of cooperation, and even outright hostility.

STRATEGIC BUSINESS ANALYSIS CHECKLIST

"Ready, Willing, and Able to Change" Assessment

The idea of the "ready, willing, and able to change" assessment is not to discourage an implementation. Resistance to change exists in even the most progressive organizations. The assessment should be used to evaluate the comfort level of the organization to eventually accept any recommended changes and to gauge its understanding of the significant effort required to make these changes.

If the readiness assessment determines the acceptance of change is low, additional education and training efforts may be required. This additional time required to complete additional education and training may extend the project time frame. Conversely, a company with a progressive culture used to change might require less education and training. This could accelerate the implementation time frame.

Unfortunately, the levels of readiness, willingness, and ability to change are very subjective measures. Responses cannot be extracted with duress. The difficulty of ascertaining this intangible information does not excuse the need to do so. The responsibility for assuring an accurate assessment of readiness relies on the skill and ability of the individual project manager as he or she gathers information through the interview process.

Application of the following general techniques can often help uncover critical issues within the company:

- Describe your view of how your day-to-day activities will be different when this project is successfully completed.

- Explain why this project is paramount to the organization.
- What are some of the major challenges project participants are facing in their individual jobs? How does this project relate to these daily tasks?

To discover even more detail, listed below are a series of specific interview questions to help determine if a manufacturer is "ready, willing, and able" to make the changes necessary to transform to a Lean manufacturing facility.

The persons being interviewed by the Lean champion or project leader are referred to as clients. Client is an accurate term to describe the relationship of the project leader or champion with the ultimate users of the Lean manufacturing system.

Overall Motivation and Drive

- What is the motivation for this project? Is the client enthusiastic? Passive?
- What kind of resistance is there to this project? Does the motivation seem to be different in different groups within the total organization?
- What is the client's view of the possible gains?
- Who wants change to take place? Who is against change? Who doesn't care?
- Does the project address a goal everyone says is important, but on which people seem reluctant to work?
- Are there any other motivational issues?

Resource Allocation and Commitment Level

- What is the client's view of the time, energy, and internal support that will be required to carry out the project?
- Does the client expect to participate in the work? Is the client ready to do his or her part?
- Are other resources required (i.e., labor or machines from other departments, etc.)? If so, have they been secured?
- Is it clear what the budget will be? Does the client's view of an appropriate budget match the consultant's view?
- Are there any other resource issues?

Climate for Change

- What kind of pressure for change exists in the client organization? What are the sources of such pressure?

- Where does the project fit in the client's hierarchy of concerns? Is it a top-priority issue or just something the client organizations feels it needs to deal with?
- Will the organization's climate support the kind of changes the project requires?
- Are there any other climate issues?

Client's Flexibility and Change Management Skills

- What is the client's capacity to implement innovative solutions? What do recent experiences suggest about the client's ability to carry out the changes the project will require?
- Does the client have firsthand experience or prior knowledge about the project?
- Are there any other knowledge and skill issues?

Client's View of Project Manager or Lean Champion

- Does the client have recent experience with other projects? How did they work out?
- How does the client feel about these recent project experiences? What can be learned from them that will strengthen this project?
- What is the client's overall attitude toward the individuals who will be working on the pending project?
- Are there any other client–project management relationship issues?

Client Understanding of the Project

- Has the client clearly defined expected project outcomes? What will the measures of success be?
- Does the client understand the implications of the project for the entire organization?
- Who is going to use the results, and how? Do the key players understand this?
- Are there any other client understanding issues?

Scope and Pace of the Project

- How quickly must the client see some tangible results? What kind of results?

- What is the client's view of the appropriate scope and pace of the project? How big a project seems right to the client? What sort of pace does the client wish to pursue?
- Are there any other scope and pace issues?

Other Success Factors

- Are there certain solutions that will be unacceptable in the client organization?
- Do the client and consultant have a shared understanding of the terminology describing the project?
- Are there any other issues not yet addressed?

Historical Perspective

- How did the current need evolve? How long has the client been aware of the need?
- How has the client attempted to deal with the need until now? What has failed to work?
- How did the idea of starting a special implementation project arise?

IMPORTANT PERFORMANCE METRICS FOR THE SBA

Lean manufacturing methodologies focus on producing a product as close to its actual work content times as possible, greatly reducing or eliminating as much nonvalue-adding time as possible. Lean manufacturers understand that the customer-quoted lead time consists of actual work content time and time that adds no value to the finished product. All additional time in excess of the work content time is considered to be "nonvalue-added" time. The size of the opportunity is, therefore, based on the difference between work content time and customer-quoted manufacturing lead time. The current-state analysis is very effective in identifying the size of this gap.

Eliminating this time gap is, more often than not, why most companies undertake Lean initiatives. They see the value of being able to deliver their product in a much shorter time than their competitors. A shorter lead time provides a major differentiator from their competitors. Customers continue to demand a quicker response time from order placement to order shipment. This differentiation becomes a significant sales tool in a highly competitive marketplace (Figure 2.1).

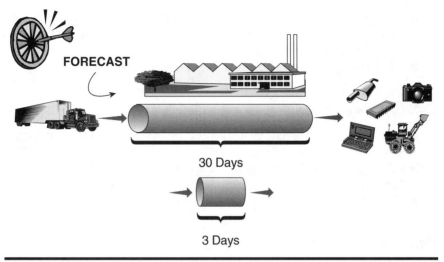

Figure 2.1 The Work Content Time Gap

Accomplishment of a reduced lead time that approaches the actual work content time becomes the basis for the other benefits sought by Lean manufacturers. By applying the tools, techniques, and methodologies of the Lean manufacturing methodologies, the future-state vision can be realized. All benefits documented in the SBA are based on the degree to which the nonvalue-added work in the quoted lead time can be reduced or eliminated.

This time gap also represents a significant inventory and working capital investment. It is then logical to assume that if the lead time is reduced, the amount of additional inventories should be reduced. Many companies are using manufacturing methods today that may be in direct conflict with the goals of reduced lead time with minimum inventories. If this is the case, the cost of maintaining existing policies and manufacturing practices must be documented in the SBA.

Current manufacturing models often cause lead time to be greater than the customer's required lead time. Rather than change the model itself, many manufacturers have concentrated on developing other solutions in an attempt to satisfy their customers' expectation. For example:

1. Tell the customer to wait the duration of manufacturing lead time offset. If a competitor can fulfill the order more quickly, the manufacturer will likely lose the business.
2. Respond by shipping products from a finished goods inventory (FGI). This works well if products are generic. However, if the product(s) are

configured or designed to order, FGI is an expensive solution, as a forecast of future demand must be made. If the forecasted demand is not sold by exact model type or during the projected period, excess inventory results.

3. A third solution is to create a partially completed work-in-process (WIP) inventory of assemblies or subassemblies that could be quickly assembled in a shorter lead time.

Supplier delivery lead times typically dictate the quantities of purchased materials necessary be kept on hand in inventory to support the desired demand flexibility. Regardless of the solution chosen to manage inventory and quoted lead times, the upstream purchasing process will also impact the overall inventory strategy. Choosing any of these solutions requires strategic inventory investment decisions to be made. What is the ideal amount of inventory?

Inventory levels are typically determined by forecasting the quantities of WIP or FGI to be held as a customer response solution. In all cases, a forecast must be used to order materials from suppliers since *no* customer is likely to wait both the supplier lead time plus manufacturing lead time.

Inventory levels can become tremendously large and costly. When this happens, the inaccuracy of the forecast is usually blamed as the cause of the problem. Manufacturing companies have spent many years and many millions of dollars trying to predict the future with sophisticated forecasting systems. Forecasts will never be right. If they are not successful at forecasting with today's technologies, there is no reason to believe they ever will be.

The following example illustrates potential financial benefits to be gained by applying the Lean manufacturing methodologies. This example shows how bloated inventory levels can be reduced. This sample analysis is based on firsthand experience derived from client interviews.

- If a company has annual sales of $150 million and its profit before taxes is 20%, the resulting cost of goods sold would be $120 million.
- Historical ratio of product cost distribution (Figure 2.2):
  - Average material cost = 60%
  - Average overhead cost = 30%
  - Average labor cost = 10%
- Applying these historical percentages to the $120 million cost of goods sold yields the following annual cost allocations:
  - Material = $72 million
  - Overhead = $36 million
  - Labor = $12 million (assume 400 direct labor employees paid $30,000 per year)

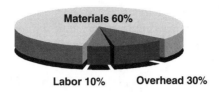

Figure 2.2   Components of Product Cost

- Based on an annual material cost of $72 million, a single day's worth of inventory = $197,260 ($72 million ÷ 365 days)

To reduce product costs, companies try many different tactics. These three components of product cost are the usual targets of such cost-cutting measures. These tactics often manifest themselves as "programs" or special "projects." Purchasing programs consist of buying cheaper material or getting price concessions from suppliers. Overhead is reduced by cutting power consumption, canceling training, reducing new equipment expenditures, reducing travel, etc. Some companies choose to pay their people less, go offshore, or lay off employees.

RESULTS OF PRODUCTIVITY IMPROVEMENT PROGRAMS

A common strategy for reducing product costs is the implementation of a "productivity improvement" program. Many companies initiate aggressive productivity improvement programs. Usually, there are no specific recommendations, and individual production managers are left to their own resourcefulness to achieve their productivity gains. Productivity on the shop floor will often take the path of longer production runs with fewer changeovers. This strategy risks the creation of excess inventory and parts shortages as purchased material is pulled forward from the MRP delivery schedule. In any event, inventory management is the responsibility of the materials group and is an objective in conflict with productivity improvement. Material shortages can also be used as a convenient excuse should productivity goals not be met.

Posters are hung throughout the plant, pep talks are given at staff meetings, a suggestion program is implemented, and a new paced line conveyor is installed. After a slow start-up, employees are soon convinced, cajoled, and threatened to work harder. They eventually achieve a 15% (a very optimistic) productivity gain.

Soon thereafter, the workforce is reduced by 15% through a layoff:

Productivity-Based Savings = $1,800,000 = 400 × 15% × $30,000

What are the trade-offs for achieving these gains? What was the impact on inventories? How has employee morale been affected? Was workmanship quality sacrificed in return for volume output? How much management time was invested to manage the smallest component of product cost? Are productivity improvement programs really the best solution for product cost reduction?

The Lean manufacturing methodologies suggest there is a better alternative to the draconian cost reduction programs traditional manufacturing models practice. Instead, what are the opportunities for cost reduction if the largest single component of product costs, inventories, could be reduced?

Contrary to typical inventory reduction programs that focus on supplier-purchased inventories, the Lean manufacturing methodologies target WIP and FGI. Lean methodologies might even suggest that raw material inventories remain unchanged or even increase in a trade for maximum flexibility in meeting daily customer demand for configured products!

Therefore, the first activity to be completed during the SBA is to quantify the inventory reduction opportunity to determine the difference between the manufacturing lead time and the actual work content time for those products to be included in the Lean implementation area. From this information, the potential inventory reduction opportunity can be estimated.

Assume one day's worth of both WIP and FGI is required to support one day of manufacturing lead time.

Current Manufacturing Conditions

Manufacturing lead time	=	30 days
Customer lead time demand	=	5 days
Wall-to-wall inventory turns	=	6
(On-hand inventory [average] at	=	$72 million ÷ $12 million
cost of goods sold, average days		
of purchased inventory)		

and the average days of purchased inventory (no labor build costs) by category is:

Current Distribution Value of Purchased Inventories

		Days	Value	
Purchased	=	30	$5,917,800	($197,260 × 30 days)
WIP	=	21	$4,109,600	($197,260 × 21 days)
FGI	=	10	$1,972,600	($197,260 × 10 days)
			$12,000,000	Average days of purchased inventory

Using a diagram of the process flow and the *actual* work content of each of the processes, sum the actual total work time of the product. This actual time required to move through the processes represents the Lean value-added response time of the product. Convert this time to days of lead time. Subtract this number from the current quoted manufacturing lead time. Multiply this difference by the cost of one day's inventory ($197,260).

After the Implementation of the Lean Manufacturing Methodologies

Lean value-added response time = 3 days
Customer-expected lead time   = 5 days
Assume zero gain in productivity (unlikely, but conservative)*

New Distribution of Purchased Inventory
After Implementation of the Lean Manufacturing Methodologies

		Days	Value	Savings
Purchased	=	30	$5,917,800	None initially**
WIP	=	5	$986,300	$3,123,300
FGI	=	5	$986,300	$986,300
			$7,890,400	$4,109,600

Lean manufacturing methodologies   = $4,109,600
one-time inventory savings

Lean manufacturing methodologies   = Increase 33% to 9
new turn rate

Annual savings in cost to carry at 20% = $820,000

This resulting amount would represent the inventory reduction opportunity. The actual work time then becomes the response time goal. The more gap time eliminated, the greater the inventory reduction opportunity.

It still takes management time to implement the Lean manufacturing methodologies. However, the return on that management time investment yields a greater return than pursuing purchasing cost reductions or productivity improvement programs. With ongoing kaizen and continuous improvement activity, these improvements and savings are just the beginning.

---

* Productivity improvement is common with a Lean manufacturing methodologies implementation, but difficult to project quantitatively during the SBA. The best conservative approach is to project no benefit unless it can be quantified.

** Until a supplier certification program can be completed, Lean manufacturing methodologies suggest that purchased material inventories cannot be impacted. Purchased material inventories can be gradually reduced over time as more suppliers are certified.

IMPACT OF MANUFACTURING LEAD TIME ON WORKING CAPITAL

A large yet frequently untapped source of savings is the reduction of the working capital required to run the business. By simply improving response through manufacturing, working capital requirements can be minimized. Far less money would be invested in inventory, and the shorter lead time response to customers would provide a tremendous competitive advantage.

The disadvantages of high inventory levels also impact overhead costs. These inventories require space on the shop floor, in warehouses, and in distribution centers. This space is not free and adds to the overhead cost of doing business. Inventory must be counted, moved, and taxed. Funds consumed by inventories are unavailable for alternative investments, so opportunity is lost. The financial implications of high inventories are simple to determine:

INVENTORIES = CASH!

As part of the SBA, consider how working capital is impacted by manufacturing lead time and on-hand inventory. The following example illustrates a likely scenario:

Recall that product cost is comprised of three components: material, labor, and overhead. Generally, material is the largest portion of product cost. Common product cost ratios are 60% material, 30+% overhead, and <10% direct labor (see Figure 2.2).

The purchased material element of product cost requires a large amount of cash to be committed for at least the manufacturing lead time. If quoted manufacturing lead time is four weeks but the lead time required by the customer is two weeks, FGI might be a strategy used to close the gap between customer lead time and manufacturing lead time. This strategy would require at least two or more additional weeks of purchased material to be tied up in FGI. This is not to mention the absorbed labor and overhead costs of partially completed WIP and fully completed FGIs.

With a four-week manufacturing lead time, a minimum of four weeks of purchased material would be tied up in WIP at any given time. There may also be purchased inventory totaling four weeks in stores because of supplier-mandated lead time.

The amount of cash invested in purchased inventory can be calculated using the following example. Substitute the numbers from the facility being evaluated.

■ Although cash-poor companies often play games with payment terms, most suppliers expect to be paid in 30 days (net 30).

■ Because of mandated supplier lead time, purchased materials are typically paid for and waiting in the stockroom before work in manufacturing begins. If the manufacturing conversion takes four weeks, this means cash is also tied up for four weeks.

■ If FGI levels are three to four weeks, then more cash is tied up for an additional three to four weeks.

■ When manufacturing is completed, products can then be shipped to satisfy customer orders. Customers can be billed at this point. Is payment always immediate? Typical accounts receivables are 45 to 50 days. More cash is tied up even longer!

At this point, the manufacturer's cash has now been invested for at least 12 to 13 weeks!

Working capital investment can be calculated by valuing purchased material plus WIP plus FGI + accounts receivable minus money owed for the materials (accounts payable):

Raw	4 weeks
In process	4 weeks
Finished goods	4 weeks
PLUS	
Accounts receivable	4 weeks
Inventory pipeline	16 weeks
MINUS	
Accounts payable	4 weeks
Working capital	12 weeks

In this lead time example, the company would have working capital turns of 4.3 (52 weeks ÷ 12 weeks in inventory). Simply stated, 25 cents of every dollar of shipped revenue must be committed to maintaining working capital requirements. Working capital requirements can cause a significant cash flow problem for any company. Companies often fail due to a lack of cash!

When manufacturing lead time is shortened, response time through manufacturing is significantly improved. The corresponding working capital reduction begins at this point. This transfer of inventory assets into cash assets increases the company's liquidity. The newly available cash can then be invested in other priorities such as new market development, capital equipment expenditure, and new plant and facilities or just added to the bottom line.

The good news is that this working capital savings is more than a one-time improvement. Resulting inventories can now be managed at significantly lower levels, eliminating overhead and inventory carrying costs, which can represent another ±20% of the value of the inventory.

The production of products using Lean manufacturing methodologies also improves productivity and workmanship quality. These may also be quantified and calculated into the final return-on-investment estimate.

THE SBA SUGGESTED INTERVIEW LIST

Representatives from the functional areas listed below should be interviewed as part of the SBA. The purpose of these interviews at this stage is to evaluate the desired benefits, the company's degree of readiness, and potential implementation obstacles and to gather the information necessary to estimate the return on investment for the implementation.

- Corporate management
  - Finance
  - Engineering
    - Manufacturing
    - Design
    - Industrial
  - Quality
  - Materials
    - Purchasing
    - Planning
  - Line managers and supervisors
  - Sales
    - Marketing
    - Order entry

PART II:
THE METHODOLOGIES
FOR TRANSFORMING
YOUR FACILITY TO
LEAN MANUFACTURING

3

UNDERSTANDING YOUR PRODUCTS, PROCESSES, AND DEMAND

DETERMINING THE SCOPE OF THE INITIAL LEAN MANUFACTURING IMPLEMENTATION AREA

A Lean manufacturing implementation should be like a good novel — long enough to cover the subject, but short enough to be interesting. A project with a manageable scope of work for the initial Lean implementation must be defined. There are several reasons for this:

1. Team members assigned to participate in the implementation project are rarely individual contributors who have no other responsibilities. Team members are typically drafted from the existing staff pool and are also responsible for routine day-to-day responsibilities. If project responsibilities become too demanding, daily priority decisions will always default to primary activities (where job performance is measured). As a team leader, it is difficult to argue with team members who can stall project activities by claiming dedication to their primary job responsibilities.

2. The project must be large enough to generate a sufficient return on the investment of time, funds, and the human resources required to make the transformation. Much of this decision depends on the size of the facility.

A smaller facility may be able to absorb a "wall-to-wall" implementation without overwhelming the staff assigned to perform the implementation. Conversely, larger facilities may require multiple implementations.

3. Determining the ideal project size must be based on a consideration of the benefits identified during the strategic benefits assessment. The size of an implementation necessary to yield sufficient benefits to justify the implementation project may require an increase in its scope. The scoping of a project is a subjective process, but a practical "rule-of-thumb" guideline is 25 products and no more than 50 processes. There may be temptation to increase the scope to achieve benefits. Caution should be exercised to assure equilibrium between return on investment and resource requirements when making these decisions. If the benefits require an inordinate amount of staff time and effort to achieve, it is possible that an implementation cannot be justified on the return of financial benefits alone. Should this be the case, more difficult to quantify but less tangible benefits such as the ability to practice "management by walking around," safety and ergonomic improvements, and enhanced employee satisfaction may be used as justification.

4. The project that never ends will eventually exhaust the energy of the implementation teams. It is easy to become excited during the early stages of any implementation project, including the commitment to implement Lean manufacturing. Teams attend meetings with free lunches, go to pep rallies, and receive recognition rewards, and the company feels a general excitement throughout. The team members are in the spotlight during this time. It can be a heady time! Eventually, the hoopla will die down, and the realities of data collection will begin. The grind of responsibility, along with the pressures of swift decision making, can bear down on them. Team members may start to re-evaluate their commitment to the project. As the project proceeds, day-to-day activities can exact the higher priority while implementation project activities are relegated to the bottom of the in-box. Therefore, the time allocated to perform the implementation should be relatively quick. Each company is different, and each has its own sensitivity to change. Depending on the defined scope, and an individual company's resistance to change, implementations should be targeted for completion in 30 to 40 days. Projects lasting longer than six months may require new or recurring justification, along with renewing enthusiasm for participating team members. Manufacturing operations are dynamic environments. Both opportunities and challenges in manufacturing are frequent and common. It is not fair to team members to restrict their participation in the operation of their company to one project. If limited to a solitary project, resistance will manifest itself in missed

due dates and a general lack of interest. A sense of drudgery must not be allowed to develop during the project. Enthusiasm generated during the project must carry over into the day-to-day operation of the system.

SELECTING PARENT PARTS FOR THE LEAN LINE

One of the first decisions to be made when initiating the Lean manufacturing implementation is choosing the products (stockkeeping unit, end-item, and finished goods inventory level) to be produced on the Lean manufacturing line. Determining the parent products to be manufactured is critical, as the implementation teams need to know which manufacturing processes and materials are required to produce those products.

Manufacturers typically offer customers numerous options for their products. These combinations of products and options often result in the proliferation of product offerings, each with an individual end-item part number. The first review of total product offerings could indicate hundreds or even thousands of products available. Manufacturers often claim that the ability to highly configure their products is what makes them "unique," differentiating them from their competitors. When selecting products for the Lean line implementation using the 25-product guideline as a basis, how does the manufacturer with hundreds or thousands of unique products scope its project so it fits into the range of a manageable project?

The answer is that it is not necessary to include all products and their permutations into the final Lean line design. To achieve a manageable number of products, a condensed listing of products can be selected from the total listing. Careful consideration must be given to which products are ultimately chosen to be included in the Lean manufacturing line design process, as they must be representative of all products produced.

Figure 3.1 shows a configured parent part number for a cold beverage vending machine. Looking at this lengthy part number with the potential amount of available options, it is easy to conclude that the number of permutations could be endless. It is likely that this company has sold many of those permutations over the years.

However, a representative group of products can be selected from even this potentially long list of products. Two important techniques are used to condense a long list of parent products to a short list that can represent the total product population for the Lean manufacturing line design.

Perform a Pareto analysis based on historical sales of these products. Vilfredo Pareto, an Italian economist, observed that a small fraction (typically 15 to 20%) of participants in a population accounts for the major portion of activity (80 to

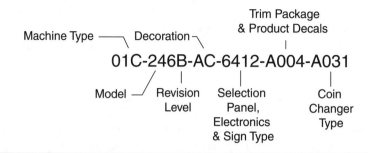

Figure 3.1 Configured Parent Part Number

85%). This law is also known as the 80/20 rule. Application of this rule when selecting product candidates for the design of a Lean manufacturing line often provides an eye-opening perspective on your products' distribution. This sorting can be done using a spreadsheet program by selecting the "sort ascending" command for the historical sales volume. Sum down the parent products until 80% of the total volume has been reached. Based on Pareto's observation, 80% of the sales volume will consist of only 20% of the total available stockkeeping units. Conversely, the other 80% of the available stockkeeping units represents only 20% of the sales volume (Figure 3.2).

For the purposes of the Lean manufacturing methodologies, a product is nothing more than a combination of its labor content and its parts. With this in mind, for each product ultimately chosen as a candidate for the Lean line, it will

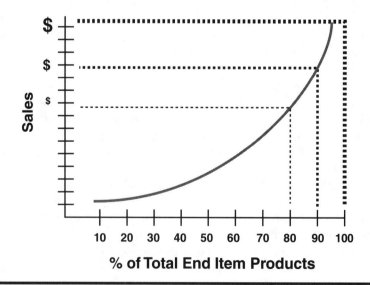

Figure 3.2 Sales Demand versus Product Mix

be necessary to document the processes where labor occurs for that product. It is critical that the final listing of products chosen to represent all products for the Lean manufacturing line include all manufacturing processes for all products. Once selected, the list must be reviewed one by one, to confirm that products identified by the Pareto analysis include all processes. An exception must be made for low-volume products where special manufacturing processes are used only occasionally. In this case, a parent product part using these processes must be added to the Lean line design part number population. It is critical that *all* processes be captured and represented in the parent product population.

The selection process for products to be included in the Lean manufacturing line population should not take into consideration production materials at this time. The focus should be on the identification of *processes* only. The purpose of selecting representative parent part numbers for line design is to make certain that all points where labor occurs are identified. Later, the material kanban system will address the materials component of a product.

The early series of numbers in a configured parent part number typically reflect the manufacturing processes, while the trailing series of numbers reflect the *parts* differences. Using these common part number conventions can help establish a parent population for line design. Using the vending machine part number as an example, Figure 3.3 illustrates that:

- The machine type "01C" designates this as a can-dispensing machine. The customer could choose a bottle-dispensing machine with a "02C" designation. Regardless of customer preference, these two choices indicate which processes are necessary to produce either the bottle or the can machine.
- The same can be said of the model designation, "246." All manufacturing processes required to produce a model 246 in can or bottle configuration are identified.
- It is possible that the revision level may indicate other processes are to be included or excluded.

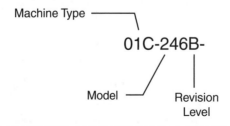

Figure 3.3 Configured Part Number for Processes

If this is the case with your configured products, parent part numbers can easily be designated by the series of numbers that identify the manufacturing processes only (e.g., 01C-246B, 02C-246B, and so on).

The balance of the parent part number configuration begins to define component part options. Product options require labor to build subassemblies. The locations where subassemblies are manufactured are called feeder processes. The feeder processes represent a required option to be manufactured and attached to the main assembly. While the parts consumed in these feeder locations are the real source of product permutation, the labor is universal.

A required option requires a selection to be made, but allows a variety of parts to be selected. In this case, each vending machine requires a trim package, but the trim package selected can consist of a wide variety of parts. The parts are optional, but the labor content is not. When optional parts can be selected, model permutation expands. Even though the number of models may vary widely, the number of actual manufacturing processes to produce these different models remains relatively static. Figure 3.4 illustrates that:

- The decoration designation indicates the color of paint. "AC" means red, "BC" means blue, "AW" indicates white, etc. The part number for the paint may change, but the process "Paint" does not. In this case, all machines must be painted. The labor time to paint a red machine and a white machine is the same.
- Greater variety can occur deeper into the configured part number. Each vending machine requires that a selection panel be installed. The customer can select a six-push-button machine or an eight-push-button machine. Parent part number configurations must change to reflect the customer's choice. Two separate selection panel parts are necessary to

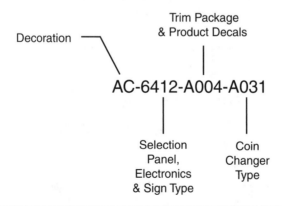

Figure 3.4 Configuration for Subassembly and Parts

satisfy the customer's choice. However, the labor content to install either a six- or eight-button panel remains the same. The process is likely called "Selection Panel Assembly." Whether a six- or eight-button selection panel part number is used makes little difference to the manufacturing process.

■ Where a product option requires additional labor, process, or separate physical location to be used (e.g., where a subassembly process is required to manufacture the option), the parent number representing that product option should be included in the part number population to identify the additional process. The individual parts used to produce the specific model do not need to be considered at this time.

If the total number of parent part numbers is small enough, the 80/20 reduction of the parent parts list as described above is unnecessary. In some cases, parent part number consolidation is obvious and the Pareto process may be unnecessary. However, for most manufacturers with a lengthy list of end-item products, applying these two techniques will help identify a condensed selection of parent part numbers that can be used for designing their Lean manufacturing line. This condensed list serves two purposes:

1. Correctly represents all the processes used to produce all the products required to meet potential customer demand. From this process identification, all locations where labor is required to produce products are identified.
2. Scopes the implementation project to a manageable project size while still assuring a sufficient return on investment for the Lean implementation.

ESTABLISHING THE CAPACITY TO MEET THE DEMAND VOLUME OF THE LEAN IMPLEMENTATION AREA

Once the decision has been made as to "what" products are to be manufactured on the Lean line, the "how many," or demand, required for each of the selected products must also be established. Quantity of demand is important, because it determines both the capacity of the Lean line and the amount of resources required to produce that demand.

Lean methodology recommends that the new Lean manufacturing line be designed with capacity sufficient to produce a level of demand greater than today's current demand. A Lean manufacturing line should be designed with the capacity to support demand one to three years in the future. It will be the responsibility of the materials team to make this future demand projection. This is often easier said than done. Many variables affect future projections of demand, and having to make that projection is often uncomfortable. Before the Lean implementation can proceed, the projection of demand must be made.

A product's expected life cycle, the volatility of technology in the industry, and the anticipated growth of market share contribute to complicate these projections. Looking into the future and plotting projected demand on a graph, the lower the slope of expected product demand, the higher the confidence in the projection of that demand. Conversely, the steeper the slope, the less confidence in the projection's accuracy.

Because of this need to project future sales and with the knowledge that the projection will be used to design the capacity of the factory, there is often much trepidation on the part of the team members whose assignment is to make the projection. Achieving consensus of future demand is one of the most difficult tasks to complete during any implementation. After several iterations in volume and mix have been tried, the Lean implementation methodology requires that the final projected demand, demand at full capacity, be authorized and signed off on by the steering committee before proceeding with the final Lean line design.

SOURCES FOR DETERMINING DEMAND

History

An obvious place to start is to use the same demand used for the Pareto analysis when establishing parent part numbers for the Lean line. This sorting of historical demand of all products has already yielded the top ±20% of products that make up ±80% of the sales revenue. From that list, further extrapolation of product knowledge can suggest a modified list of products that better represent all manufacturing processes necessary to produce all products. Because this is possible, the material team is responsible for both product definition and volume at capacity for products chosen for the Lean line design.

Deriving demand from this list of products should be straightforward. Fortunately, recorded history is not subject to interpretation. The product either was sold or it wasn't. While the quantity per model sold before today might be surprising, the fact that it was sold is indisputable. However, can the demand from historical sales guarantee the demand to be used to design the Lean manufacturing line? History alone may not be the best predictor of future demand. Other conditions may have an impact on historical sales. The following considerations can also help to identify the best level of demand for the Lean implementation.

Intuitive Knowledge

This type of knowledge is often referred to as "gut feeling" or "tribal knowledge." This is information that cannot be substantiated with fact, but instead is based on instinct. The manufacturing group is often the best source of this information. During the course of production, manufacturing can often spot trends in product demand based on the quantities running down its lines before sales and marketing see them. The group may also have visibility of requests for service and spare parts, potentially indicating a shift in customer preference from one model to another.

Intuitive knowledge alone should not be used to project the demand used for design of the Lean manufacturing line, but it should also not be discounted. When making the projection of future demand, input of intuitive knowledge should be solicited from those who have it. This knowledge could provide "eye-opening" information to the team member responsible for establishing future line design volumes.

For most users of MRP systems, forecast responsibility typically falls to the sales and marketing groups. Sometimes, because it is so good at tribal knowledge, manufacturing may have been assigned the responsibility for making production forecasts. When this is the case, manufacturing typically performs this duty by default simply because someone has to establish a production schedule. To establish a production schedule, future demand must also be established.

If manufacturing has to forecast what it will make, it must rely on the only tools at its disposal, history and tribal knowledge. Unfortunately, history and intuitive knowledge have limited visibility into the future. Manufacturing is seldom included in sales and marketing discussions and most likely has little knowledge of future marketing programs or expected shifts in the marketplace that can impact future demand. Even though information is very limited, manufacturing can still be quite accurate. Making manufacturing responsible for forecasting future demand is an abdication of sales and marketing responsibilities.

Forecast

Forecasts and forecasting are often the brunt of many jokes and provide a convenient excuse for missing performance goals. The truth is, no forecast will ever be 100% accurate. If it were possible to accurately predict the future, forecasters would be in a more lucrative line of business than predicting future sales. At the very least they would be paid the going "market rate" for the ability to predict the future. With all the forecasting tools and computer modeling programs available to manufacturers today, the science of forecasting is likely as good as it is ever going to be.

Those responsible for making forecasts are not wrong intentionally and do not like being the brunt of constant jokes. They take their responsibility seriously and do the very best job they can with the tools and information available to them. When developing the future demand for the Lean manufacturing line, forecasters usually have the most objective information available. Instead of relying solely on history and intuitive information, as does manufacturing, forecasters have valuable empirical data on which they can rely.

The forecasters typically reside in the sales and marketing group. They participate in key planning sessions, discussing new product strategies, shifting customer desires, and future corporate sales initiatives. Unlike manufacturing, they have better visibility into the future, knowledge of future marketing programs, and knowledge about potential shifts in the marketplace. Because they possess this knowledge, the forecasters' input on projected future demand for the Lean manufacturing line is crucial.

Two primary variables make forecasting an inaccurate science:

1. Accurate projection of future demand is nearly impossible when countless end-item product permutations are available for sale. Accuracy is increased if limited to product families rather than end items.
2. The longer the lead time and the longer the forecasting horizon, the less accurate the forecast.

If a forecast is used to predict all the permutations in sales for tomorrow, it is likely to be highly accurate. If that same forecast is used to predict that same product mix six to eight weeks (customer-quoted lead time) into the future, it is likely be highly inaccurate.

So how can the sales demand projection for the Lean manufacturing line 12, 24, or 36 months into the future possibly be accurate enough to design the Lean manufacturing line? The key to making a more accurate projection of demand into the future is to use *less* detail in defining products. Parent part numbers for line design were selected as the result of an 80/20 rationalization process. It is not uncommon to reduce thousands of end-item part numbers down to only a few part numbers or product families. Once again, the primary criterion to remember when reducing the product list is to be sure that all manufacturing processes are represented. Forecasting demand across a limited population of common products or families increases the accuracy of the forecast.

Using the Lean manufacturing methodologies, a product is defined as the sum of its labor content and its materials. The Lean line is ultimately designed based on a volume and mix of demand with the factory floor physically laid out with the required manufacturing resources to meet the projected demand. Volume can impact a line design, but if the actual product mix changes from the projected mix, how much different will the actual work content between the different models be? It is true that both mix and volume can affect materials, but changes in mix cause little impact on the work content used for the line design.

This is a great feature of the Lean manufacturing line as it offers maximum flexibility to produce any model of any product on any day constrained only by parts availability. The manufacturing resources of the Lean line are static and can be allocated on a day-to-day basis to produce any product.

Marketing Intelligence

Forecasting is begun by reviewing historical data and extrapolating that information into the future. Historical data are very objective in nature. Such data simply record the history of sales by product mix and volume. Other subjective and quantitative information affecting future demand is developed and is used to modify historical information to develop the best forecast. Usually the quantitative, absolute data are given more credence than subjective information. Marketing intelligence is an important component for projecting future demand. This intelligence is crucial when determining the future capacity of the Lean line. Marketing has more visibility into the future than any other group in the organization. However, even with the best possible forecast information available, rarely is it 100% accurate.

Since the Lean line is designed for demand 18 to 36 months into the future, changes to the mix of products or volume are guaranteed. Most companies develop strategic plans for the future. Based on their knowledge of the company's customer base, and the general direction of the market, sales and marketing can better predict potential mix and volume changes in the parent part number selection process. They also have knowledge of promotions, sales campaigns, competitive intelligence, and market strategies.

While marketing intelligence can be subjective and may not be weighted the same as historical data, looking at the list of parent part numbers and corresponding demands with this information in mind can be valuable. Doing so might reveal information that leads to additional modification of the final list.

Because the list of products and future demand is so critical to the design of the Lean line, the final list must be approved and signed off on by the steering committee.

DOCUMENTING THE PROCESS FLOW
AND ESTABLISHING MIXED PRODUCT FAMILIES

Process

A process is a physical location where a logical grouping of resources performs sequential work tasks. A process in manufacturing can be a combination of resources (people and machines) that perform work to change the form, fit, or function of materials as they are converted toward the completion of a product.

Once the parent part numbers for the Lean line and their corresponding demands have been defined, the processes used to manufacture these products must be identified and documented. The documentation is a graphic representation of the manufacturing processes, drawn in the same sequence used to manufacture the selected product. This graphic representation is a *process flow diagram*. A process flow diagram must be created for every product chosen to be produced on the Lean line.

Process Flow Diagram

A process flow diagram (PFD) is a graphic depiction of processes documenting the sequence and the timed input of those processes into another required for the completion of a product.

An excellent way to create the graphic PFD is to choose a product from the completed parent part number list and go to the shop floor where the product is produced. Starting at the last manufacturing process before shipment to the customer (usually the shipping dock), begin working backward (upstream) documenting processes, concluding at the point where only raw materials enter the process and labor is added for the first time. It is helpful to draw arrows showing where the input from previous processes is consumed.

With the Lean manufacturing methodologies, a product only consists of its labor content and its parts. When creating the PFD, do not consider its purchased materials. Even though differences in purchased parts may create a different parent part number, the purpose of the PFD is to document the processes where labor or machine time is consumed in the manufacture of the product. Identification of purchased parts used to build products is the function of the kanban system.

When documenting of processes has been completed, the final drawing should resemble a "fishbone" drawing (see Figure 3.5). Attach names of the processes to the drawing to help visualize the point where the completed output of a process is consumed into another.

When documenting the process flow, it is important to determine the specific

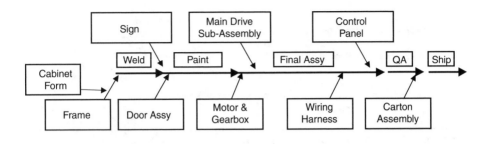

Figure 3.5 Household Appliance PFD

point in the process where the output of another process is consumed. The PFD visually shows the sequence of processes required to manufacture a product, as well as the relationship of one process to another in the completion of the product. Looking at the household appliance PFD in Figure 3.5, it is easy to visualize that the motor and gearbox subassembly is installed into final assembly before the main drive subassembly. The wiring harness subassembly is then installed, followed by the control panel subassembly.

The graphic PFD also indicates the chronology of the individual process where other processes are "consumed" into main assembly. For the household appliance PFD, these processes are subassembly processes. The Lean manufacturing methodologies refer to these subassembly processes as "feeder" processes. The careful location of feeder processes is important, as the work performed in a feeder process is being done in parallel with the main assembly processes. Completing work in parallel instead of sequentially is a major factor in reducing total manufacturing lead time.

Some products may exhibit a more linear manufacturing process flow, as shown in Figure 3.6. Others may be more complex, indicating additional activity, as shown in Figure 3.7.

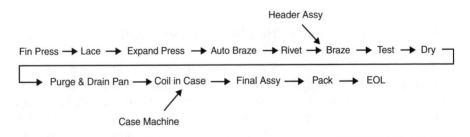

Figure 3.6 Linear Product Flow Diagram

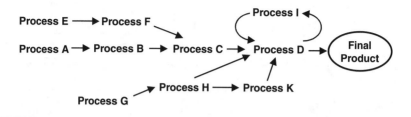

Figure 3.7   Complexity of Process Flow

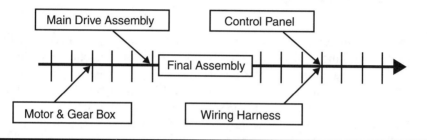

Figure 3.8   Documentation of Individual Tasks

When the individual tasks required to complete the work in the process of final assembly are documented as in Figure 3.8, it will be easy to see at precisely what point during the final assembly process the gear motor, main drive assembly, wiring harness, and control panel are installed. The ability to accurately document these work tasks will be critical when assigning the work tasks by workstation (workstation definition) and in completing the facility layout.

The same will also be true for all feeder processes. Developed at a later time, individual work tasks and their time elements for each process are not considered during the creation of the PFDs.

FACTORS IMPACTING THROUGHPUT VOLUME

A PFD must be created for each parent part number selected for the Lean line design. The expected volume at full capacity has also been established for each of the parent part numbers. The PFD assumes that the demand volume chosen for each parent part number is the demand volume throughput for each of the processes documented on the PFD. However, there are reasons why volume can change during manufacturing. At each process where the volume is less or greater than 100%, the cause and amount of the change must be documented.

Changes in throughput volume can affect the number of manufacturing resources necessary to produce the desired line volume.

Throughput volume is a crucial factor for accurately calculating Takt time. Takt time is the denominator of the calculation that identifies the number of resources necessary to achieve the throughput volume for each process. Takt time is discussed later.

Scrap and Rework

When product moves through a manufacturing process and subsequent inspection reveals a defect, two dispositions can be used for the defective item.

Rework

The product may be returned to a previous process, sent to an off-line process, or remain at the workstation (where the defect was discovered) to be repaired or reworked. Upon completion of the rework, the product moves downstream or is returned to the line to repeat a process or a series of processes. The volume of each process where rework or reprocessing occurred has now been changed. The anticipated amount of this change, stated as a percentage, must be documented on the PFD. At every process where rework occurs, four items must be noted: (1) At which process does the defect occur? (2) What is the historical (i.e., anticipated) percentage of rework? (3) At what process is the defect reworked? (4) At which process does the reworked product re-enter the Lean line?

The rework PFD is drawn as shown in Figure 3.9, where process D = process where defect was discovered, historical rework = 10%, process I = process where product is reworked, and process D = process where reworked product re-enters the line.

In this example, if the desired output of process D is 100 and the historical rework is 10%, this means that for every product that enters process D, 10% of that volume will require rework and will be sent to process I. Therefore, the volume of process I will be 10. Because 10 units are subsequently reworked at process I and returned to process D to be processed a second time, the volume through process D (throughput) is now 110 units. A 10% rework means that it

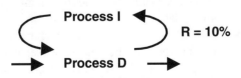

Figure 3.9 Rework Loop

requires 110 units to achieve the output goal of 100 units. This documentation is called a *rework loop*.

Reworked products may re-enter the line several processes upstream from where the defect is discovered. This is common in quality inspection processes. When that is the case, the throughput volume of each downstream process must also be increased by the rework percentage to account for the reworked volume being processed a second time.

Rework is always considered nonvalue-added work and can significantly impact the amount of resources necessary to produce the desired demand volume. The long-term answer to eliminating rework is the elimination of the defects that cause the rework to occur in the first place. *Kaizen* is an excellent technique for reducing or eliminating rework. The final resolution of some of the more difficult problems uncovered by kaizen may require changing company procedure and policy. These solutions usually require more investment in time and are best resolved through the application of the continuous process improvement techniques.

Rework and scrap are touchy subjects for most manufacturers. There is not a manufacturing facility in the world that does not have some level of each within its four walls. Unless rework and scrap are documented and recorded, most manufacturers opt to ignore them, choosing to blend them right back into the daily production counts at the end of the day. On a daily basis, if the time required to process rework is not considered, it can only be subtracted from the daily time available to produce scheduled demand. Recurring significant amounts of rework unaccounted for on a daily basis can cause missed schedules, late shipments, and overtime.

It is not uncommon for manufacturers to hedge statistics or downplay the fact that rework processes occur in their facilities. While aware of rework issues, they are often embarrassed to acknowledge their existence or the extent to which they impact their operations. If a manufacturer can successfully rework or scrap materials with impunity without impacting efficiency or utilization measurements, searching for solutions to the root cause of problems may never occur. Bringing nonvalue-added rework into the sunlight is the first step in eliminating it. Lean manufacturing seeks to eliminate waste.

Rework loops must be documented on the PFD. As tempting as it may be, no effort should be made at this point to resolve the causes of rework. The PFD simply documents its occurrence and establishes the magnitude. The PFD is used to identify processes where labor or machine resources are utilized and where throughput may be impacted by demand less or greater than 100% of demand.

Note that the rework process can be defined as separate from the normal processes required to make a product. The PFD should identify where labor or machine work is consumed for the production of products and volumes. Because

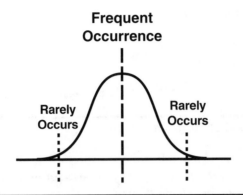

Figure 3.10   Representative Rework Percentage

many manufacturers overlook rework, the rework processes are often not thought of as "regular" processes. Manufacturers tend to think of them as anomalies or exceptions to normal production. When creating the PFD, do not overlook the rework processes. Even though nonvalue-added, rework requires resources to perform the work.

An often used argument for not documenting or even acknowledging rework is that rework volume can change every day based on a variety of changing conditions. How can a rework percentage be applied to a moving target? Depending on the type of rework, even the processes affected can be different every day. While these arguments are true, the PFD must identify the most common scenario and document it if the manufacturing resources for the Lean line design are going to be correct.

Rely on a normal distribution (i.e., bell curve) to identify the most common scenario (Figure 3.10). Avoid "analysis paralysis" by trying to make a precise estimate. If the rework throughput is overestimated, the worst case will be that required resources will be overstated. If the rework throughput is underestimated, the required resources will be underestimated. A wrong estimate is better than no estimate. If reality later proves the estimate to be incorrect, the rework throughput can be adjusted.

Scrap

For most products found to be defective, an initial effort is made to either repair or rework them to correct the defect. Rework is typically completed at the workstation, returned to an upstream process, or sent to an off-line process. If the rework is successful, the product is returned to the line to continue downstream toward completion. In some cases, the repair or rework cannot be com-

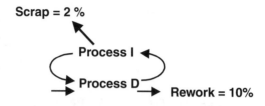

Figure 3.11   Scrap Resulting from Rework

pleted or may be financially unfeasible to perform. The alternative to rework is scrap. The product is either destroyed or disposed of in a way that reduces the output of the line or individual processes. Like rework, the volume of each process where scrap has occurred is also impacted. The difference is that with scrap processes, not only has the volume changed at the process where the scrap occurred, but the volume of all processes upstream is affected. Because scrapped units must be replaced to achieve the desired output, additional units must be input through each process. The historical scrap amount, stated as a percentage, must be documented on the PFD at the point where it occurs.

Scrap is indicated in the PFD as shown in Figure 3.11. In this example, the desired output of process D is 100 units and has a historical rework of 10%. Process I yields 2% scrap, so process D must now generate a throughput of 112 units to accommodate both the 10% rework and the 2% scrap rate (100 units demand + 10 units that will be reworked + 2 units that will be scrapped).

The process upstream from process D must now produce an output of 102 units because 2 units will likely be scrapped at process I. Subsequently, each upstream process must generate two additional units to compensate for the scrap loss at process I. If any additional scrap occurs at an upstream process, the number of units grows incrementally in relation to the amount of scrap at that process. All scrap is cumulative upstream to the gateway process. To achieve an output of 100 units at the end of the line, with cumulative scrap occurring upstream through multiple processes, the required input quantity could be significant.

Like rework, scrap represents additional work that must be done in excess of the work required to meet the required demand. Unlike rework, where only a few processes are typically impacted, scrap can be insidious. Scrap can impact all manufacturing processes, extending back into the fabrication processes. The management process for scrap disposition can represent a significant investment of management time — all nonvalue-added.

In addition to the higher cost of materials caused by scrap, the labor expended to offset it is nonvalue-added work. This extra work can significantly impact the amount of resources required to produce the desired customer volume. Once again, kaizen is an excellent technique for reducing or eliminating scrap.

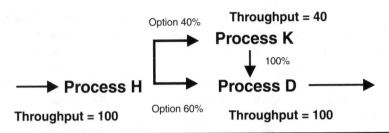

Figure 3.12   Throughput Affected by Optionality

Options

Some products moving down the Lean line may not go through some processes some of the time. Because these processes are not used in a one-to-one relationship to meet customer demand, the throughput volumes of these processes are affected. For example, consider manufacturing a car with a desired output volume of 100. Customer demand indicates that only half (50%) require the installation of a CD player. Therefore, the volume through the CD subassembly (feeder) would be only 50 units. The volume of cars on the main line remains 100.

If the time required to produce a car and a CD player were the same (hypothetically), the car would require twice as many resources to produce the volume in the same time period.

Consider the PFD shown in Figure 3.12, where

- The desired volume is 100 units.
- Process K is an optional process.
- Sixty percent of the output from process H goes to process D.
- Forty percent of the output from process H goes to process K.
- The volume of process K is 40 units.
- One hundred percent of the volume from process K goes to process D.
- The input volume from process D remains 100.
- The output volume from process D is 100.

When creating the PFD, be certain to document the optional processes and record the historical percentages. Based on the volume of product through the optional processes, the amount of resources can be impacted.

Establishing Multiproduct Families

The capability to produce multiple products on a single line provides many advantages for the Lean manufacturer. A multiproduct line allows the production of a variety of products that share the same shop floor footprint. This can be important to the Lean manufacturer that wants to delay or avoid the costs of bricks-and-mortar expansion as product volume or model proliferation grows.

It also means that separate Lean lines are not necessary to produce multiple products. Even as different products have different PFDs, they can generally be manufactured using the same manufacturing resources. The shared resources of a Lean line reduce or eliminate the need for redundant labor, machines, component parts, planning, purchasing, and supervisory support. Duplicated resources are waste and should be eliminated.

Many manufacturers produce products by grouping them into families. Products are often assigned to family groupings based on customer types, colors or customer branding, special features or applications, or sales territory. These family designations often define which products are run on which production lines. If of sufficient volume, family designation can dictate the dedication of manufacturing resources to specific products and production lines. In most companies, family definitions are not assigned by manufacturing. Defining product families is reserved for the sales, marketing, or financial groups, with little regard for the actual manufacturing requirements of the product. Manufacturers seldom challenge family designations even if it means maintaining redundant resources to accommodate their production.

Lean manufacturers also produce products using family definitions, but take an active role in assigning products to a family. Family selections for multiproduct Lean lines are based primarily on the commonality of their processing paths, as defined by their PFDs. Further selections are based on similar work content times and the commonality of work steps and materials used. Lean production lines are optimally designed to produce a "family" of similar products, which share common manufacturing processes and materials. By grouping products in this manner, all products that make up the family members can advance through their required resources one unit at a time.

It is not unusual for different products to have different demand patterns and sales cycles. If product lines have been dedicated to a few product types, their alternating demand patterns can lead to the "hiring/firing" of employees in an attempt to match production capacity to customer requirements. Lean lines operate best when making a variety of products on a single line. The more products run on a single line, the less the impact of alternating demand on valuable manufacturing resources.

A visual representation of a mixed-product PFD should be developed. This multiproduct PFD is the basis for the conceptual layout of the manufacturing facility in a Lean configuration. Rather than being constrained to department configurations, the mixed-product PFD conceptually visualizes the eventual layout of the factory that will facilitate the desired one-piece flow of product.

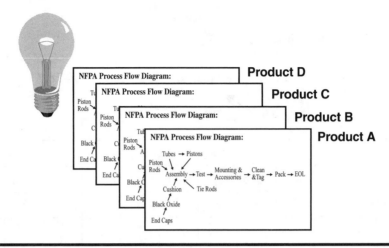

Figure 3.13   Product Variety with Process Similarity

The PFD should not consider physical size or color of the part numbers used to produce the product. Identifying processes where work occurs is the purpose of the PFD. One way to visualize a family of products capable of moving down the same line (and sharing the same footprint) would be to overlay one PFD on top of the other and hold them up to the light. Doing so would then show the location of both all similar processes, rework and optional processes and special seldom used feeder processes (see Figure 3.13).

This technique would provide a visual preview for the relational location of the manufacturing processes in a facility. However, the usual large number of parent products chosen for the line design precludes the application of this method. A more practical way to develop this mixed-product model is to create a *common processes process map*. The mixed-product PFD can be used to visually locate all the processes in the Lean manufacturing line.

The process map (Figure 3.14) is a simple matrix with a horizontal axis and a vertical axis. The format is the same as found in spreadsheet programs. A spreadsheet program is the ideal tool for creation of the process map.

List the part numbers of the products chosen for the line design on the vertical axis. On the horizontal axis, list the processes identified from the PFDs created for the line design. Beginning with the first part number, and referencing its PFD, place an "X" in the cell where the parent product and the process intersect. Continue in this manner until all parent part numbers have been matched with all processes on the process map.

When completed, the process map will visually show which products share the same processes — without regard to size, color, standard time, or current

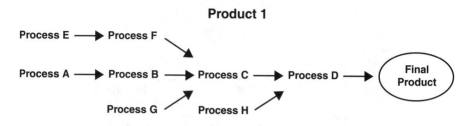

Process Map									
	Proc. A	Proc. B	Proc. C	Proc. D	Proc. E	Proc. F	Proc. G	Proc. H	Proc. I
Product 1	X	X	X	X	X	X	X	X	
Product 2									
Product 3									
Product 4									
Product 5									

Figure 3.14   PFD to Process Map Relationship

family designations. This matrix will confirm the commonality of processes for establishing families based solely on the processes used to produce them. Processes not 100% common across all products will be established as optional processes on the Lean line. When completing the line layout, the process map can be used to identify where these processes are to be physically located on the Lean line.

Using the completed common processes process map (Figure 3.15), a visual mixed-product PFD (Figure 3.16) can then be drawn. This can be done manually with pencil and paper or with software such as Word, Excel, Visio, or CAD (among others). Even a white board with dry markers will work.

Starting with the first parent product, redraw its PFD using a designated color line. Different colors are optional but useful. Select the second parent part number and redraw its PFD in a different color. There is no need to redraw processes included in the first parent part number. When a new process that has not previously been drawn is utilized, draw that process with a designated color different than the one used to draw the PFD. Continue drawing all parent part number PFDs until all processes on the mixed-product PFD have been included. The resulting mixed-product PFD is a conceptual layout of the new Lean line.

Common Processes Process Map									
	Proc. A	Proc. B	Proc. C	Proc. D	Proc. E	Proc. F	Proc. G	Proc. H	Proc. I
Product 1	X	X	X	X	X	X	X	X	
Product 2	X	X	X	X			X	X	
Product 3	X	X	X	X	X	X		X	X
Product 4	X	X	X	X	X	X	X	X	
Product 5	X	X	X	X	X		X	X	
Product 6	X	X	X	X	X	X		X	X
Product 7	X	X	X	X	X	X	X	X	
Product 8	X	X	X	X	X	X		X	X
Product 9	X	X	X	X			X	X	X
Product 10	X	X	X	X	X	X	X	X	X

Figure 3.15   Completed Common Processes Process Map

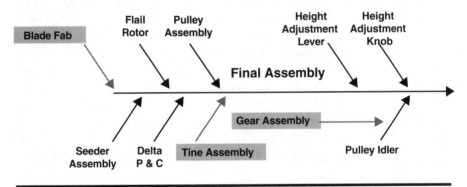

Figure 3.16   Mixed-Product PFD for Lawn Care Products

IDENTIFYING PROCESS DEMAND LEVELS AND ESTABLISHING TAKT

Balance is the key to the success of a Lean manufacturing line. When the Lean line operates, all processes complete work at the same rate. Even though individual manufacturing processes may require different work times, the Lean line breaks all work times into equal amounts of work. Achieving balance among a variety of processes with different work times is accomplished by adding or subtracting the number of manufacturing resources to the process. When balanced, no one single process has more capacity than another. Balance is at the heart of every Lean manufacturing line.

The concept of balancing work is not new, but the approach of the Lean manufacturing methodologies applies the concept of balancing differently. Instead of balancing lines based on physical considerations such as line length, the Lean manufacturing methodologies balance work based on the throughput volume of demand required on a particular process. Once throughput volume has been defined, the manufacturing processes are divided into equal amounts of work. While each manufacturing process for each product may have a different work content time, the Lean manufacturing methodologies establish balance using a time/volume relationship called *Takt*.

Takt is calculated as follows:

$$\text{Takt} = \frac{\text{Work Minutes per Shift} \times \text{\# of Shifts per Day}}{\text{Throughput Volume per Day}}$$

where work minutes per shift = *amount* of time available for a manufacturing operator to perform work each shift, # of shifts per day = how many shifts per day per process, and throughput volume per day = a total of demand volume, including the impacts of any rework, scrap, and optional volume considerations.

Takt is an expression of frequency of demand. Because it is an expression of demand over a defined time period, it is also an expression of *rate*. Takt states that if a volume is to be produced in a stated time period, then one unit must be completed every X minutes. For example, consider an eight-hour shift working one shift per day. The total available time would be 480 minutes. If the required throughput of the process is 240 units, *the Takt time rate is 2 minutes*, or 1 unit has to be completed every 2 minutes of a 480-minute day to produce a demand volume of 240 units. Takt time is typically expressed in terms of minutes.

Takt time is often designated as a "target" or "goal" rate of a process. Due to the amount of optionality, rework, and scrap of each process in the PFD, each process can have a different throughput volume. Because the throughput volume can be different, each process must establish its own individual Takt time rate.

Once the Takt rate for each process has been established, the "flow" of a product is accomplished by physically relocating the resources of each manufacturing process, balanced to the formulated Takt rate, adjacent to the Lean line where the output is consumed directly into the finished product. Total time is grouped into work elements equal to Takt time. Manufacturing processes divided into equal elements of Takt are balanced regardless of the total time necessary to produce the subassembly or final product. A single unit of work (a Takt time's worth) is performed by a person and/or a machine. A partially completed unit equal to the Takt time is then passed to the next resource downstream, where another "Takt" worth of work tasks is performed. The unit

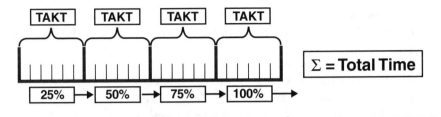

Figure 3.17 Work Content Time Grouped by Takt

of work progresses in a flow through all manufacturing processes until the sum of the required work has been completed (Figure 3.17).

Balancing work to Takt and physically linking manufacturing processes together allows the completed output of one process to be directly consumed by another. This dramatically reduces inventories and cycle times. Because manufacturing processes are simply divided into equal elements of work, the grouping of similar labor and machines into "departments" is no longer necessary. Only the resources required to produce the process volume at capacity are located on the line.

It is common for manufacturers to refer to the "Takt" time of the Lean line as a single entity. In reality, the Takt time of the whole "line" is really just the Takt time of the very last process of the line. This misuse of the term Takt can be overlooked as long as the manufacturer understands that each process has its own Takt time based on the throughput volume of the process.

NUMERATORS AND DENOMINATORS OF TAKT TIME

The Takt time formula is straightforward, but there are important elements to consider when performing Takt time calculations.

Work Minutes per Shift

While there are exceptions, the most common shift length for most manufactures remains eight hours. But are those eight hours 100% dedicated to the production of products? On a daily basis, workers engage in a variety of activities that subtract from their time to perform touch work on a product. Activities like breaks, lunch periods, required training sessions, periodic employee meetings, and continuous process improvement (kaizen) meetings all take time away from operators for producing products. These times must be identified and deducted from the total amount of work minutes available per shift.

For example, one shift that begins at 7:00 a.m. and ends at 3:30 p.m. has 8.5 hours available to perform work. However, the following must be deducted:

- 0.5 hours for lunch
- 0.5 hours for breaks (two 15-minute breaks)
- 2 hours (12 to 15 minutes) for weekly kaizen
- 0.05 hours one day per month safety meeting

That leaves 7.25 hours or 435 minutes per day as the actual work time available.

Variations to the work time are different for every company. The activities that are deducted from total time available are different for every company. Some companies work four ten-hour shifts, while still others may work a rotating five-day schedule, with nine hours per shift. Every company is different, but the need to determine the actual work time available for operators to perform touch work is mandatory.

When subtracting the minutes per shift not available to perform work, it is tempting to also discount the available time by personal fatigue and other related factors that cause productivity loss. The Lean manufacturing methodologies do recognize the existence of these elements of time but suggest that they not be considered in the work minutes per day Takt time calculation. If these elements are discounted in the Takt time calculation, they will be embedded in the Lean line design and invisible to future improvement initiatives. If productivity loss is measured, the causes can be identified.

If calculated separately, these elements of time will be exposed as candidates for later continuous process improvement or kaizen events. The Lean methodology recommends that a "productivity factor" be added to daily staffing requirements to accommodate the realities of productivity loss. Productivity losses can then be measured, with the causes identified and subsequently improved. When built into the line design, the factors that cause productivity loss go unseen, unmeasured, and unimproved.

Number of Shifts per Day

Select the number of shifts the process operates each day. For Lean line design purposes, it is often simpler to use one shift as the factor in the Takt time calculation and extrapolate the necessary resources by using simple multiplication and division.

A goal of a Lean line is to produce all demand on one shift, if possible. Aside from the overhead costs saved by not operating the second and third shifts, the line design will yield additional capacity up to 100% by allowing the addition of extra shifts in response to increases in demand. A Lean line runs like a light switch — either on or off. However, this option is not always available. For processes where one shift operation is insufficient to maintain the Takt rate, other solutions to achieve Takt balance should be considered.

Throughput Volume per Day

Demand volume is important because it ultimately determines the amount of resources required to produce that amount of demand. Lean manufacturing methodologies requires new Lean manufacturing lines to have capacity sufficient to produce a level of demand volume greater than current capacity. A Lean manufacturing line should be designed with the capacity to support demand volume one to three years into the future. Projected future demand establishes a baseline volume for determining the final throughput volume of each manufacturing process. There are several activities that can alter the baseline demand volume of a process. These activities must be accounted for in the calculation of demand volume for each process.

Optional Process

An optional process is a discretionary process where throughput volume is less or greater than a one-to-one relationship to the finished unit. The optional process is used only when customer demand requires its use to provide a feature or special functionality to the finished product. Examples of such options include painted versus unpainted, installed versus uninstalled, or one piece versus two pieces per unit. For optional processes that exceed 100% (i.e., products that require two per unit), the option percentage would be stated as 200%, three per would be 300%, etc. For less than 100%, the percentage is stated as 75%, 60%, 50%, etc.

The volume of an optional process is calculated using the following formula:

$$(Tp) = (Tp_{OUT} \times \text{Option } \%)$$

where Tp_{OUT} = throughput out of the process upstream of the option processes and Option % = percentage of Tp to downstream process.

Rework Process

A rework process is a process where defective manufactured products containing absorbed work content are repaired or where identified defects are corrected.

Identified rework material can be returned to a previous process, sent to an off-line process, or remain at the workstation where the defect was discovered. Repair or rework increases the volume of each process where rework occurs. It also increases the throughput volume of each process it passes through when re-entering the Lean line. The magnitude of this change stated as a percentage is reflected on the PFD. The volume will be increased at each process (based on the historical percentage) noted on the PFD for the process where the defect occurred, at the process where the defect is reworked, and any additional process where the reworked product re-enters the line.

The new volume caused by rework is calculated using the following formula:

$$Tp = Tp_{OUT} \times (1 + \text{Rework \%})$$

where Tp_{OUT} = throughput out of the process where the rework occurred and Rework % = historical rework percentage indicated on the PFD for that process.

Scrap

For products found defective, efforts are made to either repair or rework them. Rework can be completed at the workstation, returned to an upstream process, or sent to an off-line process. If successful, the product is advanced or returned to the line to continue downstream toward completion. In some cases, the repair or rework cannot be completed, or it may be financially unfeasible to perform rework. If product cannot be reworked, it must be scrapped. Scrapped material is either destroyed or disposed of, resulting in the reduction of the output of the line or individual process. Not only is the volume of each process where scrap has occurred changed, but the volumes of all upstream processes are also affected. Because scrapped units must be replaced to achieve the desired output, additional units must be input through each process. The historical scrap amount, stated as a percentage, is identified on the PFD at the point where it occurs.

The required volume for all processes upstream from the point of scrap is calculated using the following formula:

$$Tp = (Tp_{OUT} \div \text{Yield \%})$$

where Tp_{OUT} = throughput out of the process where the scrap occurred and Scrap % = historical scrap percentage indicated on the PFD for the process where scrap occurs. This percentage must then be calculated for all processes upstream of the scrap point.

Option Process Map										
		Proc. A	Proc. B	Proc. C	Proc. D	Proc. E	Proc. F	Proc. G	Proc. H	Proc. I
Product 1	55	55	55	55	55	55	55	55	55	
Product 2	45	45	45	45	45			45	45	
Product 3	16	16	16	16	16	16	16		16	16
Product 4	25	25	25	25	25	25	25	25	25	
Product 5	24	24	24	24	24	24		24	24	
Product 6	30	30	30	30	30	30	30		30	30
Product 7	31	31	31	31	31	31	31	31	31	
Product 8	33	33	33	33	33	33	33		33	33
Product 9	36	36	36	36	36			36	36	36
Product 10	5	5	5	5	5	5	5	5	5	5
TOTALS	300	300	300	300	300	219	195	221	300	120

Figure 3.18 Throughput Volumes for Optional Processes

Another useful tool that can be used to identify and calculate these quantities is the process map. In the process map displayed in Figure 3.18, note that the line design total for this product family is 300 units. Several of the processes have total quantities smaller than 300. While these products are in the same family, they do not use every process. These processes are optional processes. Therefore, their volume is different than the volume designated for the total product family. Because the volumes are different, the Takt times will also be different for those processes.

After the optional processes process map has been created, similar process maps can be constructed for the rework and scrap processes, applying the rework and scrap percentages and resulting throughput calculations to the process map quantities. Note that the greater the quantity, the smaller the Takt time. The converse is also true: the smaller the demand volume, the larger the Takt time.

In a typical factory, grouping similar types of work and machines creates traditional departments and work centers. This grouping of work and machines assists with organizational control and facilitates the collection of performance, routing, and inventory reporting data. In most cases, the similar work and machines are then physically located in one area of the facility. In most cases, this grouping of work or machines provides little consideration for the equal distribution of capacity. This unequal distribution of capacity can create imbalances between manufacturing processes. These imbalances are often manifested in pools of excess inventory.

Lean manufacturing lines overcome this imbalance problem. By eliminating the imbalance of capacity between departments, pools of work in process cannot accumulate, greatly reducing work-in-process inventories. In addition, the grouping of similar labor and machine resources into departments is no longer necessary. Only the required resources necessary to produce the future demand volume are located and utilized on the Lean line. Remaining resources are redundant. A Lean line uses a facility layout that allows standard work tasks to be completed in a systematic, sequential manner. Where possible, all the processes necessary to produce a product are physically linked together. The physical arrangement of the resources is important because it allows work tasks to be accumulated, distributed, and balanced evenly throughout the entire manufacturing cycle.

The Takt time at each process is a crucial component of implementing a Lean manufacturing line. Takt is the denominator in the formula for determination of resources for each process. Often, Takt is thought of as drumbeat, cadence, or rhythm. Takt time sets the pace of the manufacturing operations. With a Lean line, Takt time does not change until the designed throughput volume is exceeded. Changes in daily throughput volume are addressed by modifying the staffing of the process. The Takt time remains unchanged.

Lean manufacturers can choose to change the output of the line to match the volume of customer requirements each day. With a Lean line designed to produce products using a formulated Takt time, a manufacturer has the ability to regulate the output of the line. The output of the line can be regulated by reducing the amount of manufacturing resources assigned to the line on any given day. Output is adjusted every day based on that day's customer requirements.

Using Figure 3.17, work is completed in four equal Takt times. If each Takt time were staffed with an operator, the designed demand volume used for the Takt calculation would be produced each day. If, however, staffing were reduced to three operators, then only three-fourths of the demand would be achieved, as operators take turns completing two Takt times to complete one unit. Effectively, every fourth Takt time would be missed. By intentionally causing Takt times to be missed or gained, the rate of production can be adjusted with a simple staffing decision — the number of labor resources assigned to the line that day.

This ability to change output to match fluctuations in actual customer order demand is a powerful tool for managing both work-in-process and finished goods inventories. With this capability, manufacturers are no longer forced to commit their manufacturing resources to a schedule driven by an unreliable forecast of future demand.

Manufacturing to forecast requires staffing for the maximum possible demand. The Lean manufacturer can change the output of the line every day to match the actual sales demand every day. Whenever true customer demand is less than forecast, manufacturing has two choices to respond:

1. If overhead absorption is the driving performance measurement, continue to produce at capacity, resulting in the production of unsold inventory or finished goods storage for sales at a later date. Productivity is embedded in units produced in excess of sales. The impact of this storage is contingent on the amount of time products are stored. If the shortfall in actual customer demand occurs frequently, the amount of stored inventory will continue to grow. The productivity measurement will look great, but the inventory turn rate will be diminished. Over time, less than expected customer demand can create potentially significant amounts of costly finished goods inventory. When true customer demand does meet or exceed forecast, it is likely that stored inventories will not match the new demand required by the customer.

2. Modulate the manufacturing throughput by intentionally suboptimizing the staffing resource on the Lean line. This requires determining the staffing requirements of the line each day based on the true customer demand for that specific day. Matching manufacturing throughput with true customer demand will eliminate the need for stored inventory (finished goods inventory). Optimization of the labor resource should parallel true customer demand. When true customer demand is less than forecast, labor will be the underutilized resource rather than the continued production of expensive finished goods resources.

With materials as the largest cost component of a product and labor the smallest, the Lean manufacturing methodologies prefer choosing intentional underutilization of labor in favor of the production of inventory to offset variations in customer demand. Of course, when productivity, measured as efficiency and utilization, is the primary performance measure for a manufacturing facility, accepting suboptimization of resources presents a major conflicting objective to the individual manufacturing manager.

On the other hand, the person responsible for inventory turns is delighted. This major conflicting objective is the single biggest reason for the failure of the ongoing operation of Lean manufacturing lines within a manufacturing facility after the initial implementation. Management of this conflict falls squarely on the shoulders of the top-level manufacturing executives, as they must provide the clarity of direction for the entire organization.

DOCUMENTING PROCESS WORK ELEMENTS AND QUALITY CRITERIA

A Lean line provides numerous benefits to the manufacturer. The basis of these benefits is the ability to produce products one at a time in a continuous flow. A Lean line is capable of signaling the production of one unit at a time, pulling product along from the downstream point of consumption. The ability to produce products one at a time is accomplished by achieving balance at every workstation on a Lean line. To achieve balance at each workstation, equal amounts of work must be assigned to each location regardless of the process type. As each unit progresses sequentially through the workstations on the line, an additional Takt time's amount of work is completed. Every time a 100% completed product exits the Lean line, all remaining uncompleted units ratchet one workstation downstream toward the point of completion. The established Takt time of each process indicates the rate at which the products flow downstream.

The processes and how work is performed sequentially to manufacture products have been identified with the PFD. The production rate necessary to meet customer demand for these products has been established with the Takt time. Measuring the standard time required to complete the work of each process identified for each of the products of the Lean line is the next information needed. The individual tasks and corresponding time required to perform these tasks for each process for each product must be documented. Because every product may require different tasks and/or times, each product and its process combination must be examined.

The tool used to document these work elements is a sequence of events (SOE). The sequence of events template (Figure 3.19) must be developed for the Lean implementation and can be created using a spreadsheet program. The template can also be used for all future implementations. This template is used for documenting the work performed at each process. Most companies already have similar documentation in place, such as routing files or process sheets, and some of that information may be used to complete the SOE. Different than most existing routing or process sheets, the SOE requires a greater level of detail when documenting the process on a task-by-task basis. Work tasks documented on the SOE are used to establish the precise elements of work tasks, by Takt time, to be completed at each workstation. Detail is important.

1. Product ID

Identify the product for which the SOE is being developed. The SOE establishes baseline work task information. Once documented, the SOE is a primary record

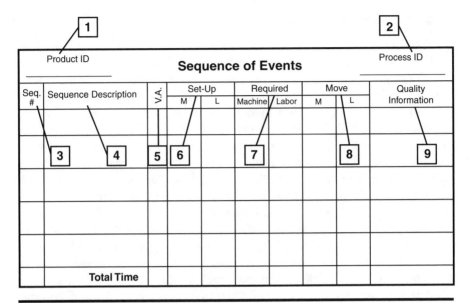

Figure 3.19 Sequence of Events

of how a specific product is manufactured at a specific process. With enough detail, the manufacturing and design engineering departments can use the SOE as a reference source for future product design improvements.

2. Process ID

Identify the process being described. The names used for the processes should be the same as those used in the PFD. Naming convention is not nearly as important as naming consistency. (For example, which is the preferred nomenclature: "Assy" or "Assm," "Grind" or "Grnd," "QA" or "QC"?) As process improvements are made due to kaizen efforts, the SOE can be used to record these changes.

3. Sequence Number

Document the sequential order of the manufacturing tasks within a specific process. Rather than a "1...2...3...4..." numbering methodology, a numbering convention similar to the familiar one used in the routing file (010...020...030...040...) is recommended. This numbering methodology allows the insertion of additional tasks as they are developed (i.e., 015...025...035...045...).

4. Sequence Description

Describe the task in detail as close to a single motion as possible. The design of the Lean line requires balancing the work being completed in a process by dividing that work into groups equal to a Takt time. Keeping the tasks in small elements will later facilitate the assignment of tasks to specific workstations. For repetitive tasks such as attaching a series of fasteners (screws), it is suggested that one sequence be used to document the work, with the next task describing the number of times it is repeated in the series. Elements of work less than approximately six seconds, or one-tenth of a minute, should not be documented separately, nor should an entire process be reduced to one large, single task. Continue documenting each task until all tasks for the process have been identified.

In Lean, work elements are divided into three categories of work type: setup, required, and move. Each of these categories defines two further levels of work types. Work can be performed by a machine or by a person and must be designated on the SOE. Sometimes a person can do work at the same time as a machine (i.e., in parallel). Where man/machine work occurs in parallel, each is listed, with the smallest element of time placed in brackets. The SOE requires documentation of each category and type of work being performed. Once setup and move work are documented, they are easily isolated from value-added tasks and become candidates for kaizen and poka-yoke. Long term, the goal is to eliminate all nonvalue-added work.

For each of these categories and work tasks, a measurement of the time required to complete the task must be documented. Balancing of the Lean manufacturing processes relies on balancing the work documented on the SOE. The work defined on the SOE will be divided into groups equal to the Takt time. Time measurements must be made for each sequence description and recorded by work category and type in the designated column on the SOE. Existing time standards may already exist but reside in separate files or alternate locations. When using existing records to develop the SOE, be certain the time elements and tasks of the routing or process sheet are 100% current and align sequentially with the process tasks and descriptions for both products and processes of the SOE. Also assure that existing time standards are realistic and reflect current time observations.

A review of existing standards may reveal that unrealistic or incomplete times may have been developed to facilitate the establishment of efficiency measurements. They may be out of date, not reflect the current methodologies, or set while timing the fastest or slowest operator. With a few exceptions, labor cost is the smallest of the three components of total product cost (Figure 3.20). Engineering standards commonly used for the development of routing files focus only on the required work category, frequently discounting the setup, move, and quality inspection times. Even though discounted, this work must still be performed by someone (or something).

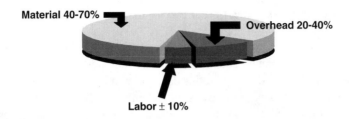

Figure 3.20 Components of Product Cost

The Lean manufacturing methodology requires all work elements, whether value- or nonvalue-added, to be documented on the SOE. It is not the function of the SOE to pass judgment or attempt to solve the causes of nonvalue-adding work elements. Its purpose is to document where it occurs and how much time is consumed when performing the work. Resolving causes and developing solutions for the elimination of nonvalue-adding work are the responsibility of kaizen and continuous process improvement committees.

The Lean manufacturing methodology requires that generous but realistic standard time be used for the SOE. The final line design will be based on an average weighted time for all products identified within a product family. There is no need to split hairs or record labor times out to the fourth decimal place when documenting standard times. The final Lean line will ultimately be staffed with people of varying skills, working at various speeds. An analysis of the work times of a group of different people performing the same task will reveal a normal distribution. Analysis will show a fastest person and a slowest person, with a majority of people clustered around the mean.

The Lean line should not be designed using the observed standard time of either the fastest or the slowest worker. It should be designed so the average person can be successful and productive. When recording standard times for the SOE, the following formula is used for documenting SOE work task times:

$$\frac{(1)\ \text{Optimistic} + (4)\ \text{Most Likely} + (1)\ \text{Pessimistic}}{6\ \text{Observations}}$$

5. Value Added

The Lean manufacturing definition of value-added work is simple. Whether or not work adds value can be determined by asking a question: Given the choice, would the customer be willing to pay for the time required to perform that element of work? Does the work add value for the customer by changing the form, fit, or function of the product, or is the work being done to reassure or confirm that the work done in a previous manufacturing process was done correctly?

Once categories and types of work have all been documented, a decision to determine if an individual sequence task is a value-added step or a nonvalue-added step must be made. Initially, this decision will have no impact on the work tasks that will be balanced for line design. When the Lean line starts up, all work documented on the SOE must be performed regardless of its status as value-added or not. If work has been designated on the SOE as nonvalue-added, it becomes a candidate for later reduction or elimination through kaizen. Each nonvalue-added sequence description on the SOE must be denoted with an asterisk (or other indicator) in the V.A. column to highlight it as a process improvement opportunity. The continuous process improvement or kaizen teams can then prioritize candidates for elimination from the nonvalue-added work elements identified on the SOE.

6. Setup Work

Setup work is defined as work done in preparation to perform other work, such as placing a unit into a workstation in preparation to begin required work. Required work is characterized as work that alters the form, fit, or function of a product. Setup work does not meet that definition. Because it does not change form, fit, or function, it is always considered nonvalue-adding work. Until eliminated through kaizen, it still remains work to be completed and is documented on the SOE.

Two separate types of setup work can be done, and this difference should also be documented for future study. The first is *dynamic*, meaning that it is performed each time a unit is produced. The second type is *static*, which indicates that the manufacturing process must stop while setup is performed. The static setup will typically be amortized over a preset quantity of products. A machine or a person can perform setup work. Dynamic setup for a machine is the time to place material in the machine each time a cycle is run. Dynamic setup for labor is the work done each time the required work is performed.

7. Required Work

This is work that alters the form, fit, or function of the unit being manufactured. Such work must be completed to transform raw materials into a product suitable for customer use. A machine or a person can complete this work. If work is done in parallel (at the same time), each task should be recorded as a separate sequence description, with the smallest time component designated by "[ ]."

8. Move Work

This type of work is done to relocate completed work to the next workstation for further processing. Once again, a machine or a person can perform this work. Like setup, move work does not meet the definition of required work, but must be documented as a candidate for kaizen and eventual elimination.

Move work can be dynamic or static. It is dynamic if it is performed each time a unit is produced. Static work is work that is not performed until a predetermined amount of product is accumulated. If a transfer conveyor is indexed each time a unit is moved to the next workstation, this is dynamic machine time. It would be static if a predetermined pallet quantity must be reached prior to moving to the next workstation. For a person performing the move, the same would be true if using a pallet jack each time a unit is completed or accumulating a full pallet before moving.

9. Quality Information

It is common for manufacturing processes to have some degree of variability. Processes are rarely designed to be completely fail-safe and capable of being produced only one correct way. When confronted with variability in a process, the individual operator must interpret how to proceed with the work, choosing the one correct way to perform the task. If experienced and very good, the operator may likely make the right decision and produce a good unit. However, an inexperienced or poorly trained operator might make the wrong interpretation, producing a defective unit. Engineering staffs work diligently to locate and design variability out of manufacturing processes. It is unlikely that all variability will be removed from the manufacturing processes, and until processes can be created that are 100% fail-safe, the only practical alternative for managing the variability is to perform an inspection.

For each sequential task description on the SOE, the single correct way to manufacture the product must be documented. Interpretation should not be left to the operator. The operator may not be in the best position to know the one correct way. It is up to the management team to define the preferred, one correct way to produce a unit at every workstation. The time required to perform the inspection must also be documented on the SOE.

NONVALUE-ADDED ACTIVITY AND QUALITY CONSIDERATIONS

Collecting information to complete the SOE requires a significant investment of both time and resources. However, collection of this information often yields surprising revelations about the manufacturing processes. Many of the items uncovered can be resolved quickly and intuitively with little cost (i.e., "low-hanging fruit"). Many others will require time, ingenuity, and expenditure of resources.

- **Setup and move:** These elements of time should always be considered nonvalue-adding. As such, all setup and move times are candidates for reduction or elimination. Often, the realignment of manufacturing processes so the output of one is consumed directly into another forces elimination of some of these elements as they are relocated adjacent to one another. Other setup and move time reduction challenges may require further study (i.e., single-minute exchange of dies, etc.) and kaizen programs.

- **Quality inspections:** Inspections for variation designated as quality criteria on the SOE should be considered nonvalue-added work. However, until the sources of variation can be eliminated from the process, inspection work must be completed to assure the one correct way has been used for production. Does this inspection work meet the definition of value-added work? Once again, ask: Given the choice, would the customer be willing to pay for this inspection work to be performed? Customers do not demand that this specific work be done. They simply require the product to perform as advertised. How that is accomplished is left up to the manufacturer. It is the manufacturer that chooses inspection as a method to overcome process variability. Kaizen and poka-yoke projects can help make a process fail-safe.

- **Design engineering:** "Engineering throws it over the wall and manufacturing figures out how to make it" is a manufacturing lament that is often a legitimate complaint. It is possible that many of the SOE tasks are performed because of engineering's lack of understanding of the manufacturing process. It is not uncommon for the design engineering department to be remotely located from the manufacturing facility. This complicates the access often required to see firsthand how a product is actually manufactured. Design engineers are focused on designing an individual product or its components, often without knowledge of how the entire product will be assembled in the manufacturing facility. Without good communication between manufacturing and engineering, by default manufacturing will improvise and interpret how to put a product together based on its own experience. Designing a product for manufacture on the shop floor without the benefit of engineering expertise is usually done with added steps and added inspections. When completed, SOEs should be made available to design engineering. This allows designers to improve upon existing manufacturing process to overcome nonvalue work elements with improved design for the next generation of products.

SUMMING THE TOTAL TIME OF THE PROCESS

Once the sequence descriptions, quality criteria, and times have been documented, sum all of the times collected for each work element (Figure 3.21). The machine and labor times are to be kept separate. The total of the labor and machine times represents the total time required to produce the identified product in this process. This time must include even the nonvalue-added times. Nonvalue-added times are the setup, move, and inspection times. Given the choice, any manufacturer or its customer would elect to not perform nonvalue-added work. Manufacturers know that the time required to do nonvalue work simply adds time and cost to their products. Too much time and cost negatively impact a company's ability to compete effectively in the market. While a manufacturer may elect to pass these costs on to the customer, there is a threshold where customers are unwilling to pay for costs that do not add value to their products and will place their business with a competitor.

Product ID Widget		Sequence of Events							Process ID Final Assembly
Seq. #	Sequence Description	V.A.	Set-Up		Required		Move		Quality Information
			M	L	Machine	Labor	M	L	
10	Retrieve dolly and unit frame	*		2.75					Match frame with sales order
20	Set frame on stand	*		1.3					
20	Seal all weld joints on back of frame with sealant					2.1			Seal must cover all areas
30	Place bolts through frame and dolly					0.6			
40	Attach torque gun and tighten bolts					1.3			Torque 40 PSI
50	Transfer to packing	*						1.0	Check for Serial #

$$\Sigma\ CT = 9.05$$

Figure 3.21   Sum of All Times: Value- and Nonvalue-Added

Painful as these nonvalue-added work elements might be to admit, somebody on the shop floor must nonetheless continue to perform the work. Unless it is low-hanging fruit and easily designed out of the process, the work must be documented and included in the initial line design. Because it is documented on the SOE, the magnitude of nonvalue-added work currently being done is highlighted. Continuous improvement is an ongoing objective. A manufacturer must deal with the elements of waste without placing blame on operators, supervision, engineering, or previous organizations.

Engineering standards do not typically recognize these elements of nonvalue-added work. Nonvalue-added work is usually broadly lumped together, proclaimed as "nonproductive," and accounted for as a variation on efficiency reporting. While sometimes subjective, nonproductive work is often cited when justifying additional head count or purchase of new equipment to leverage higher head count or machine projections. Campaigns to improve productivity are often initiated, with little idea as to where to begin. The SOE may actually be the first time nonvalue-added work has been documented and quantified.

The sum of the total time including setup, required work, move, and quality criteria will be used to determine the standard time used for resource calculations.

LINE LAYOUT AND WORKSTATION IDENTIFICATION WITH PROCESS LINKING AND BALANCING

Up to this point, information collected has identified the processes, their associated demand, and the effective minutes available to do work. With this information, Takt time can be calculated. Takt time defines the rate at which the line must run to achieve the desired daily output. The sequence of events (SOEs) have been developed. These SOEs document the individual tasks in sequential order, the time required to complete the identified tasks, and the quality criteria at the individual task level. The next consideration is how many resources will be required to achieve the capacity of the line.

What is a resource? Resources can be any of the following:

■ People
■ Workstations
■ Machines
■ Inventory

The Lean manufacturing methodology proceeds with the assignment of resources differently than does the MRP order launch methodology. MRP assumes infinite capacity is available in the manufacturing processes or in the

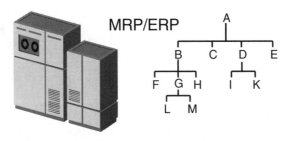

Figure 4.1   MRP Requires an Indented Bill of Material

"departments." Orders are periodically issued to meet demand based on the explosion of demand by the master schedule. Once MRP performs the time-phasing routines, the "load" in each of these departments is determined. Priority of the released orders is assigned according to the due dates and the available capacity in the department. As long as the order load does not exceed the stated capacity during the assigned time period, the plan is good.

To establish the correct start and due date for these orders, which in turn establishes the load in each department based on the net requirements, an indented bill of material (BOM) is required. The indented BOM is a key component for MRP system operation. The BOM lists the parts and quantities required to build a product. It also captures the lead time offset information for each level in the BOM necessary for time-phasing calculations that establish start and due dates for MRP-generated orders (Figure 4.1). Total manufacturing lead time of the finished product is also determined by summing the lead times for each process sequentially through all levels in the BOM.

This BOM offset function electronically communicates to the MRP system how a product is manufactured and is the basis for production schedule development. The different levels of the BOM represent the sequential build of the product through the manufacturing facility, much as a "goes into" chart. On a department-by-department basis, the sum of all orders released by due date establishes the load on that department for that period.

The indented BOM can also impact the organization of manufacturing departments. The manufacturing department shop floor layout in many factories often resembles the levels of the BOM. Similar functions or manufacturing processes are intentionally grouped together in departments to mirror the levels in the BOM. Early MRP implementations frequently promoted organizational structures that reflected the structure of the indented BOM.

The demands for maintaining and operating an MRP system require the involvement of a diverse and knowledgeable skill base. Coupled with the Sloan model of individual manager responsibility for the return-on-investment in each respective department, the installation of MRP systems contributed greatly to modern-day organization charts. In addition to facilitating execution of the production schedules, it also seemed quite logical to create and consolidate MRP maintenance responsibilities in functional organizations within the company.

Most MRP companies today assign responsibilities for BOM creation and maintenance to design engineering, forecasting to sales and marketing, planning and inventory management to materials management, and routing file management to manufacturing engineering. Fragmentation of this knowledge into functional departments for its creation and maintenance dovetails comfortably with the justification for departmental growth.

THE CONSEQUENCES OF IMBALANCE

Even with the advent of modern planning systems and the impact they have had on departmentalization of the shop floor and organization of the administrative areas, very little attention was paid to ensuring that the manufacturing departments were created equally with equal capacities. Resources are assigned to departments simply based on their similarity. The resulting unequal capacity creates many of the problems seen on shop floors today. Many of the activities on the shop floor today can be traced to attempts to balance order loads with department capacities.

Think about the activity on the shop floor today. If a released order load falls below the stated capacity of the department, additional orders are often requested from the production control group. When this occurs, production control may have to release firm planned orders in advance of their release date. Pulling orders forward in the schedule can cause future shortages. Shortages cause excessive expediting activities and the related costs.

As released order load approaches stated capacity, orders can begin to miss their due dates. Falling behind schedule generates either late orders or overtime. To complicate schedule adherence issues, manufacturing supervisors are usually measured by the efficiency and utilization (absorption) of their assigned labor and machine "resources." A common way to optimize these performance measures is to keep as many resources as possible as busy as possible. This translates into fewer changeovers, with longer runs of products used to amortize changeover inefficiency. Pulling orders ahead of scheduled due dates to group like work together in order to maximize utilization or reduce efficiency loss due to changeover is a typical solution for maximizing absorption performance goals. This grouping of work is commonly referred to as *batch manufacturing.*

Using batch manufacturing methodologies, run quantities are based solely on machine productivity considerations. Batch manufacturing allows machines to become productive when large quantities of a product are built. Through repetition, even labor resources become more efficient with longer runs of the same products. In some cases, the absorption goal takes precedence over customer satisfaction goals. Where absorption goals are most important, actual market demand often receives second priority after efficiency and utilization.

This focus on productivity has pitted manufacturing departments against sales and marketing departments for years, regardless of industry. This conflict exists today in many manufacturing companies. Batch processing becomes especially problematic when trying to build a dissimilar mix of products. What is the optimum amount? How much is too much? Which order has the highest priority? Resolution of these issues is a major contributor to costly day-to-day expediting activities.

Natural balancing does evolve to level off the absorption demands of each department. This balance takes the form of buffer inventory. Department managers soon get very smart about maintaining enough inventories or released orders in advance of demand to smooth demand fluctuations and still achieve their absorption goals. While manipulating orders by grouping them together helps to optimize department performance measures, this methodology always results in excess inventories, parts shortages, missed due dates and late orders, and high working capital inventory investment.

The costs of batch manufacturing are significant. Aside from the large shop floor square footage that must be dedicated to store buffer inventories, machine and labor capacity is prematurely consumed to produce orders incorrectly prioritized just to satisfy absorption goals. The resulting inventory produced in advance of forecasted demand solely to achieve departmental efficiency and utilization metrics often becomes excess or obsolete when actual demand does not materialize.

Because of imbalanced capacities and the need for maximum efficiency and utilization, manufacturing departments with excess capacity will always seek work from the upstream departments. If the department is the gateway work center, work is in the form of released shop orders from the planning system. If the request for additional work is in excess of what is recommended by the planning system, orders will be "pulled ahead." The practice of pulling orders ahead assures a vicious cycle of material shortages, expediting, and a series of changing due dates.

For departments with excess capacity to have the same opportunity to maximize productivity with the amortized changeovers of long runs enjoyed by other departments, they must usually find additional work to do. On the surface, overcapacity seems like a good problem to have, but department managers with excess capacity spend much of their time seeking additional work to keep their department running at full utilization. Unless they can keep their resources consumed, they will always look "nonproductive" or underabsorbed when compared to other departments. In addition to the squandered capacity, the resulting inventory allowed to accumulate downstream is always at high risk of becoming excess or obsolete.

Undercapacity departments on the downstream side of feeding departments with excess capacity experience just the opposite problem: work piles up. As work continues to backlog, the usual solution is to increase capacity. Short of capital expenditure, the only way additional short-term capacity can be created is by adding extra hours or shifts. If real capacity remains unchanged long term, overtime costs are a certainty as the department is constantly bombarded by expediting requests and the reprioritization of production orders.

If the department downstream from the undercapacity department has higher capacity and the same need to maximize productivity, pressure to change priorities in the undercapacity department to satisfy the downstream department's need for productivity will be relentless. These activities go on daily in many manufacturing facilities today. Unfortunately, they have become a way of life in those facilities. Entire organizations dedicated to expediting exist solely to deal with this daily rebalancing act on the factory floor.

THE LEAN APPROACH TO ACHIEVING BALANCE

Lean manufacturing considers all of this expediting and scheduling activity to be a waste of time, human effort, and money. Large, undisciplined, slow-moving buffer inventories are also considered waste by Lean manufacturing. Because extra activity and excess inventory add time and cost to the product, they should be eliminated. Lean manufacturing methodologies overcome these imbalance problems. The Lean manufacturing methodology is an alternative operating system that defines balance by utilizing only the resources necessary to meet customer demand. The ideal level of resource utilization to meet customer demand can mean the suboptimization of existing resources. For this reason, the Lean methodologies often conflict with the current measurement system of resource absorption.

Lean lines are progressive production lines established with a facility layout that allows standard work tasks to be accomplished in a sequential and progressive manner. Where possible, all the processes necessary to produce a product are *physically* linked together. This physical linkage of the resources permits work tasks to be distributed, accumulated, and balanced evenly throughout the entire manufacturing cycle. When a unit is sold, the entire line "ratchets" the next unit downstream. The Lean line is designed so that all processes work at the same speed. Because products are produced one piece at a time at the same rate, this type of line is often referred to as a "flow" line" (i.e., like liquid flowing through a pipe).

The Lean methodologies approach the utilization of available capacities much differently than the MRP model. The Lean manufacturing methodologies project required future capacity, calculate the resources for each process, and arrange the facility so these resources are located adjacent to one another. Because all resources work at the same rate and are physically linked together at their point of consumption, the batching or grouping of work to achieve efficiency and utilization by individual department is unnecessary. A daily sequenced listing of customer demand is necessary, but MRP-generated shop orders are not required to schedule the processes of the Lean line. The Lean manufacturing methodologies concentrate first on achieving balance among the manufacturing processes, with the need to achieve departmental efficiency, utilization, and absorption as secondary goals.

The Lean manufacturing methodologies are line-balancing techniques where the identified SOE labor and machine times are simply divided into parts equal to a Takt time. Balancing to Takt and physically linking manufacturing processes enables the completed output of one process to be directly consumed by another. This dramatically reduces inventories and cycle times. Because manufacturing processes are simply divided into equivalent elements of work, the grouping of similar labor and machines into "departments" is no longer necessary. Only the resources required to produce the demand are located on the line.

When no longer constrained by the rules of imbalanced departments, pools of work-in-process buffer inventories are not permitted to accumulate. Once manufacturing processes are balanced and linked together and manufactured in sequence, products can be produced nearer their actual work content time. Only one unit is ratcheted at a time through all processes and off the end of the line for every Takt time (Figure 4.2). The wait and queue times necessary for the normal routing of products through the different manufacturing departments in batches is greatly reduced or eliminated.

Takt time is a time–volume relationship. It is calculated by dividing the amount of time available to perform work by the desired throughput volume for each process. Takt establishes the rate at which a process must operate to achieve the designed output.

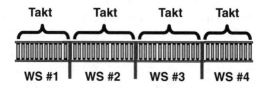

Figure 4.2   Takt Production of Work Content Time

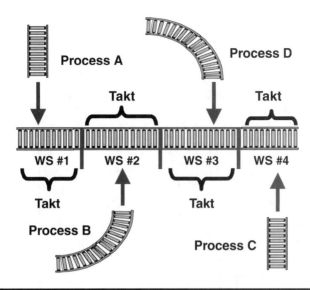

Figure 4.3   Processes Balanced and Linked Together

The goal of Lean manufacturing is to establish and design a manufacturing line capable of sequentially producing multiple products, one at a time through the processes necessary to produce the product. The Lean line can achieve this goal using only the amount of time required to actually build the product. The actual work time required to produce a product through its various manufacturing processes is almost always shorter than the time required to route batches of products through a factory. The techniques of Lean manufacturing eliminate the nonvalue-adding wait time and reduce scheduling and queue times (Figure 4.3).

The Lean manufacturing methodologies cause products to be produced one unit at a time, at a formulated rate, without wait time, queue time, or other delays. Product is *pulled* through the line using a signal from a downstream process, as opposed to being *pushed* by the planning system with a launch of orders. Time spent making products with no customer demand is considered "nonvalue-added" time. Application of the Lean manufacturing methodologies eliminates nonvalue-added time (Figure 4.4).

CALCULATING RESOURCE REQUIREMENTS

To determine the amount of resources (people, workstations, machines, or inventory) required to achieve the throughput volume for each process identified

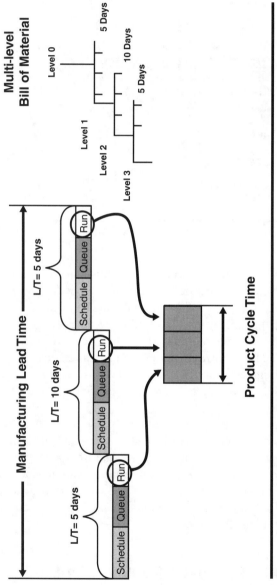

Figure 4.4 Production in the Work Content Time

Product ID Widget			Sequence of Events						Process ID Final Assembly
Seq. #	Sequence Description	V.A.	Set-Up		Required		Move		Quality Information
			M	L	Machine	Labor	M	L	
10	Retrieve dolly and unit frame	*		2.75					Match frame with sales order
20	Set frame on stand	*		1.3					
20	Seal all weld joints on back of frame with sealant					2.1			Seal must cover all areas
30	Place bolts through frame and dolly					0.6			
40	Attach torque gun and tighten bolts					1.3			Torque 40 PSI

$$\Sigma \text{ All Times} = 9.05$$

Figure 4.5   Sum of All Times: Value- and Nonvalue-Added

on the process flow diagram, two mathematical values are necessary. The first figure (the numerator) is the standard time identified on the SOE. The SOE time is the sum of all labor and machine categories of work. This includes the nonvalue-adding times of dynamic setup, rework, and move and the quality criteria inspection times. Summing these times with the value-added time elements for each process defines the total work content time for that specific product/process combination (Figure 4.5). Labor and machine times are summed separately.

The denominator of the resource calculation is the Takt time for that process. Takt time may be different for every process based on the throughput volume of the process. Factors that affect throughput volume per process are scrap, rework, and options.

$$\text{Takt} = \frac{\text{Work Minutes per Shift} \times \text{\# Shifts per Day}}{\text{Throughput Volume per Day}}$$

The basic resource calculation formula is:

$$\frac{\text{Standard Time}_{SOE}}{\text{Takt}} = \text{\# Resources}$$

Products	V_c	Processes							
		A	B	C	D	E	F	G	H
Product 1	25	2.6	6.6	4.0	10.5	1.5	30.0	10.0	12.0
Product 2	31	2.7			11.0	1.5	27.5	10.0	14.0
Product 3	50	2.5	4.5	4.0			25.0	10.0	11.0
Product 4	6		7.0	4.0	15.0	2.0	32.0	10.0	16.0
Product 5	12	2.9	5.5		13.0		29.5	10.0	13.0
Product 6	6	3.5		4.0	14.0	1.8	31.0	10.0	15.0
Σ of Total Volume = 130									

Figure 4.6   Different Products Have Different SOE Times

where resources are people, workstations, machines, or inventory. Takt time is a measurement of *rate*. SOE time is a measurement of *time*.

While the resource calculation is straightforward, it is seldom calculated using only one standard time. In a mixed product family environment, the standard times for each of the products chosen to run on the Lean line can vary. The resource calculation with only one standard time is appropriate only for one product using one process. Very few manufacturers produce only one product. Most manufacturers produce a wide variety of products with many options, with many different products using different processes. With many different products, it is not uncommon for each product to have a different SOE time through a process. Reviewing the standard time process map reveals this dynamic characteristic.

With so many products, each with a different SOE time, selecting a single time to populate the numerator of the resource calculation is not so straightforward. For process F in Figure 4.6, which time should be selected for the resource calculation? The times range from 25.0 minutes to 32.0 minutes. The best solution is not to pick the fastest or the slowest time. The average SOE time must be calculated to determine the standard time to be used for determining resources for manufacturers producing multiple products.

The volume at capacity (V_c) of product 4 is six units per day. If the line were designed for the highest number, 32.0 minutes on average, but only six units per day are produced, it is possible that resource requirements would be overstated, as the bulk of the remaining products require less than 32.0 minutes to be completed in that process. If 32.0 minutes were used to design the line, when making product 3 the line would run faster than required to produce the throughput volume.

Considering the Takt time formula, producing product on the line faster than the SOE time would result in the daily output being completed sooner than the effective work minute per shift of the Takt formula. Instead of completing work in the 435 minutes with the greater SOE time of 32.0 minutes, the daily rate could be completed in 340 minutes. In reality, operators will not maintain the speed for the entire work day just to finish early, but would more likely use the 95 minutes to pace their output to match the daily rate.

Neither choice is acceptable, as the Lean line prefers to produce at a steady rate throughout the day for the entire time of the planned effective minutes. Conversely, if the Lean line were designed using 25.0, the line would run too slowly not only when producing product 6 but for all products with an SOE time greater than 25 minutes. The better solution is to develop a production sequence of products with a mix of both high and low SOE times run throughout the day as a way to balance the line.

When products were chosen for inclusion in the line design, a grouping of products representative of all potential products and all volumes was selected. It would be an incredible coincidence if this exact product mix and volume chosen for designing the line actually occurred as the daily requirement. Knowing that to be the case, the Lean manufacturing line is designed for a product and volume mix most likely to occur on any given day.

The same logic can be used when choosing a representative time to be used for the resource calculation. An average time must be determined to perform resource calculations for each process. However, additional information is needed to make this time estimate even more accurate. A better estimate would be to weight the times to match the products that are produced most often in the process. Therefore, additional calculations are necessary for each process to establish a standard time weighted (ST_w). Using the times and volume at capacity (V_c) from the standard times process map, the standard time weighted calculation is

$$\frac{\Sigma \ V_c \times \text{SOE Std Time}}{\Sigma \ V_c} = ST_w$$

where the numerator is calculated as

Process F

Product 1 V_c 25 × SOE 30.0 = 750
Product 2 V_c 31 × SOE 27.5 = 852.5
Product 3 V_c 50 × SOE 25.0 = 1250
Product 4 V_c 6 × SOE 32.0 = 192
Product 5 V_c 12 × SOE 29.5 = 354
Product 6 V_c 6 × SOE 31.0 = 186

$$\Sigma \ V_c \times \text{SOE} = 3585$$

and the denominator is

$$\frac{\Sigma \text{ of } V_c}{\text{Volume for Process F}} = 130$$

The ST_w is

$$3585 \div 130 = 27.6 \text{ minutes}$$

Takt time is

$$\frac{7 \text{ hours} \times 60 \text{ minutes} \times 1 \text{ shift} = 420 \text{ minutes}}{\Sigma \text{ of Total Process F Volume} = 130 \text{ units}} = 3.23 \text{ minutes}$$

Substituting the newly calculated standard SOE time of the basic resource calculation with the new standard time weighted, the number of resources for process F is calculated as

$$\frac{ST_w}{\text{Takt}} = \# \text{ Resources}$$

Therefore, the number of resources for process F is

$$\frac{27.6}{3.23} = 8.54 \text{ or } 9 \text{ resources}$$

The number of resources is rounded up to the next whole number. This makes sense, because it is not possible to have a portion of a person, workstation, machine, or amount of inventory. If the fractional value is 0.1 or greater, the number should always be rounded up. If less than 0.1, the number may be rounded down, which would translate to one less resource. Consider the rounding down carefully, as it is better to have too many resources than not enough. Resources can always be adjusted after the line is operating smoothly.

Always remember that the standard time is a weighted average and Takt time is based on an estimated product mix and volume. These numbers represent *averages*. Attempting to achieve precision when making rounding decisions on an average number often reaps diminishing returns. The decision to round up or down is subjective, based on knowledge of the particular process. To be conservative, the Lean methodologies suggest erring on the high side by rounding up.

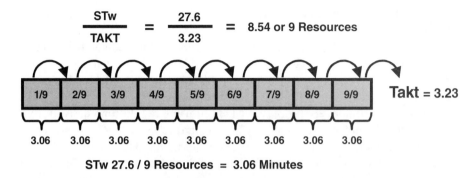

Figure 4.7 Balanced Workstations at Takt

With most products, the lowest component of product cost is labor. A resource can always be removed, but adding a resource later can be more difficult. In the end, the goal is to make the Lean manufacturing line as successful as possible to produce product in the Takt time. The rounding up of resources can provide extra latitude when it comes to achieving the Takt time targets. This is particularly true when defining human resources. Humans are not machines, and their productivity can vary from day to day. Rounding up resources should be considered when designing the Lean manufacturing line. If an error is made by including the cost of one additional labor resource, it will still have little effect on the total product cost.

If the ST_w is divided by the rounded-up number of resources (9 in this case), the resulting work content time at each resource will be 3.06 minutes (27.6 ÷ 9 = 3.06 minutes). This time is less than the Takt time of 3.23 minutes. The difference in time gives some leeway to the operators and helps to assure the Takt time target can be met (Figure 4.7).

The number of required resources must be determined for every process identified on the process flow diagram. The resource calculation is an expression of the amount of resources per process required to produce the throughput volume identified in the identified process Takt time.

The resource calculation is the line-balancing component of the Lean manufacturing methodologies. This technique is profoundly simple both in concept and practice. Consider the value of being able to balance all manufacturing processes required to produce a product or subassembly so they are completed at the same time! This ability to balance manufacturing processes is the major difference between Lean manufacturing and the MRP launch of orders into manufacturing.

The balancing of work is the key to producing product in its work content time. When the nonvalue-added elements of wait and queue time have been eliminated from the manufacturing lead time, significant lead time reduction results. Working in balance is also the key for significantly reducing or eliminating work-in-process inventories that will ultimately lead to the reduction of finished goods inventory. The less time products spend in the manufacturing process being manufactured, the easier it is to manage customer orders. Overhead costs are reduced due to the elimination of expediting and planning system transactions.

Because work in every process is balanced using a Takt time derived from required throughput volume, the varying standard times of different processes are of little consequence. The number of resources required to meet the Takt time target goal is the important factor. The Lean methodologies seek to achieve Takt at each process. The resource calculation identifies the amount of resources needed to achieve that Takt time goal.

DEFINING RESOURCES

Now that the *amount* of resources needed has been calculated, defining the physical attributes of the individual resource is required. If the standard time used to determine the amount of resources is the labor time from the SOE, then the resource calculated first will be the number of required people. The resulting resource figure is the number of persons required to produce the throughput volume for the time identified on the SOE.

While other factors will impact the final number of people needed to staff the Lean line, initial resource calculation should provide a "sanity" test for accuracy and an indication of productivity opportunities. The calculated labor resource head count for the Lean line future volume should be in proportion to the current head count and current volume. Comparing the two validates the results of the resource calculations. Wide fluctuation in the head count/volume comparisons may require an investigation of the SOE times used for resource calculation or the causes of productivity loss.

If the SOE times are valid, then by summing the number of people identified as resources for the future throughput volume and comparing it to the existing head count, the scope of productivity improvement can be estimated. SOE times assume 100% productivity, and the final resource calculation may need to be increased by the current productivity factor. Compare this number to the current head count. If current head count is greater than the calculated resource, the difference is the amount of productivity improvement available to the Lean line. Compare only processes that are similar before and after the implementation.

After the number of persons required to staff the Lean line has been determined, each person will require a physical location from which to perform the work defined for that process. Therefore, the resource calculation simultaneously defines both required people and the number of physical workstations. Individual workstations can take various forms. If the process is *assembly,* and the product is a kitchen appliance, the workstation is likely to be a workbench. It could also be a flat surface, a roller conveyor, or a ball transfer table. For a larger product, the workstation could be a painted location on the shop floor sized to the dimensions of the product. Depending on the product, the manufacturing process could be a combination of several different types of workstations. However, the total number of workstations must match the number of resources calculated for each process.

As part of the final line design layout, each workstation must be defined by its physical attributes and the dimensions of its footprint on the shop floor. Every effort should be made to keep the footprint as small as possible to optimize the amount of valuable shop floor used. If the physical dimension of the product is 12 inches wide and 6 inches deep, a 6-foot-wide workbench is not really necessary to complete the work. An alternative to one large bench might be to paint a line down the middle to separate the table into two 36-inch workstations that will still accommodate the work just as well. If possible, two workstations (resources) can occupy the same space as one workbench. If the product is only 6 inches deep, a 48-inch-deep workbench is not really necessary. Lean methodologies consider excess workstation space as wasteful. Often, creativity is required to size the workstation to the work to be performed.

If the SOE time for the process is a machine, the resource calculation will be the number of machines required to meet the Takt time target. As with the workstations identified for the labor resources, a footprint of the machine resource is necessary. This would include the footprint of any support equipment or ancillary tables, benches, die carts, etc. needed to operate the machine.

If the amount of machine resources required exceeds the number of machines available, additional resources must be added. These resources can take the form of additional machines, multiple cavity dies or stations, additional inventory, or additional shifts. The Lean methodology only determines the amount of resources required to achieve the Takt time target. The Lean methodologies cannot create capacity where none exists. As part of the line design layout, the physical placement of all required resources must be established.

A common method for achieving balance to Takt time on a machine is to build additional inventory to accommodate the differences between Takt time and the cycle time of the machine. Rather than just estimating the amount of inventory to build, the Lean methodology requires that the appropriate quantity be calculated. The correct amount of inventory is calculated using the resource calculation. For a machine process, the formula would be:

$$\frac{\text{Cycle Time of Machine}}{\text{Process Takt Time}} = \text{\# Units of Inventory}$$

If a machine process similar to *paint* requires 60 minutes to continuously travel the conveyor length through a drying tunnel, and the Takt time is 3.23 minutes, the units of inventory would be 19 units. In this case, the 19 units of additional inventory would be the number of paint hooks attached to the conveyor on which 19 units are hung, each spaced to exit the tunnel every 3.23 minutes. Even though it takes a single unit 60 minutes to travel the distance through the paint process, the 19 units in the tunnel will support a 3.23-minute Takt time for the Lean line.

Another common machine time is a "burn-in" process similar to the ones used in quality procedures. If the burn-in is 120 minutes with a Takt time of 3.23 minutes, the units of inventory would be 120 ÷ 3.23 = 38 units. The machine time indicates that 38 burn-in stations or connections are required, where one unit starts the burn-in process every 3.23 minutes and another completes it every 3.23 minutes. For line design layout purposes, the footprint for the physical location of these 38 units must also be considered.

THE PHYSICAL LAYOUT OF RESOURCES

After resources have been quantified and their physical attributes defined, configuring the resources into a factory layout that facilitates visibility and movement of products must be completed. During SOE development, two items were identified as always being nonvalue-added — setups and moves.

The new factory layout should reduce or eliminate significant amounts of move time for product and materials. In addition, the physical placement of feeder (subassembly) processes at points in the line where that material is consumed into the downstream product assembly will reduce both move and wait time.

A paper simulation of the new facility should be created to relayout the factory into the Lean configuration. A paper simulation is preferred over a CAD drawing for two important reasons:

1. **Team participation:** A relayout of the factory to take advantage of the benefits of the Lean implementation should be a team activity. Many members of the company may have excellent ideas about how to improve the flow of product through the factory. The factory relayout is a good time to test the theories of team members. Participation should include shop floor personnel who work in manufacturing every day. Relayout of

the factory on a conference room table using a large sheet of paper invites contribution by all members. It is easier to work around a table for this activity than to lean over an engineer's computer monitor while creating a CAD drawing of the layout.

2. **Low cost:** The most effective line layouts are the result of numerous layout iterations. These iterations should be encouraged to achieve "buy-in" from all the team members. These iterations occur as individual team members around the table offer their own ideas or suggest changes to previous ideas. Good debate over optimum solutions for layout issues usually results in consensus. Iterations and debate often take the form of the relayout and movement of resource facsimiles. Using properly scaled paper cutouts of the resources facilitates the debate. Moving paper representations of resources around on a paper model is faster and cheaper than representing every idea in a computer system.

Begin the process by creating a large paper layout showing the perimeter of the new Lean area. The larger the paper, the better it will be for allowing team participation. Indicate all unmovable objects ("monuments"), such as power tunnels, roof supports, drains, large expensive-to-move equipment, and other permanent building structures. For each of the resources identified, prepare a paper cutout of its footprint, scaled to match the perimeter drawing.

Beginning at the point closest to the customer (usually shipping) and working upstream, lay out the calculated resource paper cutouts following the mixed-product process flow diagram. Test all ideas that minimize movement and optimize the flow of product from one workstation to another. Create footprint cutouts for all supporting fixtures, racks, and carts used to manufacture product even though they are not manufacturing resources themselves. Be sure to set aside space to accommodate required material movements, such as lift truck aisles and large material containers. Design workstations to be compact, but as ergonomic as possible for the operator.

The optimum line design should not be constrained by current legacy work flows. With monuments in mind, the layout should assume a clean slate with no barriers in preparation of the ideal line layout. The best line layout may suggest traversing an existing aisle. An aisle is not a monument! Keeping OSHA regulations and environmental and safety considerations in mind, the shop floor layout of the optimum Lean solution should take precedence over any previous arbitrary obstruction placements.

If money were no object, it would be possible to move anything and everything. As a practical matter, there are some items that may be too cost prohibitive to move. For some moves, the return on investment to do so does not justify relocation. Examples include heavy machine tools mounted on engineered concrete pads, dirty and dangerous processes, EPA processes that require special venting or maintenance requirements, or loud processes. It does not make sense to relocate such processes next to an assembly process. The final line design should recommend practical and cost-justified solutions to maximize the Lean methodologies and reflect common sense.

All of these examples should be considered when finishing the layout. When completed, all team members must agree to the final line design. The steering committee must also approve and sign off on the new Lean line layout. The paper layout with the resource cutouts should then be converted into a formal facility layout drawing, usually with a CAD system, by the manufacturing or facilities engineer. From the final layout, a facility plan for installing the line must be created. This usually involves dropping air and electrical lines, relocation of workbenches, and contracting with riggers and other contractors. If the new layout requires that production be shut down for a period of time, a schedule for the shutdown and relayout must also be developed.

ASSIGNING TASKS FOR EACH WORKSTATION

Once the number of resources has been determined, and each process has been balanced to a Takt time target, the exact work and quality inspection to be performed at each workstation must be defined. The SOE documents the sequential tasks for completing the work of each process. The individual work tasks to be completed at each workstation are defined by summing the time elements of the work tasks listed on the SOE until an amount equal to a Takt time is reached (Figure 4.8).

THE IN-PROCESS KANBAN SIGNALING METHODOLOGY

Very seldom is it possible to make a perfect cut-off on the SOE at the exact Takt time target. Because summing the tasks rarely equals a perfect Takt time, there will automatically be minor imbalances in the workstation definition. To overcome these minor differences in time and the natural imbalance between persons staffing the line, *in-process kanbans* (IPKs) are placed on the downstream side of the workstation. The IPK provides a temporary "parking space" for units that are completed faster than the downstream workstation can consume them.

An IPK is also used to signal when it is time to start production of the next unit in sequence. For the IPK signal to work, operator discipline is required. Only one partially completed unit of production is allowed in an IPK at a time. Units are not allowed to stack up. Work cannot commence at a workstation until

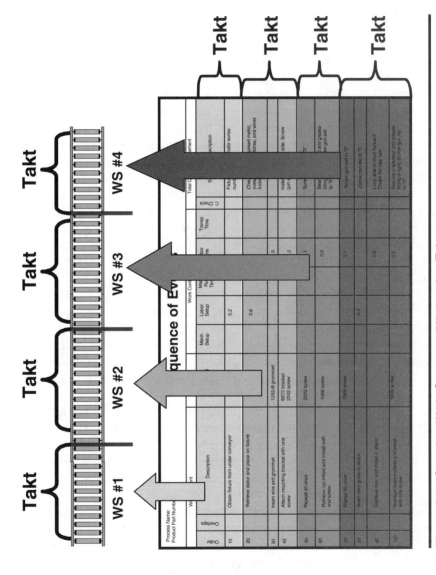

Figure 4.8   Grouping Work Content to Workstation Takt

its IPK becomes empty. The only way an IPK can become empty is for the unit to be consumed by the downstream process. The empty IPK is the signal and is the communication to the operator in the upstream workstation to begin work on the next product.

Once the IPK signal is received in the workstation to begin work on the next unit, the operator "pulls" the next partially completed unit from the upstream workstation, thereby creating an empty IPK signal for that operator. Response to the IPK signals located at each workstation throughout the Lean line and upstream into the feeders is what gives the Lean line the appearance of flowing downstream. When all workstations are balanced, the entire line ratchets every Takt time an IPK signal is received (i.e., a drumbeat or cadence).

The IPK is critical to the operation of the Lean line. IPKs control the speed of the line and help to smooth factors that cause imbalance. Different operators work at different speeds, some units take a little more time to complete at the workstation, or the component parts do not fit together well. If there were no way to control these causes of minor imbalance on a Lean line, faster workstations would just accumulate large piles of work in process as a solution for overcoming imbalance. Enforcing IPK discipline is the secret to making the Lean line flow and causing the operators on the line to work as a team to produce product at the same rate.

Scheduling production in the Lean factory is considerably simplified once factory layout and IPK signaling discipline drives the flow of work through the factory. Production scheduling on the Lean line begins at operation #1 of the Lean line, at the finished goods level. Because products are manufactured one unit at a time, they can be sequenced to move down the Lean line in the same order the customer requirement was received. The planner has only to determine the order of manufacture.

Products are introduced into the Lean line one unit at a time following predetermined sequencing rules designed to assure a balanced rate on the mixed-product line. Upon receiving an empty IPK signal, the operator in the first workstation of the Lean line simply pulls the next customer order into production by following the preset sequence the planner has chosen. This assures a first-in–first-out priority sequencing of customer orders.

Subassemblies are produced in feeder processes following the same IPK signaling methodology. With a balanced line and using IPKs to signal production, there is no need to order launch and schedule batch subassembly production. The output from these feeder processes is consumed directly into the downstream processes, and subsequent production in the feeder is initiated using the IPK kanban as a signal for replenishment.

In special cases, such as configure-to-order custom products, a sales order configuration document may be required to be sequenced along with the product.

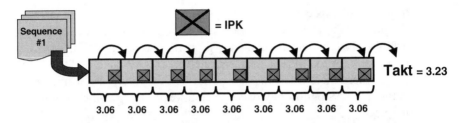

Figure 4.9   Sequence Customer Demand versus Schedule Production

This "configuration traveler" moves along with the product as it advances through manufacturing. The traveler indicates to the operator which parts are to be used to build the special configuration. The feeder process must also be sequenced in the same order as the consuming downstream processes (Figure 4.9).

DISCIPLINE FOR MAINTAINING WORKSTATION BALANCE

Because balanced processes are so critical to the success of a Lean line, periodic rebalancing is necessary to fine-tune the line. The Lean manufacturing line constantly seeks to achieve perfect balance to the established Takt time target. However, many problems can cause a line to become unbalanced. Over time, line operators can pick up bad habits. When imbalances are not corrected immediately, the Lean line will eventually fail. Management should look for the following signs of imbalance and correct them immediately:

- **Nest building:** An individual operator has decided to take ownership of a workstation. Some of the signs are personal items such as calendars, pictures, radios, and other creature comforts. This is a common habit that indicates an unwillingness to respond to the IPK. Because this person is unwilling to move in response to an IPK, he or she unilaterally decides when and where to do work. The rule on the Lean line is that people move to work; work does not move to the person. Don't wait until personal items accumulate at the workstation. Correct nest building as soon as the first item appears.
- **Stash cache:** Always ready for a rainy day, this person maintains his or her own private cache of parts. The justification for hoarding parts is usually a story about a parts shortage that occurred years ago. On a Lean line, operators build and material handlers provide parts! The same can be said for tools. Justification also includes a tale about needing a certain

tool to build a special model many years ago. Tools necessary to produce the products at every workstation should be provided by the company. Tools and equipment are company property and belong at the workstation. Look for tool boxes, drawers, shelves, file cabinets, and any other place where tools and parts can be stashed for future use. Continually enforce the 5S philosophy of "a place for everything and everything in its place."

- **I'm special:** Because of company tenure, longevity, or special skills, this operator feels he or she has earned the right to choose the work he or she will do. If uncorrected, such operators will cherry-pick only the units they prefer to work on. Sometimes they also establish nests and initiate a stash cache where they can be left alone to work only on the products of their own choosing. When observing the Lean line, pay attention to the product mixes in the IPKs. Confirm that the daily sequence selected by the planner is being followed on a first-in–first-out basis.

- **The better idea:** Operators usually have great ideas and suggestions for improvement, but they cannot be allowed to incorporate those individual ideas unilaterally. If one operator acting alone decides to stop using a piece of equipment or to reshuffle work, it can throw the entire line out of balance. Operators must be encouraged to channel those ideas appropriately. Demand the use of continuous process improvement and kaizen meetings as the forum to channel these suggestions. New ideas and process improvements impact the entire line and must be managed.

- **Speed trumps Takt:** Prior to the implementation of the Lean manufacturing line, operators were always instructed to build as much product as possible as fast as they could. In companies where absorption has always been the primary performance measurement, the ability to do this was a sign of an individual's value to the company. With the Lean line, these same operators are now instructed to produce only one unit at a time in response to an IPK signal. When work is completed, it moves to the IPK. The new Lean environment will feel unnatural to them, and their old habits will not disappear simply because management wishes it so. Assure compliance to IPK signals. The IPK is the secret to maintaining one-piece flow, and management must maintain the discipline of one-piece flow. Do not allow operators to place more than one unit in an IPK. If there is a line balance problem, it will manifest itself as a breakdown at the IPK. Do not ignore this important warning sign. Employ the balancing techniques to resolve the problem.

One of the primary reasons Lean lines become imbalanced after their start-up is management indifference to these warning signs. Lines do not fail in one day. They fail over a long period of time as a result of a series of small actions that never get corrected. After spending so much time designing the Lean manufacturing line, it is easy for team members to think of reasons to shift responsibility for operation and maintenance of the line to someone else. Allowing indifference to flourish is the first step in returning to the old practices that caused transition to Lean manufacturing methodologies in the first place.

Silence is acceptance. Monitoring the Lean line is the responsibility of all managers. When a member of the management team observes a violation of Lean methodologies and chooses to do nothing, the message received by operators that their current behavior is acceptable is reinforced. Managers must correct operator violations immediately by explaining the violation and providing training in the correct methodology. All the work required to convert the facility to Lean can be lost if the new line is not maintained and improved. Always practice "management by walking around" (MBWA).

Another common mistake is assuming that the company's conversion to Lean manufacturing is merely a project of the month with a beginning and an end date. In a successful Lean implementation, nothing could be further from the truth! Lean manufacturing must become a way of life and the chosen manufacturing methodology for operating the facility. Factory conversion to Lean must be championed as a "top-down" activity, with the expected benefits articulated and weaved into the fabric of the company culture. Sponsorship from the grass-roots level only will jeopardize long-term success.

As the workstations achieve balance, always move any remaining imbalance to the final workstation. Then, by applying a series of balancing techniques, work to eliminate the imbalance at the final workstation. Always seeking ideal balance on the Lean line requires continuous process improvement discipline throughout the organization (Figure 4.10).

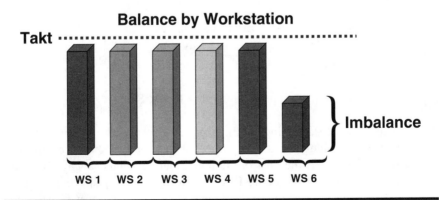

Figure 4.10 Seek Balance to Takt at Each Workstation

There are some simple techniques that can be used to overcome imbalances in the workstations. Use of these techniques should be implemented in the order presented. The first techniques are the simplest to apply and have the lowest cost. Each imbalance should begin with the first technique and progress through the additional techniques until the imbalance is resolved. Use the following techniques to continuously solve workstation imbalance:

1. **Look for work that can be eliminated:** Dynamic setups and moves are *always* candidates for elimination. Moves and setups have been identified on the SOE. Using continuous improvement techniques, exploit all opportunities for eliminating nonvalue-added work. Quality inspection work is also a candidate for elimination, along with process improvements that simplify work. Quality criteria and process improvement may require assistance from quality assurance and manufacturing engineering.
2. **Relocate work from workstation to workstation:** Relocation of work is one of the most common techniques for achieving workstation balance. Using the sequence of events, relocation is accomplished by reassigning work tasks from the SOE from one workstation to the next. Make sure the relocation of work is technically feasible and will not adversely affect quality.
3. **Add IPKs to the imbalanced workstation:** IPK = Inventory = $ Investment. If the addition of IPKs is necessary, make certain that all efforts to eliminate nonvalue-added work and all opportunities to relocate work have been completely exhausted first. Adding additional IPKs also means that additional production time will be required to manufacture the additional units. Avoid the temptation to guess the correct amount of IPK inventory to keep at the workstation. The correct amount of IPK inventory to be added is calculated as follows:

$$\frac{\text{Effective Minutes per Day}}{\text{Takt}} - \frac{\text{Effective Minutes per Day}}{\text{ST}_w \text{ of Process}} = \text{IPK Quantity}$$

$$\text{Extra Time Required} = \text{IPK} \times \text{ST}_w$$

4. **Add resources:** Adding machine or labor resources is often the most expensive solution to solving line imbalances and should be the last resort. However, the cost of adding resources should always be compared to the cost of adding IPK inventories. When justifying a capital expenditure request to purchase new equipment, the cost to carry the

calculated daily amount of IPK inventory along with the cost to carry and manage the inventory can be compared to the cost of purchasing new equipment. Make the best business decision for your company based on these costs.

5. **Sequence properly:** On a mixed-product line, the order of manufacture can have an impact on the balance of the line. Avoid sequentially running products with identical work content times. If possible, follow long work-content-time products with short work-content-time products. Mixing the sequence of products on the line throughout the day will help achieve the desired daily rate.

Seeking perfect balance at each workstation is a never-ending activity as mix and volume change. Balance is also affected as processes are improved. Lean manufacturers never achieve perfect balance. However, this does not mean that it should not be pursued. As optimum balance is achieved, the capability to produce product in its work content time is also achieved. This reduces the total manufacturing cycle time, which leads to the reduction of response time to customers and reduction of inventories. A manufacturer's capabilities to reduce response time and the total cost of production are powerful weapons for increasing market share.

Lean manufacturing is a completely different way of operating a manufacturing company. It is no magic bullet that will miraculously correct a long legacy of problems, but it does provide a set of operating techniques that yield immediate benefits. Continuing successful operation of your Lean manufacturing lines requires a commitment to seek continuous improvement using all the methodologies learned during the transformation process. For many companies, this dedication will require changing the company culture. All the hard work will be rewarded with all the benefits of Lean manufacturing.

DESIGNING 5S INTO THE LINE DESIGN

Order and neatness are critical elements of the working environment. All material locations must be clearly marked. Only the necessary tools, fixtures, gauges, and other resources should be present at the workstations. No clutter or mess should be tolerated on the Lean line. There is no need to rely on the output of a shop floor control system to determine the location or progress of an order.

Implementation of the Lean manufacturing methodologies supports the concepts of 5S. The elements of 5S and applied Lean methodologies are complementary.

Sifting (Seiri)

Remove items not used to manufacture products on a regular basis.

1. A major component of the Lean manufacturing line implementation is the removal of items identified as unnecessary for the production of product. Such items include tool boxes, file cabinets, lockers, tables, stools, personal items such as microwave ovens, desks, tables, shelves, and drawers. These items offer temptations to accumulate unwanted materials such as parts, tools, books, and other items not required to manufacture product.
2. The temptation to accumulate these types of items is part of the human condition. There is a comfort level that comes with surrounding oneself with familiar objects. This comfort level may be based on past experiences like parts shortages, the unavailability of tools and fixtures, or a need to know how to produce infrequently demanded products. Operators like to create comfort with a "home away from home," made up of a collection of personal items. Often, these personal items are accumulated in a personal workstation. The establishment of personal workstations conflicts with the Lean manufacturing concepts of balance and flexibility.

Sorting (Seiton)

Identify and arrange items that belong in the area — a place for everything and everything in its place.

1. In addition to the physical location of workstations where work is actually performed, there are always tools, fixtures, and parts that must be located so the operator can easily access them. Each of these required items should have an assigned location either at the workstation where the item is used for daily production or adjacent to the point of usage. Suggestions include silhouette boards for tools and fixtures located within operator reach, painted squares on the floor, suspended air and electrical lines, and kanban racks and containers.
2. For all materials not used directly at the workstation, assigned locations are also important. Such materials include pallet jacks, forklifts, cleaning materials, trash receptacles, and any other portable material-handling fixtures. A "parking space" should be placed adjacent to the workstation where the item is used most frequently. The space should be painted, and material handlers must be disciplined to return the item to its parking space when not in use.

Sweeping (Seiso)

Maintain order, sweep, and clean.

1. The reasons for maintaining a clean workplace are obvious. Operators should take pride in their workplace, and that pride is reflected in the product they build. Just as important, a clean workplace also provides an early warning system of problems. A cluttered workplace can hide problems such as rejected materials that indicate a defective quality process, spare parts that may indicate a faulty kanban system, or incomplete units that indicate an imbalance on the Lean line. A clean Lean line environment helps to make these potential problems conspicuous.
2. Time to perform these cleaning activities can be built into the Takt time calculation. A statement of minutes per shift makes up the numerator of the Takt time calculation. Time needed to perform cleanups at the beginning and end of each shift can be built into this calculation. Since resources for Lean manufacturing lines are based on the Takt time calculation, incorporating this activity into this calculation will provide the time necessary to do this work every day.

Standardize (Seiketsu)

Practice management discipline.

1. Making the most of Lean manufacturing methodologies requires the minimization of individual interpretations when decisions must be made. Much effort has been invested in the design of the Lean line so that operators can maximize the time spent building product, with less time spent making decisions. Operators have been trained to respond to decisions using the Lean manufacturing methodologies. All operators should follow the same rules.
2. A key benefit for the Lean manufacturer is the ability to perform MBWA, management by walking around. Walking through a Lean facility, it is very easy to see what is happening in manufacturing. The IPK product flow indicates what to do and when to do it. The supervision required can often be decreased, because of the simplicity of the Lean line design.

Sustain (Shitsuke)

It is management's responsibility to reinforce and demonstrate leadership.

1. Monitoring work conditions is the responsibility of the managers as they perform MBWA. When a member of the management team observes a violation of rules and chooses to say nothing about it, operators assume their behavior is acceptable. Operators are limited to individual interpretations at their workstations. Management must take ownership of solving problems on the Lean manufacturing lines. Managers have the advantage of seeing the bigger picture of the whole line. This is MBWA.

   ■ Monitor work conditions. Use newly established housekeeping policies as a management tool to focus on details. Small details are the first to deteriorate on the line. Look for items that do not belong. Solve problems immediately.

   ■ Monitor operator flexibility. The ability of a Lean line to vary mix and adjust its volume on a daily basis, based on actual daily demand, is a key differentiator of your Lean line and batch manufacturing. This ability provides a competitive advantage to your company. Flexible employees are key elements of Lean manufacturing.

   ■ Monitor overtime. The need for overtime should always be a temporary condition. It should be used for unanticipated spikes in demand, for only a short period of time. If overtime is permanently required, it may be time to rebalance the Lean line with a new volume capacity.

   ■ Monitor teamwork. Encourage team performance. Request ideas for continuous improvement. Allow people to have control over their own destiny. Be certain the teams focus on the performance of the line. Make certain teams have a simple and accessible kaizen or continuous improvement mechanism for improving the product or its processes.

   ■ Monitor the line's performance. The proof of success is performance. Establish performance measurements for the line. Track them and publish them. Post performance measurements on the line to display the daily production target, along with progress of actual production.

   ■ Monitor in-process quality. Establish and continue emphasizing the value and importance of inspecting for quality criteria. The final objective is for all defects to be caught and fixed before they ever reach the quality assurance final inspection process, the last point of rejection, or the customer. Perform spot checks on the lines. Have a team leader or manager pick a unit at random from a conveyor or IPK and verify that the work at that point is no more or less than it should be and that it is done correctly. Do this frequently and in plain sight!

   ■ Monitor training. Employee training is critical to ensuring a consistent and repeatable flow of product every day. The better trained employees are, the more flexible they are. The more flexible employees are, the better the line will flow.

2. Operation of the Lean manufacturing methodologies requires a shift from the way work was done in the past. Lean manufacturing methodologies are powerful, but they require support and maintenance. The benefits received from the implementation of the Lean manufacturing methodologies will be in direct proportion to management's commitment to making them work on the shop floor. When members of the management team do MBWA, they must be observant for any violation of the Lean rules (quality checks, teamwork, flexibility, and IPK compliance). Make corrections immediately. Doing nothing condones the behavior.

5

THE KANBAN
STRATEGIES

The Lean manufacturing methodologies separate product into two components: its labor or work content and the component parts. Lean manufacturers seek to achieve balance with the work content and physically link the manufacturing processes together so that the output of one process is directly consumed into the next downstream process. Resources are then staffed to match the daily customer requirements so that demand is met without the accumulation of finished goods inventories.

Work content represents only half of what is necessary to produce any product. Component parts are also required for the manufacture of a product. The Lean manufacturing methodologies recommend using a kanban material-handling strategy to make necessary components available to the manufacturing processes.

The most common usage of kanban is the "two-bin" material-handling system. Two-bin systems have been around for a long time. Lean manufacturing did not invent the two-bin system. Their use is not a new invention. However, as with many manual noncomputerized systems, they fell out of favor with the advent of modern MRP systems. Japanese manufacturers can be credited with resurrecting and improving upon the earlier two-bin systems by putting them to work in their post–World War II noncomputerized manufacturing systems.

In a two-bin system, when the first container becomes empty through consumption by production, the empty container itself becomes a "signal," indicating that the container needs to be refilled or replenished. During the time required for replenishment of the first container, the second container remains at the workstation, continuing to supply manufacturing. In those cases where the "container" was impractical to move or act as the signal itself, a card was adapted to serve as the replenishment signal.

If there is one single word in the entire manufacturing lexicon that has been misunderstood, misused, and misapplied, it would have to be the word kanban. Since its rediscovery by Western manufacturers in the 1970s and 1980s, the two-bin kanban system has arguably been applied incorrectly more than any other system.

The term kanban is often attached to any material-handling method that just happens to use small containers at a workstation or cards to reorder materials. The term has even been used to describe the manufacturing line itself (i.e., the kanban line). Just as knowledge of kanban systems evolved from the first days of observing Japanese applications, so too has the evolution of its correct application over time.

Current applications did not begin with the misapplication of original system concepts. Previously installed kanban systems usually are modified or compromised with small changes over long periods of time usually to accommodate other systems or methodologies. In a dynamic fast-paced manufacturing environment, the voice of a kanban system champion can easily be drowned out by new voices. Eventually, the original designers of the kanban system move on, and the only residual of the original kanban system that remains is often the term itself.

Kanban is a Japanese word that defines a communication, a signal or card. It is a technique used to advance products and/or pull materials to a Lean manufacturing process. There are three basic types of kanban systems, each with a specific application for a specific purpose. In Lean manufacturing, kanban may have several variations based on specific application:

- **In-process kanban:** A clear and visible signal placed on the downstream side of an operation to signal the upstream operation to perform another Takt time amount of work. An in-process kanban also serves as a signal for an operator to flex to waiting work.
- **Single-card Kanban:** A two-bin material replenishment methodology using two equally sized containers that contains quantities based on the time required to replenish the material. As the first container is emptied, it becomes the signal for replenishment while the second continues to supply the point of consumption.
- **Multiple-card kanban:** A material replenishment technique that uses separate multiple signals, move and produce, to communicate replenishment. Multiple signals are typically used in shared manufacturing processes or independent cells where long setups and great distances that require long replenishment times are present.

THE IN-PROCESS KANBAN

The first type of kanban system is the in-process kanban (IPK). The IPK is used on the manufacturing line to "signal" when it is time to produce another Takt time unit of production. The IPK has three purposes:

1. To accommodate minor imbalances on the Lean line
2. To maintain the correct sequence of production to meet customer demand
3. To alert the operator when it is time to "flex" to the next workstation to help achieve balance on the Lean line

Because human beings are not machines, achieving perfect balance for each Takt time on the Lean line is difficult, if not impossible, to accomplish. Variabilities in individual people, parts, products, and models happen all day long during the operation of the line. To overcome minor imbalances of these variables, IPKs are placed on the downstream side of the workstation. The IPK provides a temporary parking space for units completed faster than the consuming workstation.

Another use of the IPK system is to signal the next unit of production on the Lean line itself. An IPK is used to signal the next unit to be produced in sequence. Work cannot commence until the downstream IPK becomes empty. This signaling generates the communication to the shop floor as to when to begin work on the next product. Products are introduced into the Lean line one unit at a time in a specific sequence to help assure a balanced "flow" of work through the factory or to meet the priority of sales demand established by the planner.

Because products are manufactured one unit at a time, they can be sequenced to move down the Lean line in the same priority as the customer requirement was received. The planner has only to determine the order of manufacture. The operator in the first workstation of the Lean line, upon receiving an empty IPK signal, simply begins production of the next unit in the same order the planner has chosen. A first-in–first-out methodology must be followed.

The ability of operators to be flexible by moving up and down the line is a requisite for achieving productivity on the Lean line. Lean lines are restaffed each day based on the amount of product to be built that day. If the volume of product to be sequenced on the line is less than the designed capacity of the line, the output rate is modified by staffing the Lean line with only the number of operators needed to meet that day's production.

Changing the staffing daily to match the demand volume requires the intentional "suboptimization" of the Lean line. If line capacity is designed for 10 operators with 10 workstations to produce 100 units, but daily sales are 80 units, Lean would require staffing of only 8 operators at 8 workstations. Throughout the production day, any product remaining at the two unstaffed workstations sits idle for a Takt time. After each Takt cycle, operators would then be required to "flex" into the unstaffed workstation and perform the required work on the idled material.

Suboptimizing the line by staffing to meet daily demand causes two dynamics to occur: (1) A "hole" in the line is created. In the example of ten workstations with eight operators, two holes are created. On the first Takt cycle, two units receive no work. These units require an extra Takt cycle to be completed. (2) The holes in the lines move up and down to workstations on the line all day. When a hole reaches the last workstation on the line, a Takt cycle is missed and one unit is not packed off as a finished unit.

At the end of the day, 20% of the capacity remained underutilized in the form of missed Takt time cycles, while 80% of the capacity was utilized to meet the required demand of eight units. Even though the capacity was suboptimized, this was the intended result. The only remaining issue with suboptimization is the utilization of the two unused persons. Lean manufacturing recommends operators become as flexible as possible for reassignment to other processes if not required on any given day.

To allow this flexing of operators to work, IPK signals are required at the downstream side of each workstation to place incomplete units. These incomplete units or empty IPKs serve as the signals to indicate to operators where and when it is necessary to move.

THE SINGLE-CARD KANBAN SYSTEM

The most common usage of kanban in Lean implementations, or the method most often referred to when referencing kanban, is the two-bin single-card material kanban system. In the single-card two-bin kanban system, two identical containers are filled with an equal amount of parts. Both containers are placed at the same location where the material is used. As material is consumed on a first-in–first-out basis and the first container is emptied, the empty container becomes the "card" or "signal" for replenishment. Single card refers to the card attached to each container advising the material handler of the replenishment location and the container quantity to be refilled.

The second container remains at the workstation, allowing manufacturing to continue production. Its card is identical to the first container. The containers are then refilled at predetermined replenishment locations or points. Individual parts can have multiple usage and replenishment points. For purchased materials, final replenishment points ultimately terminate with the supplier's location.

While this replenishment cycle for the first container is occurring, the second

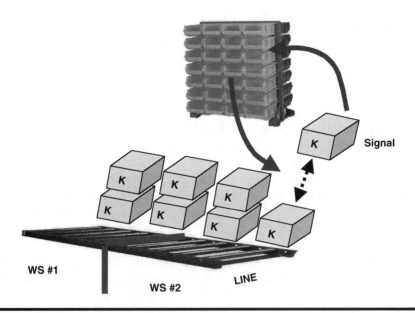

Figure 5.1 Kanban Replenishment Cycle

container remains at the consuming location, providing parts to continue production. Eventually, the material in the second container is consumed. If the container quantities are correctly sized with the appropriate amount of inventory, the last part in the second container will be consumed just as the first container is returned from being replenished, or before the passing of one additional Takt time (Figure 5.1).

The key to any kanban system is the creation of a "signal." As individual parts are consumed and container supply is exhausted, *a signal must be created.* In the case of the two-bin system, the first empty container serves as the signal. This signal demands replenishment for the resupply of that specific part. If that signal is overlooked or ignored, a stock-out situation could occur at the consumption point.

As the supply of parts at the point of consumption is exhausted and a signal occurs, the location where that part can be resupplied must also be designated. The first usage for a part is the workstation where it is installed into an assembly. This usage is the "point of consumption," or "point of usage." For every point of consumption, there must also be a predetermined location where the parts for replenishment can be stored and retrieved. This is referred to as the "point of resupply" or "replenishment point."

While specific operations or workstations can be identified as separate points of usage, creating individual nomenclature for each combined with its points of replenishment can create an exponential proliferation of pull linkages. The common name for the consumption point in the assembly process is *line*. By using the generic term "line," most kanban system users find this generic designation to be sufficient for most applications. This common nomenclature intentionally limits the number of pull sequences to simplify maintenance of pull sequences and pull chains.

The relationship between the consumption point and the replenishment point must be identified. This relationship of consumption and replenishment points is referred to as a *pull path, pull code, pull sequence,* or *pull link.* Each part number selected to be included in the kanban system must have the individual consumption and replenishment points identified. Both points of usage and resupply need to have a name designation. A common name convention for the point of usage where the part is ultimately consumed into an assembly is called *line.* This is because the part is being installed into an assembly built on or for the Lean "Line." It is also common practice to give the "line" designation to any other location where a part is installed where no additional work will be done on the part (e.g., a feeder process or a service parts center).

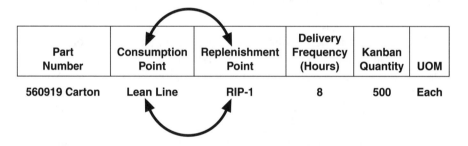

Part Number	Consumption Point	Replenishment Point	Delivery Frequency (Hours)	Kanban Quantity	UOM
560919 Carton	Lean Line	RIP-1	8	500	Each

The physical replenishment point for material used on the production line should be located within a short distance from the line. The pull sequence is established to identify the "consumption" and "replenishment" locations. This information is provided to facilitate the material handler responsible for performing the actual replenishment. Empty kanbans are then refilled from the replenishment point location. In turn, replenishment point kanbans are then refilled from either stores or the supplier directly. If suppliers are certified for reliability and dependability, materials can be delivered directly to the replenishment point location, bypassing the stockroom. Suppliers, as members of the supply chain, can be notified by receiving these signals electronically (via the Internet) based on real-time shop floor usage.

The point of resupply for line materials is commonly called a *RIP*. RIP is the acronym for raw and in-process materials. The RIP is the primary replenishment location for the storage of materials used for refilling parts to the "line."

Another commonly used term is *supermarket*. Supermarket is a more descriptive term for the line materials replenishment cycle. Supermarket is the metaphor for the simplicity of resupplying household items used on a day-to-day basis from the local supermarket. Much like the local supermarket, a kanban RIP or supermarket requires a wide variety of items in close proximity to the point of usage with ample inventories to meet unforeseen demand.

Rather than keep large amounts of materials tied up in inventories in the home pantry (i.e., the line), the frugal chef is happy to let the local supermarket (RIP) maintain sufficient inventories to supply his or her recipe (product) requirements. When an ingredient is required, a short trip is made to the local supermarket to purchase only what is needed as close to the point of consumption as possible. Inventory of ingredients (materials) is kept to a minimum yet is in close enough proximity to supply production needs on short notice.

As with the local supermarket, the more frequent the replenishment, the greater the turn on materials. The same dynamic would be true in manufacturing. Inventory residing on the line should be rapidly consumed with a very short replenishment time, or a faster turn rate, while RIP inventory quantities are sized so that replenishment occurs more infrequently. The use of either term to describe the replenishment inventory location is acceptable; however, the term RIP is most frequently used to describe this inventory.

There is no set rule for the number of supermarkets or RIP locations, but it is not unusual to see several "supermarkets" in a manufacturing facility. The number of supermarkets required is based on the total number of parts, the desired replenishment velocity, and the size of the individual facility. As with "line" designations, creating too many supermarket locations can proliferate the quantity of pull links. Careful consideration should be given to the use of multiple supermarket designations, as overuse can cause diminishing returns on the investment of time required to maintain them.

Using the same two-bin configuration as with the line location, the RIP location contains inventories of duplicate parts used at the line location. While identified as the replenishment point for the line pull sequence, it is also a consumption point for inventory consumed to satisfy the replenishment on the line. Therefore, the RIP inventory is both a consumption point and a replenishment point. As with the line inventory, a signal for material replenishment must be generated when the first container is emptied. The empty container serves as the kanban signal for replenishment. Just as with the line kanban, the RIP replenishment point must also be identified.

Replenishment of the RIP location can occur at two possible replenishment points. The first is a stockroom location where purchased materials from suppliers have been stored. Purchased materials are delivered to the stockroom from the supplier. The supplier delivers material based on the required due date in

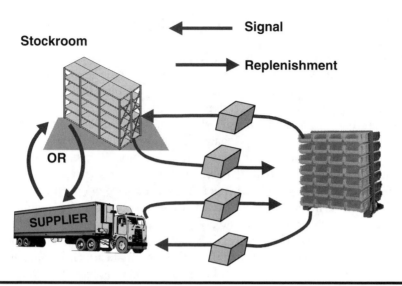

Figure 5.2 RIP Replenishment Points

quantities planned by the planning system. The delivery date established for the supplier is based on forecasted demand of future requirements captured by the planning system (Figure 5.2).

Another location for replenishment to the RIP location is directly to the supplier. At this point, rather than sending an empty physical container, the signal would more likely be in the form of an electronic signal (e.g., fax, bar code, Internet, or even a phone call from the buyer).

Today, new opportunities are emerging with the electronic and e-commerce technologies. The ability to connect businesses via the Internet and enable them to buy and sell goods and services among each other is an exciting concept. Real-time communication, elimination of the middleman, instant order processing, tightened kanban inventories, and other efficiencies offer a company the opportunity to transform obsolete procedures and reduce costs. The pull sequence routine is a critical link to and provides the required platform from the shop floor to the supplier in the electronic kanban communication.

Because a high-speed Internet connection can transmit information at the speed of light, there is an even greater need for a system to be in place to assure that information is as correct as possible. The two-bin kanban system provides the platform to make e-commerce transactions accurate and meaningful for both the manufacturer and suppliers. With balanced and linked manufacturing processes capable of producing products one at a time in their true manufacturing lead times, material kanban systems will only generate material replenishment signals based on real consumption rather than forecast. Internet transactions can now consist of pull chains that extend, electronically, beyond the four walls of manufacturing, linking the customer to manufacturing through to the supplier.

Without this platform in place, what is the basis for supplier transactions? Will it be the MRP action item report transmitted at the speed of light only to be retransmitted with the next iteration of MRP? How many cycles of changed dates and quantities transmitted at the speed of light will it take for a supplier to pronounce the end of its participation in your electronic experiment?

Ideally, the preferred replenishment point for a RIP location would be directly to the supplier. However, the most popular replenishment point for most manufacturers remains the stockroom. The primary reason for this preference is a lack of confidence in the supplier's ability to deliver products on time reliably while meeting dependable and repeatable quality criteria. The risk of shutting down a manufacturing line due to a shortage of purchased material is just too great a responsibility to be left with a supplier! This fear is a primary cause for the accumulation of "just-in-case" inventories.

In reality, it is unfair to apply these reliability and dependability fears to all suppliers. If these fears could be overcome, the amount of purchased materials residing in the stockroom could be greatly reduced or even eliminated. Developing reliability and dependability criteria for a supplier so deliveries can be made directly to the RIP location, bypassing the stockroom, is the best justification for a supplier certification program.

The Replenishment Time

Once consumption and replenishment points have been established, the time required to physically perform the replenishment must be determined. The replenishment time is defined as the time required to retrieve the signal container, transport the container to the replenishment point, refill the container, and return the container to its assigned location at the consumption point. The time required to complete this replenishment cycle will determine the amount of inventory remaining in the second container to sustain line production while the first container is being refilled.

Because replenishment time is used to establish inventory quantities of material containers, it is the crucial element for determining inventory investment and turn rate on the shop floor.

The amount of material for each container at each consumption point is calculated as:

$$\frac{\text{Daily Demand} \times \text{Replenishment Time}}{\text{Package Size}} = \text{Container Quantity}$$

where

- **Daily demand** = The average daily rate of demand for a part number. Daily rate can be determined by establishing the demand of all the parent part numbers using that part and multiplying by the required demand established by the bill of material (BOM): [Σ Demand × (Quantity BOM)]. This calculation is the product of the MRP system "explosion" routine for parts requirements generation. Kanban does not consider the time phasing of MRP.
- **Replenishment time** = The time required to retrieve the signal container, transport the container to the replenishment point, refill the container, and return the container to its assigned location at the consumption point. Replenishment time is typically stated in days or percentage of days (i.e., 50% = one-half day of material requiring replenishment twice per day). If daily demand is 100 and replenishment time is 0.5, the quantity of material in the container would be 50 pieces.
- **Package size** = Some materials may be supplied in packages (e.g., hardware, small parts, partitioned parts, and fragile items). These components are usually difficult to handle on an individual basis. Because the part number is supplied prepackaged with a set quantity, the kanban formula will calculate for the number of packages required to cover the replenishment time. If no package size is designated, the default is one. Package sizes are usually seen at the RIP and stores replenishment points.

When establishing the kanban system for the first time, there may be a temptation to squeeze the replenishment times to make them as small as possible to increase material velocity and reduce inventory investment. However, this strategy does have a cost. Increased velocity of material movement means increased material-handling costs, more material handlers, more movement, and more traffic throughout the manufacturing area. Therefore, trade-off decisions must be made to balance the inventory investment and material-handling costs. Achieving optimum balance between inventory investment and material handling costs will result with multiple iterations of replenishment time.

A common technique for optimizing inventory investment is reviewing the daily demand quantity for the kanban calculation. Recall that a daily demand quantity must be established to calculate Takt time and determine the quantity of manufacturing resources to meet that demand. Because Lean lines are designed with the capacity to meet future demand, future desired capacity is established to consider a volume greater than current demand.

This projected increase in volume may represent a significant increase (up to 50%) over current demand volume. When operating a Lean line, reducing the staffing of the line to suboptimize the output can regulate variations in daily sales volume. Once in place, there is no mechanism in kanban to accommodate a daily variance in demand. Signals are created when containers are emptied. If the quantity in the kanban container is sized for a daily demand volume based on significant future sales, the replenishment signal can exceed the desired replenishment time. Inventory quantities will be too large and inventory turn rate slower than expected.

The kanban system may be operational several years in advance of achieving the projected sales volumes of the demand of factory capacity. To accommodate any linear growth in demand volume, daily demands used for kanban calculation can and should be modified to reflect sales volumes at the time of system implementation. Therefore, if the Lean line is designed for a future volume of 150 units, but current sales volumes are 100, the kanban containers should be sized at 100. If sized at 150, replenishment will take 50% longer to occur. Material will remain in inventory 50% longer than desired.

Linked combinations of pull sequences are referred to as *pull chains*. A pull chain must be established for each part used in the kanban system. The pull chain identifies the complete series of consumption and replenishment point relationships for each part managed by the kanban system. Each pull sequence in the pull chain must also have a replenishment time identified.

Consumption Point	1 Day	Replenishment Point	3 Days	Replenishment Point	10 Days	Replenishment Point
Lean Line ———→		RIP-1 ———————→		Central Stores ———→		Supplier

The pull chain is also a policy statement as to the amount of inventory that will reside in the kanban system. Because inventory quantities are based on stated replenishment time, inventory investment can be managed by managing the replenishment time between pull sequences.

Setup and Day-to-Day Operation of the Single-Card Two-Bin Kanban System

After the pull chains and inventory investment decisions have been made, it is time to fill containers, consider the presentation of kanban materials, and begin operation of the system. The initial setup of a kanban system can represent a significant amount of work. Many companies underestimate the time and physical labor necessary to get the system in place and operational. Based on a simple line-RIP-stores pull chain, there will be at least four containers that will require filling, labeling, and presenting at the points of consumption and resupply.

Multiply that by the number of parts in the kanban system and the time required adds up to a large project. However, once initial setup is completed, daily maintenance routines will be limited to mix/volume and engineering changes. The successful kanban system setup must enlist the help of as many persons as possible to assure completion prior to starting the Lean line with the material kanban two-bin operating system in place.

Sizing Containers to the Calculated Kanban Quantity

It is very important to match the physical kanban container to the calculated kanban quantity to assure inventory investment integrity. Humans have a tendency to use the space available to them. This can be confirmed by inspecting most people's basement, attic, garage, or storage locker. When it is time to decide whether to keep or dispose of something, the decision is often based on the storage space available. Operators bring this tendency to work with them.

If a kanban container is larger than necessary to hold the calculated quantity, the tendency will be to fill the container to its capacity rather than substitute a container that more closely matches the specified kanban quantity. Oversize containers will inflate the desired inventory investment. Often, there is a temptation to avoid the cost of purchasing suitable containers, opting to reuse existing containers. If existing container capacities are not sized with the calculated kanban quantities in mind, this cost avoidance may actually cost more in the long run.

When setting up the kanban system for the first time, it is imperative to remember the definition of a kanban as a "signal." A signal must be created when the calculated kanban quantity has been reached. That signal can take different forms with variations on the definition of a container. If materials are too large to be placed in a container, then the decision must be how to generate the signal when the calculated kanban quantity has been reached and an empty container cannot be used as the signal. When considering kanban container alternatives, the term container becomes figurative.

Variations on the generation of this signal can be as numerous as the imagination required to create them allows: A kanban card inserted halfway down a stack of materials, with the card signaling replenishment. A footprint for two pallets painted on the floor so that when one pallet is consumed and removed, the empty space is the kanban signal. A slanted roller rack with sufficient space for two containers, with the space for the second container painted as the signal. A sight glass on a silo indicating half full can be a kanban signal. The key is the creation of a signal.

With smaller parts that require capacity less than the smallest commercially available container, a single container can be used with a partition placed horizontally halfway in the container. When the front half of the container is consumed, the partition can be removed and used as the kanban signal. The back half of the container can be tipped forward to serve as the second container. Regardless of the solution ultimately devised, the critical element of the kanban system is the generation of a signal when the calculated kanban quantity has been reached. The remaining balance (second container) should be sufficiently sized to support production until replenishment has been accomplished.

The color of the kanban containers is not important. Color of containers is a matter of esthetics and personal taste. A single color may be preferred to project the order and discipline of the kanban system. Kanban practitioners have been known to designate certain colors for certain categories of parts or pull sequences. Unless extremely disciplined, the first time a designated container is substituted with another color, the color-coding system will become contaminated.

Remember that this is a Lean manufacturing system. Lean means the elimination of nonvalue-adding work. Are the time and effort required to maintain a color-coding system for the kanban system worth the investment? Do customers feel that color-coded kanban containers add value to the product they buy from you?

Container Labeling

Just as with the Lean line itself, the kanban system relies on the premise that systems are not designed around certain individuals. The careers of operators and material handlers of the kanban system can be fluid. People are promoted, change jobs, and retire. If the kanban system is not robust, its success will be tied to the last person operating it.

Systems are designed to meet the goals and needs of the organization. Operators using the system must exercise the rules and procedures established by the system. With Lean, the decision-making process to establish the desired results is completed before the operation of the system actually begins.

There must be room for improvement and system correction, but even that process must have structure. Be certain to provide a process like kaizen to capture and implement the good ideas generated by operators and material handlers. Users of the kanban system cannot take unilateral action to change the system as a result of their own personal interpretation. If allowed to do so, the kanban system will atrophy into an informal material-handling system with as many methods as material handlers. Unlike maintaining a color-coded container system, maintaining the discipline for operating the kanban system adds significant value to your product.

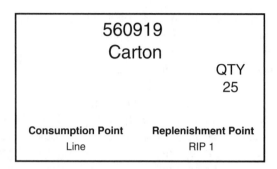

Figure 5.3 Kanban Card Label with Five Elements of Essential Information

After training, the primary way to communicate to the individual material handlers the parameters designed into the kanban system on a day-to-day, hour-by-hour basis is through the labeling of individual containers. There are five essential pieces of information that must be placed on the kanban container label to communicate the elements designed into the kanban system: part number, description, point of consumption, point of replenishment, and container quantity (see Figure 5.3). Optional additional information often included on the kanban label includes bar code, machine cell, machine die, or product grouping for machine setup.

If operators and material handlers maintain the integrity of the label elements, the desired inventory investment strategy will be achieved, BOM and item master records maintained, and customer fulfillment goals met.

If the kanban parts are small and inexpensive (e.g., hardware items such as screws, washers, nuts, etc.), a "quick-count" methodology can be used. Rather than painstakingly counting out a unit of measure of "each," a quick-count methodology would suggest a unit of measure such as a handful or scoop. Another common-sense modification might be to draw a line on the inside perimeter of the kanban container with a corresponding quick count of "fill to line." Kanban quantities and container capacities should make common sense to enhance the value-adding activities for the material handler. Again, these decisions are not to be made unilaterally by the material handler. Decisions to change kanban quantities must be made by a kanban system manager.

Material Presentation Considerations

The kanban system operates under the theory of the division of labor. This means that manufacturing operators are best utilized in the manufacture of products on the Lean line. Material handlers are best utilized refilling kanban containers and maintaining the inventory and kanban systems. For that reason, replenishment and movement of materials are the responsibility of professional material-handling personnel. Manufacturing operators are not allowed to "shop for parts" in the kanban system. Collecting parts for assembly is a major contributor to lost productivity for manufacturing operators.

The replenishment of kanban parts to the manufacturing operation works best when the manufacturing operator is not disturbed while performing work tasks at the workstation on the Lean line. Therefore, there must be a methodology in place to (1) advise the material handler that a container is empty and needs replenishment and (2) let the material handler know where to physically place the replenished material when returned to the line.

There are two methods for advising the material handler when material needs replenishment. The first is a multicolored light system. This system consists of three colored lights mounted next to one another. The typical colors are red, yellow, and green. The lights are elevated high into the air, with a switch for each color located at operator height. The lights are high in the air so the material handler can easily see the three lights from anywhere in the manufacturing area. These lights are evenly spaced and located adjacent to the manufacturing line, where operators can quickly and easily deposit empty kanban containers that have been consumed.

If all kanban containers are full, all green lights would be illuminated, indicating a full inventory condition exists. When a kanban container becomes empty, the operator is trained to move the empty container to a collection area near the light. The operator then switches the light from green to yellow. The yellow light notifies the material handler that a material replenishment is necessary at that location. The material handler then has the delivery frequency time to collect the container, replenish the material, and return the filled container to the consumption point. If the material in the second container at the consumption point is exhausted before the refilled container is returned, a stock-out condition will occur.

When a stock-out condition occurs and the operator cannot continue to produce product, the yellow light is switched to red. If the material is not replenished before another Takt time passes, the Lean line will stop upstream from that point. Work downstream from the workstation will dry up. A red light condition must attract immediate attention for resolution. Manufacturers often direct wire an additional red light into the production manager's or manufacturing engineer's office to assure immediate attention to the stock-out condition. Manufacturers can also expand the use of the red light condition to indicate manufacturing problems other than material stock-out conditions.

Another popular method is the "milk run" system. The creation of signals and the movement of containers to a central collection point adjacent to the Lean line are the same. The difference is there is no three-light system. The material handler simply has a "route" which is run periodically throughout the day. Empty containers are picked up, returned to the replenishment point, filled, and returned to the workstation with newly emptied containers picked up to repeat the cycle.

Higher volume Lean lines are more apt to use the three-light system, whereas lower volume lines usually opt for the milk run system. However, either system will work.

Placement of the kanban materials at the Lean line workstation should support ease of use for the manufacturing operator. This requirement should not be an issue if good material replenishment techniques are implemented. Interference with the operator should be avoided. Materials should be presented from the back side of the workstation. Slanted flow racks designed to feed materials to the operator are the best solution. Feeding from the back side requires labeling at the location with an additional label on the back side of the container.

When locating kanban containers at the workstation, always consider ergonomics for the operator. Locate kanban containers in front of the operator at arm's length to avoid the operator having to turn from side to side or 180 degrees to get material. Consider the average height of operators. In a Lean line, different operators will potentially be working at a workstation on any given day. Consider the Takt time of the line and consider the consequences of time and physical wear and tear on an operator making repetitive motions that many times a day. Kanban material placement is a critical element of the Lean workstation design.

Where possible, stacking containers vertically on top of one another is the preferred method. Containers placed side by side tempt the operator to use both containers simultaneously. Unfortunately, if this occurs, both containers will empty at the same time, potentially causing a line stoppage until replenishment can occur. If side by side is the only alternative, place an indicator on one of the containers to remind the operator which container to consume first.

Materials should be placed as close to the operator as possible without compromising safety and ease of movement. This will reduce the replenishment time for the material handler. RIP locations should be close as possible to the line locations. In a Lean system, all move and setup work is considered nonvalue-added activity.

Some of these solutions require creative thinking in addition to creative racks, containers, and shelving. Make sure to include material handlers and operators in kaizen activities to improve the Lean line.

Kanban Sequencing of One-Time-Use Parts

Scheduling production in a Lean factory is greatly simplified once factory layout and kanban signaling drive the flow of work through the factory. Production planning is accomplished by sequencing the Lean line with finished goods products at the first operation. Subassemblies are produced on feeder processes, with production triggered using the IPK methodology. The output of a feeder process is consumed directly into a downstream process with subsequent production in the feeder initiated using IPK as a signal.

Because products are manufactured one unit at a time, they can be sequenced to move down the Lean line and feeders in the same order as the customer requirements. Utilizing this "ratchet" effect where all workstations complete their work and move at the same time, the planner has only to determine the order of manufacture. Using a first-in–first-out IPK signaling methodology, the operator in the first workstation of the Lean line begins production of the next unit following the same order the planner has chosen. The same is true for the first operation in any of the feeders. Operators need to know the next subassembly in sequence to begin production. At the end of the feeder process when the subassembly is completed, it is consumed directly into the exact model that requires that specific subassembly.

In special cases such as configure-to-order custom products, a sales order configuration document sequenced to accompany the product through production may be required. This configuration traveler moves with the product as it advances through manufacturing. The traveler indicates to individual operators at their workstations which parts are to be installed to build the special configuration.

For standard parts chosen to be included in the kanban system, even the configured product subassembly process is simple. Parts identified on the configuration traveler are consumed directly into the product, and the normal kanban replenishment cycle is completed as needed. For products that require one-time-use parts, additional management and material handling time is required. Using one-time-use kanban routines established by the kanban for products with low and infrequent demand, special component parts are pulled into the production process only when actual customer demand is received.

On a daily basis based on actual customer demand, material handlers need to know what special parts should be picked and the point of consumption where they will be used. This information can be presented as a set of sequencing cards on a sequencing board or as a tabular report. The actual material must then be placed at the workstation in a designated location so the operator can easily install the parts when the configuration traveler reaches his or her workstation.

When designing the two-bin material kanban system, a Pareto (80/20) analysis was used to achieve part number rationalization to select parts for the kanban system. It is usually the case that most of management's time will be spent managing and sequencing the one-time-use parts. The time required to manage these parts is the reciprocal of the initial parts rationalization process: 80% of management time is consumed by 20% of the total volume. This same 20% of volume represents 80% of the total parts.

The obvious solution to this dilemma is the standardization of the product line, limiting configuration to only a few manageable variations and eliminating all one-time-use parts. As a company's product line approaches true commodity status, this may be possible. Unfortunately, for most manufacturers, this scenario may never happen. Many sales staffs are simply unwilling to relinquish even the smallest percentage of sales to achieve standardization. Sales perceives the ability to promise highly configured products as an important competitive differentiation.

Material planners must then be prepared to spend the corresponding amount of time on managing these special customer orders and their one-time-use component parts on a daily basis. A portion of the remaining management time not spent on the sequencing and material handling of one-time-use parts should be dedicated to increasing the number of part numbers that are added to the standard kanban population.

In the end, it becomes a matter of trade-off, choosing the best strategy for the company. If highly configured products will be offered at the same price with the same delivery policy as the more standard higher volume units, the cost of that policy must be understood. A policy of "all things to all customers all the time" will include the cost of carrying the individual component parts required to achieve that promise. If a company is willing to absorb these material costs and still achieve market share and profit margin objectives, this policy may be best.

The best order policy is usually somewhere in between. The kanban system is an excellent tool for making those price and service policy decisions. The initial kanban system started with an 80/20 split. What would be the cost of an 85/15, 90/10, or 95/5 split? The cost of increasing the component part participation necessary to achieve these order fulfillment goals can be easily calculated. Once the cost of each different fulfillment policy is determined, the best one to achieve projected sales or market penetration goals can be established.

For customers that continue to demand one-time-use parts for their special configurations, an alternative order policy should be established to include the lead time required to receive specified parts from a supplier and any additional handling costs for processing the order. Any promise quoting the same delivery and cost as standard items not only causes chaos in manufacturing and with the supplier but is ultimately unfair to the customer.

THE MULTIPLE-CARD KANBAN SYSTEM

A variation of the single-card kanban system is the multiple-card system. The multiple-card system is a technique that uses separate multiple signals, move and produce, to communicate a replenishment signal. Multiple signals are typically used in shared manufacturing processes or independent cells where long setups and great distances that require long replenishment times are present. The most common use of multiple-card systems is in fabrication and machine environments. Instead of a single card or a single container serving as a signal, the multiple-card system collects a series of cards until a predetermined number of cards have been accumulated. This predetermined number of cards then serves as the signal to perform a machine setup and run of the replenishment quantity.

Multiple containers are required when the replenishment quantity is too large to fit into a single container. Because the replenishment quantity cannot fit into one container, a series of containers must be used. As a container of parts becomes empty through consumption and container capacity is insufficient to hold the replenishment quantity, a method to accumulate a collection of partial signals from a series of empty containers is necessary.

Because a quantity of partial signals must be accumulated before the actual replenishment is started, the multiple-card kanban system requires that a collection point be established. The best location for the collection of the partial signals is at the machine or machine cell where fabrication begins. A "wait/work" sequencing board is used to accumulate these signals.

The Wait/Work Sequencing Board

For a machine operator in a fabrication department, there are two critical decisions that have to be made every day: (1) what parts to make and (2) how many. The great advantage of any kanban system is its ability to answer these two important questions. Receipt of a kanban signal announces the need for replenishment of an individual part number. In the single-card system, establishing the priority of replenishment is simple; replenish in the order of receipt (i.e., first-in–first-out. Where a machine or group of machines is producing a variety of parts, and multiple kanban signals are being received throughout the day, establishing the correct priority requires a system. The multiple-card system uses a wait/work sequencing board to determine what to produce, and to establish the priority of production based on consumption.

The multiple-card system is similar to the single-card system in that when a container is emptied at the point of consumption, a signal must be generated. Unlike the single-card system, the multiple-card system does not use the empty container as a replenishment signal. Containers in a multiple-card system are nonspecific.

Instead, the container has a card attached that is removed when the material is emptied. The card is simply returned to the fabrication area to be used for any material replenishment. The card removed from the parts container initiates the kanban signal. This card is called a *move* card. It is called a move card because it acts as an authorization to move material for replenishment as the consumption point.

Material for replenishment is stored in a secondary location, similar to the RIP location in the single-card system. Unlike RIP, the number of containers stored for replenishment is based on a quantity calculated to overcome the time for setup and run time of other parts being run in that fabrication machine or cell. Attached to each container in the storage location is a second card. This card is called the *produce* card (Figure 5.4).

When the new full container of parts is pulled to the point of consumption, the produce card is removed from the container and replaced with the move card. The move card is reusable and is reattached to the new full container of parts each time it is pulled to the point of consumption. After the produce card is removed from the container, it is sent to its point of replenishment. Produce cards sent to the point of replenishment are accumulated on a wait/work sequencing board.

In addition to the part number and description of the material, the produce card has an additional piece of information. The card indicates how many cards must be accumulated to equal the "signal" to authorize the setup and run in the

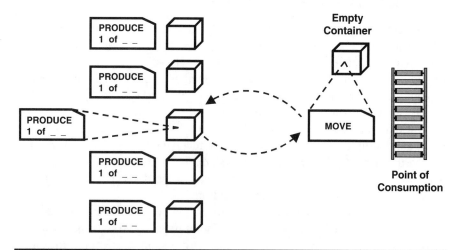

Figure 5.4 The Move and Produce Multiple-Card System

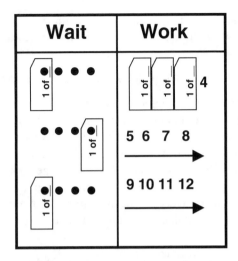

Figure 5.5   The Wait/Work Board

fabrication or machine cell. It is stated as 1 of X cards. A single produce card removed from a replenishment container represents one of a predetermined number of cards that when summed equal the authorization to commence the production of more parts. All cards must be accumulated at the wait/work sequencing board before replenishment begins.

The wait/work board is a simple board that is divided vertically evenly down the middle. Across the top on one half of the board, the word "wait" is written On the other half, "work" is written. On each half of the board are pegs, clips, or hooks for holding the produce cards that have been returned from the point-of-consumption material replenishment location. Using the wait side of the board, returning produce cards are collected randomly by part number on any peg, clip, or hook. Cards continue to accumulate until the predetermined number of cards for that part number has been received (Figure 5.5).

Once all cards have been collected, the produce card set is then moved to the work half of the sequencing board. When moving the produce cards, random location of cards is no longer allowed. Pegs, clips, or hooks on the work half are numbered left to right, top to bottom, and produce card sets are placed sequentially on the work side of the board. The cards must be placed in a first-in–first-out sequence to assure parts are produced in the same sequence in which they were used at the point of consumption.

Using the kanban discipline for the fabrication and machine cell automatically establishes the correct priority of production, while the part number and quantity to be produced are determined by the produce cards. This solves the daily dilemma of what, how many, and in what priority to produce parts. No additional interpretation is required from the machine operator.

Establishing Kanban Quantity and Number of Cards

The number of cards required to signal production in the multiple-card system must be calculated using the additional variables of days of kanban material desired plus the estimated number of wait days on the wait/work board. These additional days should include travel time required to assure replenishment to the point of consumption before a material stock-out. The formula is similar to the calculation used to calculate single-card kanban quantities.

The total quantity is then divided by the quantity per container. The resulting quotient is the number of containers and number of produce cards.

$$\frac{\text{Daily Demand} \times \text{Replenishment Days}}{\text{Container Quantity}} = \text{\# of Containers and Cards}$$

While this calculation is straightforward, the final answer can become complicated when all parts that run across a machine or machine cell are included. Additional calculations to assess the total utilization of the machine or machine cell must be made. If the utilization begins to exceed ±85%, the replenishment days may need to be modified.

It is suggested that machine utilization be assessed on a monthly basis. Factors necessary to calculate utilization include:

- Number of machines
- Run time per piece
- Work days per month
- Available minutes per shift
- Number of shifts per day
- Setup time
- Amount of preventative maintenance and downtime

For the kanban quantities, the run time per piece must be known. The total kanban quantities for each part must be calculated and added together to determine the amount of machine time required to produce the desired kanban quantity. When this required machine time is subtracted from the total time available, the difference is the time available to perform setups. Dividing this time by the time required to perform a setup determines the number of setups that can be performed per month. The total quantity of kanban part numbers to be run must not exceed the number of setups that can be made.

Based on the utilization of the fabrication machine or cell, ideal kanban quantities may need to be modified to fit the utilization model developed for a machine or machine cell. This is typically an iterative process and often requires multiple iterations to determine the final ideal kanban quantities.

6

MANAGING INVENTORY WITH THE KANBAN SYSTEM

THE ADVANTAGES OF KANBAN SYSTEMS

Simplicity of a Physical Signal

The key to the successful kanban system is the creation of a signal. This signal is notification that material must be replenished. This signal also requires that the replenishment occur in the stated replenishment time. Whether the signal comes in the form of an empty container, a card, or an empty space on the floor, the signal is a physical one. The replenishment signal is a tangible object and, therefore, difficult to ignore when received. The empty container or card simply says that material needs to be replenished. It is nonjudgmental. No interpretation of a computer-generated report is necessary. No further investigation is necessary. At the point of replenishment, no training of material handlers to research a stock-out condition is required. Material must simply be replenished in the quantity specified in the calculated replenishment time.

The use of physical signals introduces simplicity into material replenishment and handling systems. The critical issues of material replenishment have been predetermined in the calculation of the kanban. Individual interpretation on receipt of the physical signal by material handlers is not required. All that is required of the material handler is the execution of the quantity and replenishment time. Priority for refilling material containers is on a first-in–first-out basis.

Replenishment must simply occur in the stated replenishment time with the quantity designated.

Flexibility to Produce the Maximum Variety of Products Every Day

Planning (MRP) systems are order-based systems. When the planning system completes the bill of material explosion process and recommendations for manufacture are generated, an order is created in the system. The order status in the planning system changes from planned or firm planned to "released." This shop (production) order lists the product to be produced, the time-phased due and start dates, and the quantity to be produced. Component parts required to manufacture the product must be issued from the stockroom and are documented on a pick list. This is also referred to as the "kitting" of parts.

Once the required parts have been pulled from the stockroom and issued to manufacturing, the MRP system requires an inventory transaction occur to change the part location from the stockroom to a work-in-process location. Parts are then assigned or "allocated" to the specific shop order. Barring changes in the due date, quantity, or item to be produced, these parts stay with the order throughout the manufacturing process.

Unfortunately, it is not uncommon to experience changes to the production order in the form of due date, quantity, or even the item to be produced (e.g., customer cancellation or changes in forecast). Other changes include changes in the priority of released orders, customer expedites, shortages of purchased materials prior to production that delay order start-up, grouping of orders out of due date sequence to achieve productivity goals, equipment breakdowns, and labor issues among myriad other reasons.

When these changes do occur, the planning system must be made aware of the changes so that the next net requirements iteration is accurate and based on the most current information. This requires feedback to the planning system to update the status of the released order. In many manufacturing facilities, these changes are so frequent and common that the majority of a planner's daily activity can be dedicated to maintaining these changes and the feedback to the planning system. Some planners are even assigned full time to deal with the daily multitude of changes. Expeditor is a common title for the person who performs this function.

Not all part numbers are candidates for the kanban system. There are important reasons why certain part numbers should be handled on an exception basis only. Part numbers initially chosen to be included in the kanban system were determined using the 80/20 rule. Pareto's law states that 80% of the total sales are accomplished with the highest 20% of the total stockkeeping units (SKUs) or end items. By making the component parts necessary to produce 20% of SKUs available every day, the capability to meet the demand for 80% of total customer sales on any given day is available. Going beyond the 80% availability should be a financial decision based on a sales strategy for capturing market share. Providing the ability to respond faster to highly configured customer demand beyond the 20% of SKUs requires an inventory investment in slower moving parts.

Once the kanban parts have been selected and placed on the line at the designated workstation, these parts are available for any product that flows down the Lean line. Kanban parts are not allocated to any designated SKU or shop order and can be used on any product at any time.

Having parts available for usage on any product every day provides a great capability for the manufacturer with the goal of meeting customer demand with shorter response time. Parts not allocated to released shop orders allow maximum flexibility to meet customer demand. Even customer-expedited end items can be introduced to the Lean line at any time outside the product cycle time. The kanban system allows these changes to occur without the need to provide feedback of released order changes to the planning system. There is no need for deallocation and reallocation of parts to separate production orders. The parts residing on the Lean line can be used for any product.

Simplified Management of Turn Rate Velocity

Managing turn rates and inventory investment strategies is simpler using the material kanban system. Quantities of inventory and the resulting working capital investment are based on the days or replenishment assigned to the individual parts. The more time necessary for replenishment, the greater the inventory and the greater the inventory cost. The amount of this investment can be controlled by managing the length of replenishment time designated for a part. When the kanban system is initially installed, careful consideration should be given to this dynamic.

Replenishment time is a statement of the time necessary to complete the replenishment cycle. The time required to complete this replenishment cycle dictates the number of parts that must be available at the consumption point to sustain production during the replenishment cycle. A material quantity calculation must be performed for each pull sequence to project the amount of material necessary at the consumption point to assure production can continue for as long as it takes material being replenished to arrive back at the consumption point. Failure to replenish in the time established can cause a stock-out situation at the consumption point.

Part Number	Consumption Point	Replenishment Point	Replenishment Time (Days)
560919 Carton	Lean Line	RIP-1	1

The calculation to determine the amount of inventory for each pull sequence is

$$\frac{\text{Daily Demand} \times \text{Replenishment Time}}{\text{Package Size (Optional)}} = \text{Container Quantity}$$

For each part number selected to be managed in the kanban system, a pull chain must be assigned to it. A pull chain is a series of pull sequences linked together to define all consumption points and replenishment points for the material. The pull chain defines the consumption and replenishment points, along with the time required to complete each replenishment. The kanban system then uses the pull chain to "set" the inventory policy for each individual part based on the sum of its replenishment times for each pull sequence.

Consumption Point	1 Day	Replenishment Point	3 Days	Replenishment Point	10 Days	Replenishment Point
Lean Line	⟶	RIP-1	⟶	Central Stores	⟶	Supplier

When first installing the kanban system, it is recommended that the number of pull chains developed be kept to a minimum. This simplifies the management of the system until a comfort level with its operation is established. By definition, limiting the number of pull chains forces the grouping of parts into classifications.

A common grouping of parts used extensively today by many manufacturers is the ABC analysis. The ABC designation of parts is an excellent place to begin establishing an inventory turn rate strategy. In most cases, parts are assigned an A, B, or C designation based on their per-unit cost, with A items being the most expensive and C items having the least cost. Standard logic follows that different inventory strategies can be assigned to the parts based on their ABC classification. The kanban system uses this same logic to manage parts.

Pull chains should be developed with the ABC analysis in mind. Pull chains for A items should reflect fast replenishment times throughout the chain to minimize inventory quantity along with the desired inventory investment. Conversely, low-cost items assigned the C and lower designations can have slower replenishment times, resulting in greater inventory and fewer replenishments.

The result of establishing inventory policy by pull chain is that the desired velocity by part number valuation can be easily controlled simply by managing its replenishment time.

Simplified Inventory Control Routines

The requirements for inventory accuracy with a kanban system are as important as with any inventory control system. Kanban systems require fewer inventory transactions and reduce the amount of system maintenance activities normally needed to keep up with the real-time environment of the shop floor. Reducing the number of material input and output transactions facilitates high accuracy of on-hand inventories. Unless mandated by regulation, many Lean line manufacturers have greatly reduced or eliminated cycle counting and physical inventories.

The management of inventory with a kanban system is straightforward and simple. The pull chain designates the inventory accounts that must be maintained for the kanban system. The line inventory and the RIP (supermarket) inventories are materials that reside in the work-in-process inventory. *Stores* are material maintained in the stockroom. With the kanban system, the only time an inventory transaction is necessary is when material moves from one of these locations — line, RIP, stores, or supplier — to another.

When materials at the line consumption point are consumed, a signal is generated. The empty container is retrieved for replenishment and is delivered to the replenishment point, the RIP. Identical material in two containers is located at the RIP location. Using a first-in–first-out methodology, material is replenished from the first container and returned to the line location.

To encourage rapid turn rates and high velocity, line to RIP inventory transactions are not required. By design, this cycle of consumption and replenishment should happen at a very rapid pace. If the kanban replenishment time of the pull chain is sized at one day's worth of demand, this cycle will occur once a day. Recall that the kanban container quantity is calculated as daily demand × replenishment time.

If the completion of a transaction for each part number for each cycle from line to RIP for one day's demand were required, the amount of overhead expense and chance for error would increase. Also, if transactions were necessary for every part, rapid turn rates and high-velocity inventory turns would be discouraged. Simply by increasing the number of days worth of demand kept at the line location, the higher replenishment times would cause signals to occur less frequently. More inventory = less frequent replenishment signals = fewer transactions.

After repeated replenishment cycles to the RIP location, eventually the first container of the RIP location will become empty. If the replenishment time of the RIP container is sized to hold three days of demand, three days of the line/RIP replenishment cycle will be supported before the container becomes empty. Once empty, this first container in the RIP location becomes a signal for replenishment. Line production can continue and the line/RIP replenishment cycle can be supported as the second container in the RIP location contains enough material to sustain another three days of daily demand before it, too, becomes empty. This requires the first container be replenished and returned to the RIP location before three days has passed.

RIP is usually replenished from two designated replenishment points, the stockroom or the supplier. Both of these locations are typically located outside the manufacturing shop floor. Even if the stockroom is located adjacent to manufacturing, it is not usually controlled by manufacturing. Barring a midnight requisition process, it is common for the materials stored there to be unavailable to manufacturing without a material requisition. Material in the stockroom is likely to be the responsibility of the materials group (Figure 6.1).

The kanban system recognizes and encourages this ownership. Once the empty RIP container has been returned to the stockroom and refilled, a transaction is necessary to decrease the on-hand inventory in the stockroom and increase the work-in-process inventory in the RIP location. This transaction routine is also required when the RIP location is replenished directly from the supplier.

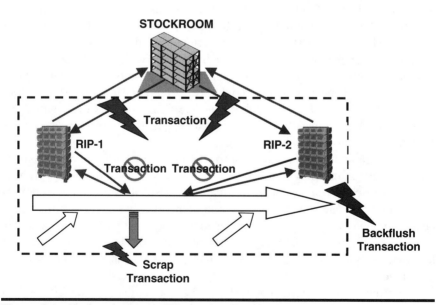

Figure 6.1 Kanban Inventory Transaction Requirements

Depending on the days of inventory sized at the RIP location, the number of transactions will be dependent on the number of parts in the RIP location. If sized at three days, each part number will be transacted every third day. If sized to five days, transactions occur every fifth day, and so on. As with the line inventory, more inventory = less frequent replenishment signals = fewer transactions.

Once material is transacted onto the manufacturing shop floor, there are only two ways for it to leave. The first is in the finished product. The second is as scrap. The scrap reporting system must be current. If there is a material review board process in place, it is recommended that scrap be reconciled each day so that the operation where the scrap occurred can be queried as to problems. Reconciliation done less frequently sacrifices the ability to determine the causes of scrap.

For inexpensive parts, a simple token system can be used. Rather than an operator taking time to complete a scrap report for inexpensive parts, discretion can be given to the operator to dispose of defective materials directly into the scrap bin. A token (e.g., a poker chip) is placed into the kanban container of the scrapped material to replace the scrapped material. When the bin becomes empty, the trained material handler responsible for refilling the bin counts the chip(s) and completes the scrap report.

Materials received from suppliers are transacted into stores or directly into an in-process location. Material is then relieved from in process using a backflush transaction. The backflush transaction reduces the on-hand inventory in the in-process location by deducting the material recorded in the product's bill of material. At the same time, one completed unit is added to the finished goods inventory.

Having entered the manufacturing area, the second way material leaves the shop floor is as a component in a completed unit. Part quantities are then reduced from the work-in-process inventory by the quantity in the bill of material through a process called *backflush*. The backflush transaction occurs after all work to build the product is finished and all required materials are consumed into the end item. The backflush transaction adds one completed SKU to finished goods inventory and reduces work in process by $1 \times$ the quantity in the bill of material. For the backflushing transaction to be effective and keep the integrity of the work-in-process inventory high, the bill of material must be extremely accurate.

Bill-of-material inaccuracies that can impact work-in-process inventory are (1) parts that are not included in the bill of material, (2) parts listed but not actually used in the manufacture of the product, and (3) inaccurate quantities of material listed. Bill-of-material errors are the primary cause of backflush errors leading to work-in-process inventory errors.

Errors can also occur if an operator makes an unauthorized substitution on the Lean line. When the correct material has been exhausted, and a substitution is made, it must be done with the approval of the Lean line team leader.

Material Shortages Become Invisible to the Line

For many manufacturers, parts shortages are a major problem. The reasons for parts shortages in manufacturing are as numerous as there are parts. Bill-of-material errors, poor inventory accuracy, late suppliers, faulty quality, lack of discipline to make required transactions, unreported scrap, hoarding, and poor file maintenance are common reasons.

When shortages are detected, heroic expediting efforts are made, often paid for in premium transportation charges from the supplier's location and late-night pickups at the airport. Threats, cajoling, and innuendoes are leveled at good suppliers. Desperation is in the air. Parts are borrowed from a staged production order and given to another with higher priority. Parts are cannibalized from finished goods inventory to continue production. Expediting is the word of the day. Everyone becomes a firefighter.

Manufacturers make valiant efforts to avoid shortages from ever occurring in the future. Alternate supplier programs are initiated with suppliers lined up three and four deep.

Parts are staged ahead of production and locked up. Safety stock programs are developed and put in place. Stockrooms are locked up at night to discourage unreported usage. Planners develop caches of hidden parts, and safety stock inventories double and quadruple. The result is that manufacturing no longer trusts materials management, which in turn does not trust manufacturing. MRP systems are blamed as invalid. Fingers are pointed and mistrust reigns.

Regardless of promises, no material system in the world can overcome all the things that can happen on the shop floor and in the administrative offices. Kanban systems cannot make such promises. No material system can overcome or predict all problems responsible for causing shortages.

The kanban system can, however, keep shortages invisible to the line consumption point by providing an opportunity for the shortage to be resolved before a line stoppage. This can be done by using the RIP inventory as a safety stock point.

Consider the pull chain of a part:

Consumption Point	2 Days	Replenishment Point	8 Days	Replenishment Point	10 Days	Replenishment Point
Lean Line ──────→		RIP-1 ──────→		Central Stores ──────→		Supplier

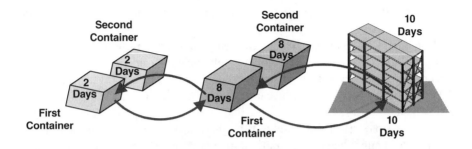

Figure 6.2   Part Number Pull Chain Replenishment Cycle

The kanban containers for this pull chain would look like Figure 6.2. Following this pull chain, the line to RIP replenishment cycle will occur four times before the first RIP container will become empty. The pull sequence for the RIP container indicates that the replenishment point is central stores. Based on the supplier lead time, there should be ten days of usage of the part number in the stockroom. With this pull chain, after the fourth line to RIP replenishment cycle is completed, the first RIP container is returned to the stockroom to be refilled. For whatever reason, if no parts are available in the stockroom to replenish the RIP container, there is a parts shortage!

In the kanban system, the effect would be as shown in Figure 6.3. Although there is a parts shortage, it has been discovered in the stockroom, not at the line consumption point. Manufacturing can continue to produce product at the line location. The parts shortage is invisible to the line location at this point. The parts components at the Line location should be able to sustain line consumption from two to four days. There should be at least a full second container that has just been replenished from RIP combined with whatever remains in the container currently being consumed, zero to two days. At the RIP location, the second

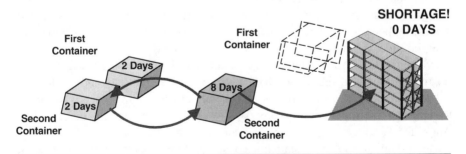

Figure 6.3   Shortage Discovered in Central Stores

container with an eight-day supply should be able to replenish the line container four more cycles.

If the first RIP container, which now resides in the central stores as a physical reminder of the shortage, does not get replenished from the supplier to the stockroom before 10 to 12 days has passed, the final cycle from the line to the RIP will occur and potentially cause downtime for any product using that component.

It is possible that a line stock-out might still occur because the reason for the shortage cannot be resolved in time to avert a line shortage. However, there is at least 10 to 12 days of buffer inventory on the line and in the RIP inventory to sustain production while a solution to the shortage is developed. While the causes and ultimate resolution of the shortage are being developed, manufacturing can continue to produce product using the buffer inventories on the line and in the RIP.

Kanban does not eliminate the causes of shortages; it channels the responsibility for the resolution of shortages to the most appropriate organizational component, materials management. In most manufacturing companies, the materials group has responsibility for purchasing, inventory accuracy, the stockroom, and receipt of material. Therefore, responsibility for resolution of a shortage will be isolated to the stockroom. All shortage resolution activity is invisible to the Lean line!

In addition to resolving the shortage, information necessary to investigate the root cause of the shortage, document the frequency of its occurrence, and develop long-term solutions to avoid repeating it in the future is made available to the materials group. Good kaizen tools including a Pareto analysis can help to focus efforts on solving the root causes of shortages and excuse manufacturing from the shortage resolution business.

A manufacturer's first reaction to installing a kanban system might be to question the need for a RIP inventory. RIP inventory does require a footprint on the shop floor and does require an inventory investment. As with any system, it must be maintained. Also, the costs of the RIP inventory must be weighed against its benefits. If the elimination of shortages on the line is an important goal, consider a kanban system without the RIP inventory (Figure 6.4).

Once the line kanban signal is generated and the first container is returned for replenishment, if there is no RIP inventory the container would go directly to the stockroom. If, as before, for reasons unknown, no inventory is available to replenish the line, for how many days can production continue before a line stoppage? With a two-day replenishment time, the remaining parts at the line location should be able to sustain line consumption for two to four days. Without the intermediate RIP inventory location, only one line replenishment cycle can be completed.

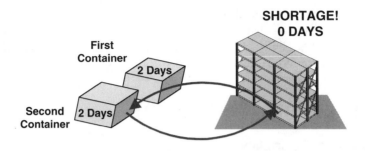

**SHORTAGE!
0 DAYS**

First
Container

2 Days

Second
Container

2 Days

Figure 6.4 Kanban Replenishment without RIP

It is possible that the shortage can be resolved in two to four days, before the line experiences a shutdown. Heroic expediting efforts and the electricity of crisis resolution can be exciting in an organization. Conversely, if short-term shortages are commonplace and frequent, what is the cost of constant turmoil in the stockroom? What is the cost to the supplier/buyer relationship? What is the quality of life for the planner in an environment of perpetual expediting?

The RIP location serves a dual role in the material replenishment cycle of manufacturing. First, it becomes the "early warning system" of a potential stock-out situation, allowing the materials organization sufficient time to respond before the shortage becomes critical enough to shut the line down. Second, RIP is a safety stock inventory. Instead of a quantity held in inventory based on a percentage of past usage, the RIP safety stock triggers replenishment based on actual usage, with an empty container serving as a flag. Rather than being based on an arbitrary quantity or percentage, the RIP signal is based on the time required to replenish the material.

RIP does provide a buffer of inventory designed to reduce or eliminate material shortages on the Lean line, and having a safety stock inventory to provide an early warning system does require investment. Kanban = Inventory = Capital. However, by managing the kanban system, achieving inventory investment goals is possible. Using a pull chain with 2 days of line materials, 8 days of RIP, and 10 days of stockroom, with 20 total days of inventory, based on a 250-day work year, the turn rate exceeds 12 times.

If the line inventory is reduced to replenishment once per day, the RIP is reduced to replenish every 5 days, and the stockroom remains at 10 days, the turn rate increases to greater than 15 turns (250 ÷ 16 days). The trade-off for higher velocity of material turn rates with more frequent replenishment times is an increase in the amount of material handling necessary.

It is possible that material-handling requirements will increase with a kanban system. The benefits of faster inventory turns and reduced working capital requirements must be weighed against the amount of material handling that must be done. In the end, a balance between replenishment frequency and inventory investment must be achieved. There are software programs available today that can perform the multiple iterations needed to achieve this proper balance.

THE DISADVANTAGES OF KANBAN SYSTEMS

No Planning Capability

The two-bin material kanban system has no forward visibility for determining demand. The initial setup of the kanban system uses historical and extrapolated information to establish the daily demand for kanban container sizing. Demand is not a static factor. It can increase and decrease based on whims of the market. Product mix and volume change over time. Technology changes and new models are frequently introduced to the customer catalogue. Older models fade away or are discontinued. To remain current and accommodate all potential changes, responsibility for maintaining the kanban system must be assigned.

Changes to standard planning systems are made using database changes required to maintain system integrity (i.e., the item master and bill of material). Stand-alone kanban systems generally do not interface with existing planning systems. Whoever is assigned responsibility for maintaining the kanban system must be included in the change control distribution list so as to manage changes in concert with the current planning system.

One way to accomplish this is to review the action item output from the planning system. Net requirements through the horizon can be accumulated and divided by the number of days in that horizon. This will give an average daily demand for that part number for that period. A percentage of demand either higher or lower (e.g., ±15%) can be established as a range. If the existing kanban daily demand falls outside the range, an adjustment can be made. Of course, all new and discontinued parts require individual decisions on a case-by-case basis.

The argument could be made that if taken to its ultimate conclusion, the output of a planning system is not even necessary to establish material demand. Suppliers could just respond to the kanban signals they receive from a manufacturer. This would be true as long as future demand could be established so as to determine the daily demand for the kanban sizing. Also, it would be necessary for all suppliers to be recognized as certified suppliers. While early practitioners had little choice but to use the kanban system to receive materials for manufacturing, it is still a stretch for most modern manufacturers to achieve that goal.

Not All Parts Are Candidates for the Kanban System

The kanban methodology is a material presentation method designed to simplify material handling and inventory management. Instead of materials being staged in "kits" and issued to production to follow the routing, materials are physically placed at the point of usage on the line and replenished only when a "kanban" or "signal" is generated by its consumption into the product.

Once parts have been designated to be part of the kanban system, with daily demand determined and replenishment frequency documented, the kanban signal generated through the pull chain "automatically" replenishes material with no input from a planner or buyer. Effectively, the only time additional input is necessary is to resolve any mix or volume issues for the part. Beyond those reasons, the replenishment cycle can go on indefinitely.

A kanban system that places material directly onto the line at the point it is consumed into a product offers a real competitive advantage to the Lean manufacturer. Because all the material needed for manufacturing is located on the line, it is available for consumption on any product that happens to flow down the line. All materials become available for all products. The best of all situations suggests that every possible part be automatically replenished by the kanban system. If this were possible, material handling would certainly be extremely simplified. However, for most manufacturers with highly configured products, including all possible parts for all possible product configurations in the kanban system could be a very expensive alternative.

Like the balance between material handling and inventory investment, trade-off decisions that make the most business sense will be necessary. One of the very early decisions to be made when implementing Lean is to choose which parent products (SKU, end-item, finished goods inventory level) should be supported on the Lean line. Determining which parent products are to be manufactured on the Lean line will determine the initial parts necessary to manage using the kanban system.

The optimum fulfillment policy for most sales organizations is "all things to all people, all the time." It is not uncommon for companies to offer their customers numerous options on numerous products. The number of products offered can swell to hundreds or thousands. This policy, formal or informal, is what most manufacturers attempt to fulfill. The permutations of options and products often result in the proliferation of product offerings each with its own individual end-item part number. Manufacturers often claim that their products are unique. What are really unique are the amount, variety, and combination of available parts and process options to the standard line of products (Figure 6.5).

This proliferation of end-item products correspondingly translates into a large number of component parts to service that demand. How, then, do manu-

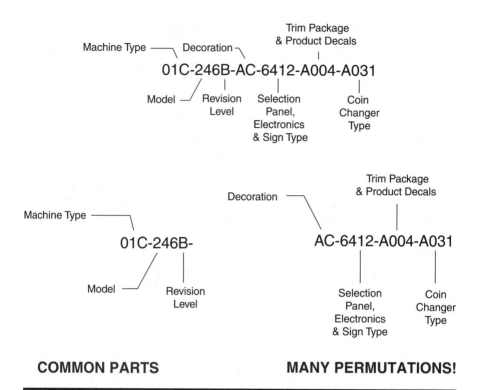

Figure 6.5 Common Parts and Configured Options

facturers that may have hundreds or thousands of possible component parts combinations decide which of those parts should be made available to meet customer demand on a timely basis.

To address this issue, consideration should be given to which products are to be included in the Lean line design process. Is it really necessary to include all parts for all permutations for all possible product configurations, or can a group of products be selected to represent the whole of all the products produced? If a representative group of products is to be selected from this potentially long list, two important concepts can be used to condense a long list of parent products into a short list that ultimately will make up the product population for the Lean line design.

Begin by performing a Pareto analysis of products based on historical sales. Pareto's Law was developed by Vilfredo Pareto, an Italian economist who was born in 1848 and died in 1923. He observed that a small fraction, 15 to 20%, of participants in a population accounted for the major part, 80 to 85%, of an activity. This law is also known as the 80/20 rule. Application of this rule when

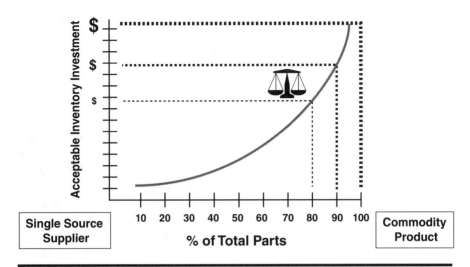

Figure 6.6 Achieving Equilibrium: Investment versus Customer Service Level

selecting product candidates and their associated parts will identify 20% of all part numbers necessary to produce 80% of total demand.

Having parts available to serve 80% of total demand upon receipt of a customer order should then become an economic decision. This means that in order to serve the other 20% of the potential demand, all or a portion of the balance of the parts that make up the remaining 80% of possible permutations must be stocked to meet all possible demands.

Making the decision to meet in excess of 80% of customer demand upon receipt of an order is a function of the level of inventory investment a manufacturer is willing to make to meet that demand. Each company must make this decision based on what is best for the company. As products approach commodity status, more than an 80% fulfillment rate may be desired. If products can be differentiated from competitors with attributes other than price, delivery, and configuration, an 80% fulfillment rate may be adequate for that market (Figure 6.6).

Determining which parts to introduce into the kanban system may lead to discussion of the customer order fulfillment policy. Is it really realistic to be all things to all people at all times? Is the company prepared to make the inventory investment necessary to support that policy? Has the order fulfillment policy even been defined? Have customer expectations evolved from the last time order fulfillment policy was articulated?

It is likely that a series of different order policies designed for different customers may be required to determine parts to be maintained in the kanban system. Once again, the Pareto analysis is a good tool for identifying these customer categories. Categories of customers can be determined based on their order pattern. Sort customers based on their total dollar sales volume and product configuration. Identify the 80% level of total sales dollars. The component parts in the bills of material represented by those product configurations should be included, as a minimum, in the kanban system.

Also, product configurations within this range (±80%) should have an order policy that guarantees shipment within the total product cycle time of that product. This will be possible because the line is designed to perform the work content and the kanban system will support the part requirements. The cost for higher service levels, above the initial 80% fill rate, can then be ascertained by the parts investment required to meet that level. Customer service policy can then be established by individual SKU.

By moving down the total sales dollar listing, additional order policies can be established based on the time required to procure the parts not kept in the kanban system. If these parts are purchased, the lead time required to purchase them from a supplier must be added to the total product cycle time.

Establishing order policy based on sales dollars often exposes many of the reasons manufacturers spend much of their time expediting orders through the factory. Is the time spent expediting products through manufacturing worth the sales dollars generated? What are the costs of processing special-order configurations in terms of overtime, premium transportation, lost capacity, and quality of life? Are the sales dollars generated by the bottom 10% of the total product configurations representative of the current business model, or does it even serve the markets the company wants to participate in? Is it possible to switch customers to products in the 80% order policy range in exchange for faster delivery?

Some parts that may not be good candidates for participation in the kanban system are very expensive, fragile, or environmentally sensitive. Other parts may be inexpensive but very large and cumbersome to locate adjacent to the Lean line. Examples include corrugated containers, large molded parts, precut insulation, and other bulky packing materials. While these materials are relatively low in cost, the footprint required for stocking numerous part number configurations on the shop floor would be prohibitive.

Instead, these materials should be handled on a one-time or as-needed basis. Materials in the two-bin kanban system are automatically replenished when depleted and a signal is generated. One-time-usage materials must be managed each time they are consumed. Because they must be managed, responsibility for their usage must be assigned to a material handler and they must be sequenced to the line matching consumption with the Lean line sequence.

Hands-On Management of Kanban System

The two-bin material kanban system is a hands-on system that requires the dedication of responsible materials professionals to design and maintain the system to be most effective. Once designed and implemented, day-to-day upkeep of kanban part numbers will be limited to mix and volume changes, engineering releases, and physical maintenance of the labels, containers, and storage racks. This required maintenance means a commitment to assure system integrity.

The commitment to a kanban system is much different than that required for a computer-driven planning system. In a computer-based system, maintenance is centered on the item master and bill of material. When the item master and bill of material are updated, the planning explosion routine generates the necessary quantity and time-phased requirement action messages. The kanban system does not rely on the output of the planning routine. The kanban system requires that a person calculate the ideal quantities for the pull chain, fill and label the containers, and present the material.

A kanban system also requires dedicated persons assigned to maintain the correct part numbers, reflecting the most current mix and volume relationships and physical effort to handle parts, containers, labels, and placement of containers in their assigned locations. For the current generation of material-handling personnel used to leaving the maintenance of materials to engineering and the planning system, the sudden requirement to take hands-on responsibility for the physical handling and integrity of production materials gives new meaning to the term "materials management."

Hands-on management of the material kanban system is especially apparent with the setup of the system for the first time. Even with the 80/20 rationalization of parts to match the projected sales volume, a significant number of individual parts can result. For each of these part numbers, a series of individual kanban decisions must be made. If the final kanban population of part numbers equals 1000 parts, then at least 1000 individual decisions must also be made.

The first decision to be made is whether to include a part in the kanban system. If not included, what is the alternative system for getting this part to the consumption point? What will the signal for replenishment be? Parts intentionally not included in the kanban system are referred to as one-time-use parts.

A common way to handle one-time-use parts is to assign them a separate planner code in the item master and plan them normally using the planning system. When action is recommended by the planning system, the planner responsible purchases the item as usual and notifies receiving. This can be done with a separate one-time-use kanban signal or card. When the part is finally consumed on the Lean line, the card is returned to the buyer for disposition. The buyer can elect to either reuse the card in the event that part is required in the future or destroy it.

The next decision is based on the desired inventory investment. Based on the per-unit cost of the part, assignment of the most appropriate pull chain representing the desired number of days of inventory must be made. If the unit cost is small, the pull chain with the greater number of days of inventory can be assigned. Conversely, if the unit cost is high, the pull chain with the smallest number of days of supply can be assigned. When assigning pull chains to part numbers based on desired inventory investment, it must be remembered that the smaller the number of days of supply, the greater the amount of material handling.

Another important consideration is the size of the part. Can the calculated kanban quantity of the part fit into a container? If so, what size a container? Most manufacturers of parts containers make them in a variety of sizes, colors, and materials. If the parts cannot fit into a container, how will they be presented to the consumption point? If the size and quantity of the parts are too large to place into a container at the workstation, can the container be placed on the floor or on the floor on a pallet? If on the floor, what will the signal for replenishment be? Every part number in every quantity included in the kanban system must be presented at the point of consumption.

Each of these decisions must be made for every part in the kanban system. This requires a hands-on approach to the management of materials. With a kanban system, these decisions cannot be delegated to an unseen administrative function. There are shortcuts that can be taken to consolidate the total number of decisions that must be made. Grouping parts by category and applying policy based on predetermined category criteria is a common approach. Common categories used for kanban decision making include ABC analysis, commodity code, and planner code.

The requirement to make an individual decision for every part number selected to participate in the kanban system introduces a whole new paradigm for managing production materials.

KANBAN MANAGER JOB RESPONSIBILITIES

Setting up the kanban system for the first time requires a lot of work and decision making. Once completed, the kanban system must be managed on a day-to day basis. If not maintained and improved, it will begin to deteriorate after the first day of operation. The term "manager" is not meant to indicate a job level. It is intended more to describe the management requirements of operating and maintaining the kanban system. More important than job title or organization level is the assignment of responsibility for the kanban system.

The kanban manager should participate in the design of job criteria for the position. The scope of the job should include the following activities:

- Develop a formal methodology to perform periodic and frequent pull sequence audits to validate that all kanban cards or signals are in their assigned locations.
- Develop procedures to assure participation in process change and engineering change order notification to validate that kanban sizing is current to reflect all bill of material and replenishment times changes.
- Audit procedures of the kanban system to assure accurate sizing to support stated inventory investment strategies. Assure accurate kanban quantities are in place in the production process as designed and the calculated kanban pull quantities are being performed by material handlers.
- Develop and lead kaizen activities for the kanban system with all material handlers to assure that best practices are being utilized and material handler recommendations can be investigated.
- Assure material handler training and certification are based on the three-light or milk run system used to signal replenishment.

The kanban manager must assure that all important elements of the kanban system are operational and maintained to make certain the system operates at peak efficiency in order to achieve the optimum inventory investment and customer delivery strategies of the kanban system.

It is important that inventory accuracy levels are high. The kanban manager must develop a methodology and enforce procedures to assure RIP inventory transactions are made when material is moved into the RIP location. This is necessary to allow component parts to be recorded as on-hand inventory available to the material-planning routines of MRP. A powerful feature of the kanban system is that component parts maintained in the RIP area are not allocated to products or orders.

A backflushing routine must be established to account for material usage out of the RIP locations. Backflushing must be a formal computer transaction designed to relieve the RIP inventory of component parts upon completion of a finished unit. The backflushing routine is accomplished by electronically relieving material and quantities listed on the bill of material. Backflushing must occur each time a finished unit packs off the Lean line.

The bills of material will need to be as close to 100% accurate as possible in order to maintain accurate inventory balances. A business process to handle the implementation of engineering changes should be in place to assure the bill of material is updated and as current as possible. The kanban manager must be in the information loop to be certain that timely changes are made to the kanban system. As with the backflush transactions, engineering changes to part numbers will need to be reflected in the kanban system to assure the most accurate backflushing transactions are recorded.

Setup of the kanban system was based on static data available at a specific point in time. However, kanban is a dynamic system that requires frequent and ongoing maintenance to reflect the current manufacturing environment. Timely kanban sizing procedures must be established so that kanban pull chains and quantities can be maintained to capture the most current engineering changes, supply replenishment times, packaging sizes, and manufacturing capacity changes.

In addition to providing the parts necessary to produce product, a goal of the kanban system is to keep inventory moving through the manufacturing process at a rapid pace to achieve inventory turnover goals. This velocity is intended to manage and improve inventory investment and reduce the working capital requirements of the business. The key to managing the turnover of inventory is the frequency of replenishment of the kanban container. Frequency of container replenishment is based on the predetermined "delivery frequency." Therefore, there is direct correlation between kanban container replenishment times and inventory investment.

The amount of inventory investment is in proportion to how often material is replenished. The longer the replenishment times, the greater the inventory investment. Conversely, more frequent replenishment means smaller inventory. This relationship between time and investment is so important that it must be carefully managed and maintained.

A good barometer for assessing the kanban velocity is the speed of container replenishment. Kanban containers being replenished too slowly are an indicator that inventory levels are higher than necessary to support production. Conversely, more frequent replenishment means more material-handling time. Rapid container replenishment is a sign that inventory savings may be offset by material-handling costs.

While it is tempting to think only of the benefits of reduced inventories, kanban systems must ultimately establish the optimum strategy that balances inventory investment with material-handling costs. Usually, this is an iterative process until optimum balance is achieved.

Kanban quantities have been calculated to support a stated number of average days of usage. There will be times when the calculated number of days of supply in the kanban system will be exceeded by actual customer demand. The indication of this will be increased replenishment cycles of the line and RIP containers. If the RIP quantity is sufficient, the kanban system can withstand short-term spikes above the daily average of customer demand. If the cycle repeats itself too many days in a row, even stockroom inventories can eventually become depleted and a shortage occurs. The kanban manager must be alert to these circumstances and investigate their cause.

If the spike in demand was a short-term anomaly, then no action may be needed other than to suggest that the sequencing planner smooth the increased demand over more days if possible. If the spike in demand proves to be the leading indicator of a new demand trend, the kanban manager must recalculate the daily rates, delivery frequencies, container quantities and sizes, material presentation attributes, and sequencing routines.

In some cases, a spike in demand may be an indicator of a customer order pattern. Using the model of an average daily usage rate for calculating kanban quantity for those parts is inaccurate. While the demand cycle is infrequent, it always occurs in that demand quantity. An important question for the kanban manager to answer is whether kanban inventories of that part in that amount should be kept on hand at all times to meet the infrequent demand. What are the cost/benefits of maintaining inventories to meet infrequent demand?

Keeping parts on hand over longer periods of time to assure customer service does increase the cost of the product. If the cost is not passed on to the customer, margin is decreased. Any decision that causes reduction of margin must be carefully considered. Does the cost of satisfying customers with infrequent highly configured demand justify carrying the parts inventory to meet that demand? Does the volume of demand deserve the same lead time delivery promise? Has the direction of your company changed so that servicing those customers is no longer cost effective? Would it be better to relinquish that business to a competitor so as to concentrate on manufacturing those products that yield the best margin for your company?

The operation of a kanban system often is a catalyst for challenging existing policy. With a goal of making the best possible business decision for the company, the kanban system is an objective cost estimate mechanism for evaluating specific order policy. While the kanban manager should not be empowered to make order policy decisions unilaterally, he or she should feel free to initiate such discussions and contribute significant value to the decisions ultimately made.

The only time two full containers should reside in the kanban locations is at the initial setup of the kanban system. After the first cycle of replenishment, only one container should be in the kanban location, with the second container being replenished. This indicates that material is always moving, either being consumed into production or being replenished. This is a balancing act that requires ongoing adjustment. Using a five-day delivery frequency for RIP replenishment as an example, material handling should take four to five days to fill and return a container to the point of consumption. If the container is consistently being filled every one to two days, inventory is potentially twice the amount of parts necessary.

Over time, the goal of the Lean system is to reduce or eliminate the need for a stockroom. Without a stockroom, a supplier would bypass receiving and the stockroom to deliver component parts directly to the RIP locations. Delivery frequency times could be reduced on the kanban pull chain by the amount of time required to receive, inspect, locate, and stock inventories.

Although the savings of a supplier-direct-to-RIP policy may be evident, there are two reasons why this policy cannot be implemented on the same day as the kanban system: supplier unreliability and undependability. If a supplier's quality has been suspect in the past and future reliability remains questionable, the last thing any manufacturer wants is to have those parts delivered directly to the Lean line only to have to stop the line because of defective quality. The same is true for on-time delivery history from a supplier. Most raw material inventory that resides in a stockroom is safety stock to serve as a cushion against undependable deliveries from suppliers.

Historically, manufacturers have dealt with suppliers at arm's length. In most cases, it is unfair to lump all suppliers together as unreliable and undependable. Most suppliers want to do an excellent job for their customers and are willing to work with them to prove their reliability and dependability. Because of the long history of this adversarial relationship, establishing trust with suppliers takes effort. Developing an open, honest, and trusting relationship to prove reliability and dependability is the primary goal of a supplier certification program. Only when reliability and dependability can be proven can a supplier-to-RIP policy be implemented.

PART III:
PROJECT MANAGEMENT FOR IMPLEMENTATION, LINE START-UP, DAILY OPERATIONS, AND PERFORMANCE MEASUREMENT

7

TEAM ESTABLISHMENT

COMMITMENT TO CHANGE

The project management team plays an active role in the Lean implementation. This team is the catalyst for change in the company and keep the project moving forward. When the initial project is completed, it is imperative that the organization take ownership of the new Lean manufacturing system. Operating the new system on a day-to-day basis will be different from what is done today! While the Lean manufacturing methodologies are the best way to run your manufacturing operation, they are just a system. As a system, Lean must be properly maintained and operated by the management team after the initial implementation. Ownership of the Lean system is imperative.

Ownership can be established by applying the following principles:

- **Education:** Establish the mechanism to provide a fundamental understanding of the Lean manufacturing methodologies. The goal of such training should be for both current and new employees to internalize the new methodologies and to incorporate the results from continuous process improvement efforts.
- **Participation:** The process of transforming any company using Lean methods requires a thorough understanding of the company's business processes. Conversely, the company must understand the concepts and principles of Lean manufacturing. The more people invited to participate in the implementation, the easier it is to create the "critical mass" needed to perpetuate the changes long after completion of the initial project.
- **Leadership:** Lean manufacturing methodologies encourage the practice of "management by walking around." The management team must ul-

timately embrace the methodologies and champion the changes implemented. Monitoring work conditions is the responsibility of managers.

THE TRANSFORMATION PROCESS TO LEAN MANUFACTURING

Achieving measurable results is the primary goal of any project. The Lean implementation methodology is designed to achieve specific, measurable results by focusing directly on improving manufacturing performance. This results-driven approach identifies specific milestones and the steps necessary to achieve the desired results. It is the project team's responsibility to provide guidance and leadership to the organization to complete the milestone tasks. The management team must demonstrate commitment to the implementation in the form of human and financial resources and support of the cultural changes that are certain to occur.

The effort required to convert from the current operating methodology to the Lean manufacturing methodologies can be significant. Implementation of the Lean manufacturing methodologies consists of a series of sequential, systematic steps included in a series of project milestones that can be timed to match your company's comfort level and ability to deal with change. The aggressiveness and the pace of change are dependent on the condition of the existing process information and the level of commitment from the management team. This implementation methodology will help lead a team of manufacturing professionals through a step-by-step process for designing a Lean manufacturing line and installing the related kanban systems.

Because the implementation tasks are systematic and sequential, the large amount of information required can be separated and assigned to teams members who have specific technical expertise. This team approach resolves two issues simultaneously: (1) Work is divided into manageable pieces. Team members assigned to the implementation project are typically not excused from performing their everyday responsibilities, even though critical information about the company must be collected. (2) Numerous team member assignments facilitate greater participation from more people. The implementation of the Lean manufacturing methodologies should not be mysterious or done behind closed doors. More participants mean more assimilation and greater acceptance of the new methodologies.

Crucial information about your company is needed to begin the redesign of the manufacturing facility. Much of this information is most likely readily available but is generally not in the form necessary for a Lean implementation. The Lean manufacturing methodologies use this information to design the manufacturing processes to resemble the process flow of products. The information collected is used in a series of formulas that provide key pieces of resource information. The results of these mathematical models lead to critical line design optimization features. As the implementation moves forward, teams should always be prepared to respond to the need for additional information as it occurs.

It is recommended that an implementation document be created as an implementation archive. When the implementation project is completed, this archival document establishes a journal that tracks and records all factory transformation activities. It should include all material and process definitions, facility preparations, team communications, team assignments, milestone definitions, and a copy of the Lean methodologies milestones and supporting documentation. This implementation document can be used as an historical reference for future implementations within the company.

The Lean implementation encourages the involvement of a wide spectrum of participants. It is mandatory that team members assigned to the implementation project receive training in the methodologies and concepts of Lean manufacturing prior to commencing their implementation activities. This level of team understanding is critical not just during the implementation but is also vital to understanding the dynamics of designing the first multiproduct Lean line. Other employees not assigned to the initial implementation should be encouraged to attend a similar training workshop as well. Individual contributors not participating as full-time implementation team members are still instrumental when creating a critical mass of employees to internalize and train others to operate and maintain the Lean manufacturing line over time.

The initial successful implementation of the first Lean line becomes the platform for achieving additional business objectives. The business objectives for the first program must be identified. If targeted by the strategic business assessment, progression toward meeting these objectives will be recorded and tracked as key measurements for the success of the program. If not established prior to the start of the implementation project, business objectives must be identified as soon as possible into the implementation process.

A Lean coordinator and individual team leaders are assigned to each team formed. These team leaders provide a focal point for communication, coordination of team resource assignments, and program performance reporting. Horizontal and vertical communication is critical to the success of any implementation.

PHYSICAL FACILITATION FOR PROJECT TEAMS

A classroom or conference room large enough to seat the project implementation teams, 6 to 15 members and 3 project team leaders, should be dedicated to the project teams for the duration of the initial implementation project. The assigned space should be able to accommodate team members working around tables. Chairs and tables must be provided in addition to the following equipment:

- Overhead projector with screen (or suitable computer projection device)
- Large easel with paper tablet and pens
- White board with erasable color markers

This room is to be used for individual team meetings, classroom training sessions, team strategy sessions among all team members, and for publicly posting implementation documentation. The room should also have a telephone and access to the Internet. If possible, the conference room selected should be located close to a common area where manufacturing personnel can have easy access. Manufacturing personnel should have an open invitation to review activities and ask questions about Lean and the team's progress.

PROJECT MANAGEMENT STRUCTURE

The project management structure defines the internal organization structure for managing the Lean conversion project. The structure is designed to provide clarity of direction for participating team members, to assign responsibility for the collection of information, to identify responsibilities for critical decision making, and to provide a path for problem resolution.

The Lean manufacturing implementation methodologies consist of a series of activities that are associated with defined milestones. Progress against these activities and milestones is monitored so that the benefits and agreed-upon deliverables result from the implementation activity. Resolution of simple issues will be accomplished at the team level. Occasionally, there may be issues that must be resolved at a higher level of management. The project management structure must assign these responsibilities and define problem resolution paths. It is suggested that the implementation journal document and record activities as they occur throughout the program. Updates to the journal should also include accomplishments, completion to plan, open activities and issues, and concerns discovered during the information-gathering process.

The Steering Committee

To ensure successful implementation of the Lean manufacturing initiatives, it is imperative that a steering committee be created to oversee implementation

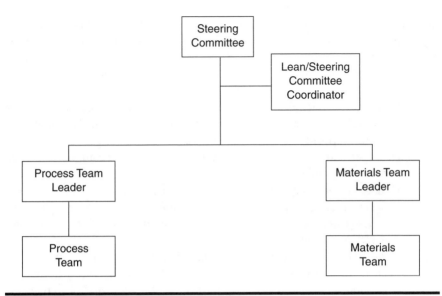

Figure 7.1 Team Structure

activities. Management-level personnel representing all major functional organizations should be chosen to serve on the steering committee. The membership of the steering committee should also consist of the managers of those employees assigned to the process and material teams. This reporting relationship not only assures upward and downward communication at the functional level on a day-to-day basis, but establishes the platform for educating the steering committee as well.

Representatives from the following functional areas should also be included as members of the steering committee. Others can be added if they add value, but these are the core members:

- President
- Manufacturing engineering
- Design engineering
- Quality engineering
- Human resources
- Industrial engineering
- Manufacturing operations
- Information systems

Metaphorically, the steering committee acts as a "board of directors" for the Lean implementation. The steering committee provides overall guidance and direction for the progress of the Lean implementation and also prepares for possible future company-wide transformation. The steering committee should meet on a regular basis to monitor progress toward the Lean manufacturing methodologies project milestones. To facilitate communication among the steering committee members and the individual teams, a steering committee coordinator should also be selected.

The primary responsibilities of the steering committee are to:

1. Commit staffing resources from each organization represented on the implementation teams. This often requires the steering committee to direct the priorities for the implementation teams.

2. Hold periodic meetings to review the progress of the implementation. Review status of action items and compliance to the Lean methodologies. Understand and reconcile the existing business practices with the modifications recommended by the Lean implementation teams. Achieve consensus among the members of the steering committee on recommended action plans.

3. Understand, reconcile, and ensure the integrity of and compliance to the Lean methodologies implemented during the project. This will demonstrate upper management's commitment to the goals and objectives established for the implementation.

4. Monitor program milestones and set priorities to maintain progress in support of the Lean implementation.

5. Assure identified supplies, kanban materials, and incremental machine and labor resource requirements are funded. Confirm organizational roles and responsibilities are agreed to and supported. Secure funding for the project as necessary.

6. Develop a communications and publicity strategy to ensure all employees, customers, and suppliers are exposed to the Lean implementation project, the anticipated benefits, and how the goals of the project support the goals of the organization.

7. As needs are identified, develop, fund, and staff the necessary training plans. Two types of training are typically needed: (1) introductory Lean methods training for existing employees and (2) Lean orientation training for new employees.

8. Assure the business objectives established for the company are being met. Monitor critical baseline performance criteria related to response, quality, inventory, product cost, floor space, and staffing. Systematically measure the program's progress toward meeting the business goals targeted.

While the implementation team members accomplish the day-to-day work, it is ultimately the steering committee that has direct responsibility for the program's progress.

Lean Manufacturing/Steering Committee Coordinator

Some team members may participate in the implementation of Lean on a part-time, as-needed basis in addition to their day-to-day activities. However, the Lean/steering committee coordinator should be assigned full time to the implementation. This person is responsible for communication upward, downward, and among all the team members. In addition to holding the teams accountable for their action items, the Lean/steering committee coordinator serves as a liaison between the steering committee and the teams to determine when communication is necessary. The coordinator must evaluate issues to be elevated to the steering committee for resolution.

The Lean/steering committee coordinator should:

1. Understand the responsibilities delegated to each team member, monitor the progress of action items, and know when to seek help from the steering committee.
2. Jointly manage the Lean manufacturing project with the process and material teams, team leaders, and steering committee members.
3. Suggest and lead the efforts for the communication and publicity strategy, making sure to publicize successes as they occur.
4. Develop a plan to educate and inform the entire company, customers, and suppliers. Develop a plan to ultimately expand the Lean methodologies throughout the entire facility or company.
5. Serve a dual role as the leader of the steering committee. The steering committee coordinator:
   - Determines the targeted product lines and implementation areas.
   - Determines the facility design capacity of the identified product lines.
   - Organizes necessary training for the implementation teams and work force.
   - Assigns and monitors tasks, responsibilities, and action items.
   - Assures milestones and goals are being met.
   - Addresses resource needs identified by the teams.
   - Supports organizational changes as necessary.
   - Champions training programs aimed at employee involvement.
   - Leads the monitoring of progress toward business objectives.
   - Provides status reports to the steering committee on implementation progress and presents issues requiring their attention.
   - Reviews budgets and presents implementation funding requirements to the steering committee.
   - Manages overall coordination of the implementation team efforts in the execution of assigned day-to-day tasks.

■ Provides resources — both human and financial — to support teams that need assistance.

Implementation Teams

An important goal of the Lean implementation is to provide your company with a new set of tools with which to operate the business. When the implementation project is completed, the new Lean methodologies must become daily routines. The gap between current methodologies and the Lean methodologies will soon be obvious after beginning the implementation process. Although trained, team members may be unfamiliar or uncomfortable with the Lean manufacturing methodologies.

There may be a period of uncertainty when challenging the current methodologies and implementing the new Lean methods. This uncertainty can be an uncomfortable feeling for most people. There may not be clear and easy solutions for some issues. Avoid the temptation to fall back on the warm and comfortable familiar systems. Work to solve issues as they occur using the new Lean methods as a guide. Over the course of the implementation, the knowledge and comfort level of each team will evolve until a thorough understanding of the Lean methods is complete. By the time the new Lean line is started, the new set of tools should feel comfortable to the team members.

This evolution begins with the implementation project. One of the best ways to effect this evolution is to involve as many employees as practical on the implementation project. A team approach is the best way to accomplish this evolution. The team approach resolves two issues simultaneously: (1) team assignment facilitates greater participation, which leads to better integration by more people, and (2) work is divided into manageable pieces.

Because Lean methodology models the current manufacturing processes, a significant amount of information must be gathered and incorporated in the Lean mathematical models. This is an iterative process that requires an in-depth knowledge of the manufacturing processes and materials strategies. The implementation will progress sequentially and systematically. The required information can be separated by manufacturing discipline and assigned to teams of people who possess the specialized technical expertise. Two teams will be established and charged with the responsibility to implement the Lean manufacturing methodologies: a process team with knowledge of the manufacturing processes and quality criteria and a materials team with knowledge of the parts and product configurations.

The participation of individual team members will be on a part-time basis, typically requiring approximately 10 to 20% of their available time. Just as the steering committee is made up of a cross-section of representatives from various functional organizations, the composition of these two teams will reflect the membership of the steering committee and the required functional knowledge. The teams work directly under the guidance of the steering committee, steering committee coordinator, and selected team leaders throughout the project.

The teams are responsible for completing all assigned implementation tasks. These knowledgeable team members will play a major role in internalizing and making the methodologies of Lean manufacturing a part of everyday life once the implementation project is completed.

Both the process and materials teams must designate one member of each team to serve as the team leader. Team leaders share responsibility for the success of the project with the Lean coordinator.

Team leader responsibilities include:

1. Assigning work tasks, agreed upon with the steering committee and Lean coordinator, to the team members. The team leader must effectively manage team resources to assure the on-time completion of milestones and goals.
2. Leading and monitoring milestone achievement, assigning responsibilities, assessing resource feasibility, and escalating issues based on frequent and periodic milestone reviews.
3. Leading the team and gaining consensus for all team decisions while reserving the right to make a final decision for the team, if necessary.
4. Motivating the team to complete assigned tasks.
5. Managing and maintaining all documentation as required for the program and providing periodic updates to the implementation journal as requested.

Because team members participate on a part-time basis, rotation of alternate members is encouraged. Rotating team members allows additional employees to be brought in to provide specific technical expertise when needed. The rotating team member method encourages involvement and helps to expand the knowledge of Lean methodologies across the organization. More knowledgeable personnel also help to create the critical mass needed to make Lean methodologies a standard part of the everyday job routine. With additional programs in other areas of production and in the back office, more rotations will occur, allowing more and more employees to become involved.

Participants who rotate into a team based on specific expertise should be managed by the core team members to ensure that only the expected contribution is obtained. While interesting and often fun, guard against peripheral discussions and going off on tangents. Caution is also advised when including casual observers from other locations, divisions, or companies who are not members of the core implementation team. With no responsibility for project scope, observers can divert attention from the task and can slow down the implementation process with extraneous questions and concerns that are not relevant to the implementation.

While full-time dedication of team members to the project is not expected, accomplishing the program objectives within specified time frames is. The effort for a successful project requires an extreme amount of focus and hard work. To support and acknowledge the extra efforts of these team members, special recognition as core members of the implementation team is recommended. These core team members possess long-term "ownership" and involvement to assure the success of the new Lean manufacturing processes.

Assignment of team members to the implementation team is a very important decision that deserves careful thought and consideration. Team members must understand the significant commitment of effort required for the implementation program. While team leaders will be responsible for achieving goals and objectives, each person chosen for the team must be able to work independently on an as-needed basis without minute-by-minute supervision. All communication about the implementation must begin with these teams. It is important that all participants receive training in the concepts of Lean manufacturing.

Once operational, these teams can be quite dynamic. As they achieve successes, team members will continue to generate enthusiasm and energy for the project. Enthusiasm will become contagious throughout the company. Excitement about the benefits will be beneficial to incorporating the Lean methodologies throughout the company. The Lean coordinator and steering committee must be active and committed to the success of the project during the implementation. Questions, doubts, and issues along the way must be discussed and resolved before proceeding. By working together, your company will soon be able to enjoy the many benefits of the Lean manufacturing methodologies.

The Process Team

The process team consists of employees who have specific knowledge of the manufacturing processes. This includes knowledge about how products are manufactured, how products differ from one another, the time required to manufacture products, what manufacturing issues exist, and facility and resource management capabilities. Typical membership of the process team includes representation from manufacturing, design and industrial engineering, production management, quality control, and scheduling.

The responsibilities of the process team are:

1. Define the manufacturing processes
   - Creation of process flow diagrams, in graphical format, for all designated parent part numbers included in the initial line design area
   - Identification of rework and scrap percentages for each process and for each product
   - Identification of optional work paths and their corresponding demand percentages, also for each product
2. Process mapping
   - Definition of product families (products that share common manufacturing processes)
   - Definition of rework, scrap, and options by product
3. Sequence of events
   - Documentation of sequential work tasks for each process
   - Identification of the actual time required to perform each task
   - Identification and documentation of any quality criteria for a work task
4. Line design for facility optimization
   - Identification of resources required to perform work by type and quantity
   - Creation of a list of discrete machine types
   - Identification of the major labor skill groups (if applicable)
   - Identification of effective work hours and number of shifts in which work is performed
   - Final approval of line design based on mixed-product calculations and methodologies
   - Management of the physical changes to facilities
5. Employee training
   - Training for line employees to work in a Lean manufacturing environment
   - Training to manufacture multiple products chosen to be produced on the mixed-product line

The Materials Team

Members of the materials team are knowledgeable about the parts, both purchased and manufactured, that are used to produce products. They understand bills of materials, data in the item master, how planning systems and subsequent order launch routines are performed, and historical usage and forecasting systems. Typical membership of the materials team includes the master scheduler, planners, buyers, distribution, warehousing, systems, and sales and marketing.

The responsibilities of the materials team are to:

1. Select parent part (stockkeeping unit) candidates used in the Lean manufacturing methodologies project
   - Establish product candidates and possible options representative of the manufacturing processes to be used in the design of the Lean line
   - Establish the demand volumes for the stockkeeping unit products selected, along with product options and percentages
2. Consolidate the bill of material databases for products selected for the Lean line design
   - Generate a comprehensive parts list to includes active products, options, and component parts that match the initial 80/20 parent parts selection
3. Develop and install the kanban strategy
   - Designing the kanban system, including pull sequences, delivery frequencies, container sizing, supplier packaging requirements, replenishment inventory (RIP) locations, and "quick-count" methods
   - Present material to the line, by securing sufficient containers for both line and RIP locations, labeling the containers, performing the initial fill of the containers, and placing flow racks and RIP storage shelving where necessary
   - Train employees how to operate the kanban system, including pulling material with replenishable and one-time-use kanbans, handling material review board materials, and sequencing one-time-use items with sales orders
4. Sequence demand to the line
   - Develop a standard format to communicate the sequence of orders to be produced on the line and prepare a sales order sequencing board (or electronic equivalent) to organize this function
   - Formalize material replenishment policies and procedures identified during the implementation

REQUIRED INFORMATION OVERVIEW

Key elements of information needed to optimize your facility and design the new Lean manufacturing line are outlined below:

- **Product/family definitions:** For all current and anticipated new products, along with their historical sales volumes and family designations.
- **Process flow diagram (PFD):** For each manufactured finished goods product included in the Lean facility optimization design. The PFD is

a graphical drawing that shows the relationship of the processes as they flow together to manufacture your products. Numerous products often share a common PFD. A single diagram showing all processes for all products will be developed and used for the final multiproduct line design.

☐ *Process:* A physical location where a logical grouping of resources performs sequential work tasks. A process in manufacturing is a combination of resources (people and machines) that convert material toward the completion of a product.

☐ *Process flow diagram:* A graphic depiction of the time-based relationship of resources that perform work tasks. The work tasks these resources perform are required to build a product or complete an administrative activity.

☐ *Mixed-product process flow diagram:* A PFD that consists of multiple products that can be grouped together based on similar manufacturing processes and standard times to produce those products.

■ **Sequence of Events (SOE):** For each process identified in the PFD. The SOE requires the detailed listing of individual tasks necessary to perform a particular process for a specific product. In addition, each task identified must also include the amount of actual time necessary to perform the work, along with any quality criteria for that task. Documenting this information represents the greatest amount of work in a Lean manufacturing methodologies implementation.

☐ *Sequence of events:* A definition of the work and quality criteria required to build a product in the specific production process.

■ **Process maps:** Using the information developed for the SOE and PFDs, create a matrix with all processes identified along the horizontal axis and all products listed on the vertical axis. At each product/process intersection, record the labor and machine times, in minutes, as identified in the SOE. Then, using the same matrix format, indicate scrap, rework, and option percentages at each product/process intersection.

☐ *Process map:* A matrix that shows the manufacturing processes derived from the PFD along the horizontal axis and the products along the vertical axis. This matrix is used to determine multiproduct families with common processes and standard work times.

■ **Required volume at capacity (V_c):** For each product. V_c is a statement of the anticipated volume of each product for the time horizon determined by the steering committee for line design. These data are usually developed as a joint effort among marketing, manufacturing, and senior management. V_c should be signed off on by the steering committee as it represents a statement of capacity for the manufacturing facility. V_c is the basic denominator for all subsequent facility optimization calculations.

☐ *Volume at capacity:* A statement of anticipated future demand for products to be manufactured on a Lean line. V_c is the denominator used for the calculation of Takt time. Takt time is subsequently used in all resource calculations required for line design.

☐ *Takt:* A time–volume relationship calculated as the rhythm, beat, or cadence for each process of a Lean line. Takt is used to establish resource definition and line balance for the Lean line.

■ **Resource listing:** Identifies effective hours and shifts and the number and type of labor resources in the facility optimization area.

☐ *Effective hours:* A statement of the amount of time available to manufacturing employees to perform the work identified in the SOE. For Lean line design, this time is stated in minutes.

☐ *Resource:* A person or machine capable of performing the work tasks required to produce a product.

☐ *Resource time available:* The work minutes available in a day from a series of Lean manufacturing resources (employees, workstations, and/or machines) to build products.

■ **Kanban pull design criteria:** Defined for all component parts chosen to be replenished with the kanban system. Pull sequences define points of consumption and of resupply, delivery frequency, and container and packaging sizes. This information will be used to establish kanban strategy.

☐ *Kanban:* A Japanese word that means a communication signal or card. It is a technique used to pull products and materials to Lean manufacturing lines. There are several variations of kanbans based on application: in-process, two-bin, single-card, multiple-card, and one-time-use kanban.

8

THE LEAN IMPLEMENTATION MILESTONES CHECKLIST

Transforming a manufacturing facility from one that uses a computerized planning system to launch batches of orders into manufacturing scheduled to be routed through a series of departments to one that produces products in a one-piece regulated flow is no easy task. It requires the complete rethinking of the current operating system and how products are manufactured today.

The information necessary to understand products, their processes and component materials, and their demand has already been discussed. Typically, the information required is either not available or is not in a format usable for redesigning the facility into a one-piece Lean manufacturing facility. The required information usually has to be gathered and developed in a format to be usable for designing a Lean facility.

Let there be no mistake about this information-gathering process. It can be difficult, time consuming, and tedious. Nonetheless, this information is imperative and must be complete before the Lean transformation process can take place. One way to capture this information would be to assign the responsibility for data collection to an individual contributor and leave him or her alone for long periods of time to focus solely on the gathering of information. This method of information gathering would get the job done, and because one person collected the information, it would also be consistent in detail and content.

Chances are the length of time required for one person to accumulate all the information would be great. In addition to the time required, the in-depth understanding and knowledge required to design a Lean manufacturing line would be limited to just one person. Broad assimilation of the Lean manufacturing methods throughout the entire organization would take more time than what was originally saved by one person doing all the work.

The better method is the Team method. Establishing teams to collect the required information not only spreads the difficult and time consuming work over several persons, it simultaneously educates and trains team members in the concepts and methodologies of Lean manufacturing. These original team members make up a significant part of the critical mass necessary to internalize the Lean methodologies throughout the entire organization.

Also, by giving the work to many team members, the speed of the implementation can be accelerated. The initial success of long drawn-out implementations is diminished when team members lose their enthusiasm and passion for the transformation project. Implementations can still be successful, but may take more time and energy to achieve maximum benefits.

After the Lean implementation teams have been established and a Lean/ steering committee coordinator has been assigned, team members need a blueprint to channel and direct their activities so as to avoid overlapping of work and creating redundant information and to maximize the efficient use of their time. Not only is the efficient use of team members' time critical, but collecting information in the correct priority is also crucial.

The Lean manufacturing methodologies use the Lean Implementation Milestones Checklist to assure the Lean/steering coordinator and the materials and process teams collect the required information in the correct priority sequence. There are six milestones, each with a series of action items that need to be completed before progressing to the next milestone. Each milestone must be completed in sequence. Because action items must be completed before moving to the next milestone, the checklist is a working document for managing the implementation project. The Lean/steering committee coordinator, working in concert with the steering committee, and the implementation teams must agree that all action items for a milestone can be checked as completed before advancing to the next milestone.

The action items for each milestone are arranged by category based on team responsibility. The steering committee and the materials and process teams are responsible for their assigned action items in the time frame determined by the Lean/steering committee coordinator. Individual implementation team leaders are responsible for assuring their team members dedicate the time necessary to collect the required information. Time or resource constraints should be elevated and negotiated by the team leader with the Lean/steering committee coordinator.

It is important the project stay on schedule to avoid team member burnout and delay of benefits.

The action item statement is concise and brief. The brief action item statement is designed to capsulize the work to be completed or the information to be collected for each milestone. In many cases, checking off an action item may require significant work effort. Unlike the Lean manufacturing lines the implementation project is designed to create, the action items and milestones are not balanced. It is not realistic to assume that all action items and team tasks will be completed at the same time. While effort to spread the work tasks evenly across the milestones has been made, processes, component materials, and type and organization of information vary greatly from company to company. Because of this variability, expect some action items to be completed faster than others. Maintain patience for teams with greater challenges for information collection.

SOFTWARE REQUIREMENTS FOR LEAN MANUFACTURING METHODOLOGIES

There is a significant amount of mathematical calculation work to be done to determine kanban and Lean line resources. For both line design and kanban, the capability to perform multiple iterations until the optimum solution is achieved is desirable. Commercial software programs available in the marketplace are designed to perform these necessary calculations. These products range broadly in price and features. However, these calculations can be programmed into popular spreadsheet programs or other commercially available programming vehicles. There is no requirement to purchase software to complete the installation of your Lean manufacturing lines.

The size and complexity of spreadsheet programs can grow substantially as the implementation project moves forward, so including a person with good spreadsheet skills as a team member is suggested. As the spreadsheet grows in size, the implementation team may want to consider limiting access to the spreadsheets to a few selected team members. The common practice of locating these programs on a corporate network could lead to contamination of the data.

MILESTONE #1
Initialization and Project Start-Up

Objective: Get implementation project started! Establish a strategic vision for the company. Select and train teams. Document an action plan. Empower teams and identify goals. Begin to collect required information for line design and kanban.

Steering Committee Tasks

1. Articulate strategic vision ☐
2. Complete executive overview ☐
3. Document master plan ☐
4. Identify team members and establish teams ☐
5. Complete materials and process team training ☐
6. Confirm target line design area ☐

Materials Team Tasks

7. Begin product identification for the target area ☐
8. Identify volume required for target area ☐
9. Begin selection of kanban candidate part numbers ☐

Process Team Tasks

10. Establish working minutes per day ☐
11. Begin creation of process flow diagrams (PFDs) ☐
12. Begin writing sequence of events (SOEs) and process times ☐

Objective

The action items listed in milestone #1 are designed to get the implementation project started. The majority of the action items for milestone #1 are the responsibility of the steering committee and must be completed before the materials and process teams can begin their activities.

Steering Committee Action Items

1. **Articulate strategic vision:** Reasons for changing the operating system of the manufacturing facility must be known, stated, and published if necessary. Stating the reasons publicly also forces the steering committee members to think carefully about their expectations of the Lean manufacturing line. Different agendas of different members of the steering committee must be reconciled among the members. The strategic vision must provide the clarity of direction to ensure that implementation team members guide the implementation process to achieve the goals of the strategic vision.

2. **Complete executive overview:** In many companies, it is unlikely that every member of the executive management staff will actively participate in the implementation project. Some of the executive management staff may be on the periphery or completely unaware of the project itself. Even though these staff members may not be directly involved in the Lean

implementation project, they should still be informed of the project in the event the implementation team members require information from their functional departments. The overview should consist of a brief educational session to explain the differences between the current operating system and a Lean manufacturing system and to provide courtesy information to their functional areas.

3. **Document master plan:** A high-level plan that states the strategic vision, the milestone action items, their anticipated dates of completion, and lists the person charged with the responsibility for completion should be created. This document becomes the "master plan" for the steering committee during the entire implementation project. The master plan must be reviewed and updated at each meeting held by the steering committee. It is the responsibility of the Lean/steering committee coordinator to provide communication from the implementation teams when changes to the master plan are required. Modifications to the master plan must be agreed to by the members of the steering committee. The Lean/steering committee coordinator must also communicate changes in the master plan to the implementation teams.

4. **Identify team members and establish teams:** Each functional area represented by the steering committee must select a person from the area to participate as a member of an implementation team. In addition to the steering committee and implementation team relationship, the team member will also have a manager/direct-report relationship. This additional relationship ensures that implementation issues are elevated and appropriate solutions are created. The manager/direct-report relationship also ensures that the necessary team member resources are available to the implementation teams. Some required team members may not have representation on the steering committee. Additional education of these team members' management may be required to secure support for participation on an implementation team.

5. **Complete materials and process team training:** Once team members have been chosen for participation, training and education in the concepts and principles of Lean manufacturing are required. This training is frequently available as an external training course or as an internal training department offering. If not available, an internal training course should be developed to train new team members and later new employees who will be working on the Lean line. Training in the implementation process is usually not necessary as the actual implementation provides on-the-job training as the team members progress through the milestones.

6. **Confirm target line design area:** Selecting the appropriate target area for the initial Lean implementation is a critical task. Using the information

from the strategic business analysis, the target area should be large enough to return a significant return on investment while being sensitive to the amount of change being introduced into the organization. Initial implementation projects should be targeted for completion in approximately four to six months.

Once the materials and process teams have been formed and have held their initial meetings, they must begin their information collection activities. The information to be collected is described in previous chapters.

MILESTONE #2
Understanding Products, Processes, and Materials

Objective: Document all manufacturing processes. Identify process throughput including options, rework, and scrap. Define product families by process. Document consumption and replenishment points for kanban parts. Establish pull chains and replenishment times. Identify one-time-use kanban parts.

Steering Committee Tasks

1. Follow up team training ☐
2. Review and update master plan ☐
3. Achieve consensus for products in target area ☐

Materials Team Tasks

4. Complete first iteration of demand volume for products ☐
5. Identify parts for kanban system ☐
6. Develop kanban pull chains ☐
7. Calculate cost of kanban replenishment strategy ☐

Process Team Tasks

8. Complete PFDs ☐
9. Quantify and document process throughput variables ☐
10. Create mixed-product PFD ☐
11. Review SOEs and process times ☐
12. Generate first iteration of resource requirements ☐

Objective

Continue the collection and documentation of the manufacturing processes started in milestone #1, including any option paths, rework loops, and scrap on the PFDs. Group PFDs into families by process similarity and create a mixed-product PFD. Continue development of the material kanban system by establishing pull chains and selecting parts to include in the kanban system. Complete first-pass resource calculations for the Lean line design layout and an initial inventory investment estimate for the kanban replenishment strategy.

Steering Committee Action Items

1. **Follow up team training:** As new team members are introduced to the implementation teams, they may require training to bring them up to speed with the current team members. The steering committee must provide the resources necessary to assure this training is provided.
2. **Review and update master plan:** Record team progress and document any modification.
3. **Achieve consensus for products in the target area:** It is not uncommon for much discussion to focus on the selection of parent parts (stockkeeping units) chosen to represent the products produced on the Lean line. However, this discussion cannot go on forever. The key selection criterion is that products chosen must represent all the manufacturing process used to produce all products. Current family designation, color, size, and configuration are secondary considerations. Discussion can still continue during milestone #2, but must eventually be finalized.

Materials Team Action Items

4. **Complete first iteration of demand volume for products:** Final demand volume to be used for the final line design layout can be very difficult to determine. Selecting the final volume capacity is an extremely important decision. Designing a Lean manufacturing facility capable of producing future demand requires a projection of the future. Many manufacturers are uncomfortable when making this projection. Team members responsible for generating the volume at capacity number are more comfortable when they are able to perform "what if" projections on different mix and volume combinations. Time should be allowed for team members to execute multiple iterations of mix and volume.
5. **Identify parts for the kanban system:** Continue identification of parts to be included in the kanban system. The initial listing should include parts that represent 80% of the total sales volume.

6. **Develop kanban pull chains:** Individual kanban pull sequences with corresponding consumption and replenishment points should be developed and completed during milestone #2. Series of pull sequences must then be attached together to form pull chains. The delivery frequency times dictate the velocity of inventory turns.

7. **Calculate cost of kanban replenishment strategy:** The kanban formula must be calculated for each replenishment time for each pull sequence in each pull chain to determine the quantities of material to be maintained in the consumption and replenishment points. Multiplying the standard cost by the kanban quantity and summing by pull sequence, the inventory investment for each consumption and replenishment can be determined. If the desired inventory investment or expected turn rate cannot be achieved with the replenishment strategy, the replenishment times in each pull sequence can be adjusted and recalculated until the desired inventory investment is achieved. This is an iterative and ongoing process and begins with milestone #2.

Process Team Action Items

8. **Complete PFDs:** All PFDs should be completed. If the materials team selects new part numbers or substitutes parent part numbers, PFDs must be developed for those parts.

9. **Quantify and document process throughput variables:** Scrap, rework, and options that affect process throughput quantities must be documented at milestone #2. Where these variables occur, volume through the process is changed and can impact Takt time and ultimately the resources required.

10. **Create mixed-model PFD:** The mixed-model PFD will provide the first indication of how the final Lean layout will appear.

11. **Review SOEs and process times:** The single largest information-gathering task is the development of the SOE. An SOE is created for every product and for every process. Even using duplicate SOEs, when added together, they can number in the hundreds. The task of writing SOEs can be even more daunting if no process information ever existed before. The size of and time required for the generation of SOE records are often abbreviated during the implementation project and limited to the collection of standard times. It is unrealistic to expect that all SOE information will be completed by milestone #2. At milestone #2, the progress of SOE information collection is reviewed to be certain the information is accurate and will be completed on time to meet the project dates in the master plan. Additional resources may be needed or the master plan may need to be modified to reflect the completion of the SOEs. If the date of completion must be

extended past the anticipated completion date of the implementation project, the decision to limit SOE information to standard times only may be made to meet project deadlines. The balance of information will be necessary for workstation definition and quality criteria.

12. **Generate first iteration of resources requirements:** Enough information should be available at milestone #2 to make a first effort to construct a common processes process map. In this process map, the manufacturing processes are listed vertically across the top and the representative parent part numbers are listed horizontally. At the cell where the information intersects, the standard time from the SOE should be listed. This process map should also list the rework and optional processes. At the base of each column, the Takt time, standard time weighted, and the resource calculations can be made. Although incomplete at milestone #2, there should be sufficient information to compare with current conditions to assess if collected information is reasonable. The process map is also a project management tool for the process team leader to determine missing SOE times for products and processes.

MILESTONE #3
Final Check

Objective: Complete all information collection activities. Achieve consensus and steering committee sign-off for products, demands, and effective minutes per day identified for the target area. Complete SOE tasks, process times, and throughput variables. Make final selections of parts for the kanban system and pull sequences for the target area. Complete all resource calculations for final line layout.

Steering Committee Tasks

1. Follow-up team training ☐
2. Review and update master plan ☐
3. Approve products for target area ☐
4. Approve product demand for target area ☐
5. Approve mixed-product PFD ☐

Materials Team Tasks

6. Complete selection of parts for kanban system ☐
7. Develop replenishment strategy for one-time-use parts ☐
8. Determine final cost of kanban replenishment strategy ☐

Process Team Tasks

9. Complete SOE, quality criteria, and process times ☐
10. Populate the final resource process map ☐
11. Complete all resource calculations ☐

Objective

All information-gathering activities must be completed. The discussions about which products best represent the Lean line product mix must be finalized. The future demand volume of those products must also be agreed upon. The mixed-product PFD must be approved as representative of the manufacturing processes. The work minutes per day must also be approved. All of these information parameters become the numerators and denominators of line design and kanban calculations. They are crucial enough to require signed approval by the steering committee.

The time required to complete milestones #1 and #2 provides ample opportunity for all participants to make a case for maintaining current conditions or to present their ideas and suggestions. Milestone #3 is the time when all these discussions must come to a conclusion. When milestone #3 is completed, a consensus must be built that begins to reflect the future operating environment in manufacturing. Building this consensus is the responsibility of the steering committee and the Lean/steering committee coordinator.

Steering Committee Action Items

1. **Follow up team training:** The steering committee must assure all team members have been trained in the methodologies of Lean manufacturing.
2. **Review and update master plan:** Record team progress and document any modification.
3. **Approve products for target area:** The final selection of parent parts to represent the Lean line is the responsibility of the steering committee. While the materials implementation team may actually construct the list of parent part numbers, it typically has little visibility of long-term product issues. Many product issues can only be resolved by members of the steering committee.
4. **Approve product demand for target area:** The demand volume is a statement of the capacity of the Lean line. Because this volume capacity is based on the projections of future demand, it is usually one of the last data elements to be decided. The implementation teams have little visibility of future business conditions and should not be responsible for making capacity decisions. Because it is so important to the design of the Lean line,

it must be approved by the steering committee before the final resource calculations are performed.

5. **Approve mixed-product PFD:** The steering committee must approve the mixed-product PFD to assure all manufacturing processes have been represented for the Lean line design.

Materials Team Action Items

6. **Complete selection of parts for kanban system:** Discussions about which parts to include in the kanban system should be completed at this milestone.

7. **Develop replenishment strategy for one-time-use parts:** Parts that are large, expensive, or slow moving not included in the kanban system require an alternative one-time-use kanban system.

8. **Determine final cost of kanban replenishment strategy:** Management of the kanban system is ongoing, but at this milestone the final inventory investment strategy for the start-up of the Lean line should be completed. Adjustments to inventory investment or turn rate goals can be accomplished by changing the delivery frequency time. Also, the kanban system should be tested for its capability to incorporate changes to part numbers, delivery frequency time, and consumption and replenishment points. The system must be robust and easy to manage. During milestone #3, exercise the system and make modifications as necessary,

Process Team Action Items

9. **Complete SOE, quality criteria, and process times:** Information from the SOE is used to perform resource calculations on the process map, identify quality criteria at the workstation level, and define work tasks for each workstation.

10. **Populate the final resource process map:** All information required to calculate resources on the process map must be recorded on the process map before this milestone is complete. Complete and accurate information from the process map is the key to determining accurate resource requirements to meet the demand volume at capacity.

11. **Complete all resource calculations:** At the base of each process column of the completely populated process map, the demand volume at capacity, the Takt time, standard time weighted (ST_w) and the number of resources required for each process are calculated. Once calculated, it is a good time to perform a "sanity" check of resources calculated. The number of future resources for each process should be in proportion to the current number of resources based on the current and future volumes when factored by

efficiency. If the resources difference is unreasonable, recheck the SOE times for accuracy and the demand volume at capacity (V_c).

MILESTONE #4
Factory Design

Objective: Create facsimile Lean manufacturing factory layout using calculated resources for the resources identified on the PFD. Identify and locate in-process kanban (IPK) and RIP locations. Develop kanban system rollout plan. Identify requirements for operator training. Develop a facility plan and a Lean line start-up strategy.

Steering Committee Tasks

1. Review organizational training requirements ☐
2. Final approval of paper line layout ☐
3. Final approval of kanban replenishment cost strategy ☐
4. Review and update master plan ☐

Materials Team Tasks

5. Finalize kanban system cost strategy for line start-up ☐
6. Develop kanban system installation plan ☐
7. Establish RIP locations on the final line layout ☐
8. Establish sequencing points for the location of one-time-use parts ☐
9. Identify material handler training requirements ☐

Process Team Tasks

10. Complete process map resource calculations ☐
11. Create paper line layout following the mixed-product PFD ☐
12. Locate IPKs and sequencing points for custom-product configurations ☐
13. Identify Operator Training Requirements ☐
14. Develop facility plan for line start-up ☐

Objective

Create the Lean manufacturing factory layout. Using a perimeter drawing of the Lean target area and cutouts scaled to match the resource footprint, lay out the Lean manufacturing line, placing the feeder processes in the correct location to facilitate the flow of product. Locate fixtures, carts, RIP racks, machines, and any other resources identified as necessary for the manufacture of product. Place all IPKs in workstations to assure a clear and visible line of sight for upstream operators. Develop the two-bin material kanban system rollout plan. Identify operator training needs, and develop a facility plan for rearranging the factory.

Milestone # 4 is an exciting milestone to complete. Previous milestones were focused on the collection of information required for designing the Lean line. Now is the time to actually lay the factory out in a design that will optimize the flow of product. Creating the paper facsimile of the Lean line layout is an energy filled experience where the pent-up good ideas from all the team members can be released on the perimeter drawing. Multiple iterations for locating the resources on the layout should be exercised. Because good ideas can be tried simply by moving a cutout around, great latitude for creative suggestions should be given. Moving resources on paper is an inexpensive way to try out all ideas without passing judgment or offending any individual on the team. Every team member's ideas should be heard and tried on the line design.

The Lean line design process can take several days, but when all ideas are exhausted and a final layout emerges, it will be one of team consensus and buy-in. Ownership of the final line design belongs to the team members and will not be perceived as just another "management" factory layout. Buy-in by the team members is important, as they will explain the logic of the Lean line design to their associates and fellow employees.

Steering Committee Action Items

1. **Review organizational training requirements:** In addition to reviewing implementation team training requirements, an assessment of training needs for all other employees who may be impacted by the start-up and operation of the new Lean line must be completed. This may also include Lean line operators who need to know how to manufacture a variety of different products. Operators will also need to be trained in the skills of flexing operations on the Lean line.

2. **Final approval of the paper line layout:** Members of the steering committee must approve and sign off on the final Lean line configuration. There can be no second-guessing after the line is installed. Requiring sign-off on the final line design assures a total company commitment to the Lean line design. If any modification is necessary, this is the ideal time to propose it.

3. **Final approval of kanban replenishment cost strategy:** The steering committee must agree as a team with the final inventory investment and turn rate strategy. Once the strategy is agreed upon, all that remains is the execution of the strategy by installing the two-bin material kanban system.

No second-guessing is allowed after the system is in place. The kanban system requires daily management and ongoing maintenance of the system.

4. **Review and update master plan:** Record team progress and document any modification.

Materials Team Action Items

5. **Finalize kanban system cost strategy for line start-up:** Sizing of container quantities based on replenishment times must be completed for all part numbers to be included in the two-bin material kanban system. The standard cost of the component parts should be applied to the calculated kanban quantities and summed in total to determine if the inventory investment and the turn rate goals can be met. Modification to the pull chains or the delivery frequency times must be made to adjust investment to be in line with stated goals. The final kanban replenishment strategy must be approved by the steering committee.

6. **Develop kanban system installation plan:** The kanban installation plan must identify the requirements for purchasing any new containers, racks, material presentation fixtures, labels, and other material-handling requirements. The plan for setting the system up must also be identified. This includes the labor resources needed to fill the containers with the calculated quantities, label the containers, and place the containers in their assigned locations. Identifying training for operators and material handlers in the operation of the kanban system is also required. Most companies underestimate the amount of time required to complete all this kanban setup work. Waiting until the Lean line starts up to begin this work will be too late!

7. **Establish RIP locations on the final line layout:** This requirement is usually difficult to complete until after the Lean line layout has been completed. It is necessary to establish a RIP footprint for the development of the facility plan and relocation of resources. Location of RIP material adjacent to the line consumption points is preferred, but is secondary to the ease of flow of products downstream on the Lean line.

8. **Establish sequencing points for the location of one-time-use parts:** Slow-moving, infrequently used, or one-time-use component parts not included in the two-bin material kanban system that require consumption into configured parent part numbers must have a designated location on the Lean line where the material is consumed. The location for this category of parts should be permanent so operators never have to look for one-time-use parts.

9. **Identify material-handler training requirements:** Operation of the two-bin material kanban system is not intuitive for material handlers used to

operating in an order-launched kit-picking planning system. They must be trained to know the consumption and replenishment cycle based on pre-established replenishment times. They must also know the replenishment routines and understand the replenishment signals as they are received from the Lean line operators.

Process Team Action Items

10. **Complete process map resource calculations:** The final resource calculations must be performed at milestone #4 to determine the resources required to meet the demand volume for Lean line capacity. All information parameters for line design calculations must be completed at this time.

11. **Create paper line layout following the mixed-product PFD:** Following the process flow diagrammed on the mixed-product PFD, physically lay out the calculated number of resources. The resources must be scaled to match the scale of the perimeter drawing. The scaled footprint can then be placed at a location where its output can be consumed into the next downstream workstation. The final layout must be approved and signed off on by the steering committee.

12. **Locate IPKs and sequencing points for custom-product configurations:** The IPK is the key to regulating the speed of the line. Operators properly trained to respond to IPK signals will assure the Lean line produces to Takt time and does not build excessive inventories to achieve balance. IPKs must be clearly visible upstream and downstream of operators so they know when to produce the next unit or flex into another workstation. The location for IPKs must be indicated on the layout. Special one-time-use parts sequenced to be installed into a configured product must have a designated space next to the workstation where they will be used. These sequencing points and physical locations must also be indicated on the Lean line layout.

13. **Identify operator training requirements:** There are two main areas in which operators must be trained when the new Lean line starts up. The first area is training for working on the Lean line. This includes responding to IPK signals, operating the two-bin material kanban, and understanding flexing assignments. The second area is individual training to produce the entire family of parts designated for manufacture on the Lean line. Prior to working on a Lean line, operators may have been trained only in the production of a few specialized products. Lean line operators are expected to produce all products manufactured on the Lean line.

14. **Develop facility plan for line start-up:** It is the process team's responsibility to develop a schedule for the rearrangement of manufacturing resources that may need physical relocation to the Lean line. In addition to

the physical equipment moves that may be required, all hydraulic, pneumatic, electrical, and plumbing fixtures must be identified. If outside contractors are necessary, they must be scheduled. Facility rearrangement is an excellent time to schedule the repair of infrastructure such as flooring, lighting, and painting. If new workstation benches, conveyors, material racks, or fixtures are desired, including these as part of the Lean line implementation is recommended. New fixtures, better lighting, and general facility improvements confirm the company's commitment to the Lean manufacturing methodologies. The steering committee must approve all facility rearrangement plans.

MILESTONE #5
Line Start-Up

Objective: Start line up. Test for balance to Takt time and flexing of operators. Validate workstation tasks and check for ergonomic layout. Confirm all IPKs are clear and visible to operators. Exercise the two-bin material kanban system. Assure all training has been completed. Develop work-in-process reduction "bleed-down" plan. Check to assure a continuous process improvement mechanism has been established.

Steering Committee Tasks

1. Assure operator training is completed prior to line start-up ☐
2. Master plan review and update ☐
3. Initiate and monitor new performance measurements ☐
4. Document follow-up items and assign responsibility for completion ☐
5. Final approval of lean line start-up operation ☐

Materials Team Tasks

6. Assure principles of 5S are in place ☐
7. Validate kanban materials presentation for ease of use ☐
8. Exercise two-bin material kanban system ☐

Process Team Tasks

9. Validate workstation layout for balance to Takt ☐
10. Confirm IPK placement at each workstation ☐

11. Assure principles of 5S are in place ☐
12. Exercise the Lean line at full and reduced volumes ☐
13. Test for operator flex knowledge ☐
14. Check for operator skills at three workstations ☐
15. Install and monitor employee qualification board ☐
16. Begin continuous process improvement activities ☐

Objective

After the physical line layout has been completed and the two-bin kanban system has been installed, it is time to start the line and test for balance and flow to the Takt time. The workstations must be designed to perform a Takt time amount of work, and the layout should be as ergonomically friendly as possible. The IPKs are in place, and operators are responding to the signals to regulate the rate of the line. Assure the two-bin material kanban system is ready to operate with filled containers located in their correct positions on the line and in the RIP.

Considerations for Lean Line Layouts

Workstation definition is accomplished by dividing the work content of each product in a process as documented in the SOE as equally as possible across the number of operations in that process. The number of operations is determined by dividing the work content of the process by the Takt time of the process. Achieving a perfect balance of work elements at each workstation in a process is unlikely. Often, the time to perform the work at an operation will be different for different products, even if the work is very similar. This is actually a benefit to the operation of the Lean line since a range of products with differing times produced throughout the day will help balance the line. Workstation balance should be observed and rebalanced if necessary.

The ideal arrangement is for all the operators to work on the same side of the Lean line. This offers operators the best chance to successfully flex up and down the line. Working from one side also allows materials to be resupplied from the opposite side of the line, eliminating the possibility of material handlers and operators interfering with one other. Chairs or stools also limit the ability of operators to flex as necessary.

Continue to monitor and make modifications to assure accessibility for flexing, and minimize the distance between operations where flexing occurs. Operations that require less than a full resource depend on resources from other workstations to flex into the workstation and perform the assigned work. When flexing from one workstation to the next, Lean line operators need to be able to move freely without obstruction. To facilitate the ease of performing this flexing, operations need to be placed as close as ergonomically possible to encourage operators to be as flexible as possible.

Line Start-Up Schedule of Events

Before the Lean line starts on the first day, the process and materials teams should check to be certain everything is in place to start the line. The line should be physically arranged to follow the mixed-product PFD. All material kanban containers on the line and in RIP are filled. Training has been provided to the Lean line operators to give them an overview of Lean manufacturing methodologies, emphasizing the manufacture of products in a one-piece flow, the use of IPK signals, and the requirement for flexing between adjacent workstations.

For the first day, at least two days of sequenced work should be released to provide a continuity of work for the line. If possible, the work sequence should be balanced with few or no "difficult" products during the first week. The line should be fully staffed in the beginning, even if it means the line is overstaffed for the daily rate. Overstaffing allows all operators the opportunity to participate in the initial line start-up. Allow some holes on the Lean line to let the operators practice their flexing skills. Feeder sequencing boards should be set up and ready for use.

Day One

Process and materials team members and the company training manager should be at each workstation when operators begin building product. At the first operation, the first Takt time amount of work starts to be produced. The team members should stand by to monitor and help operators understand the work to be completed at the operation. Instruction about the work being completed should be given as the initial product is built. The teams should continue monitoring and helping at each consecutive workstation by following the product as it moves down the Lean line.

The monitoring teams should note any problems the operators identify. If material problems occur, the kanban planner must be notified and the problem resolved immediately. Operators may want to rearrange the materials presented at the operations. This is acceptable as long as the operators on either side of the workstation and the material handler agree. Materials must still be presented within the kanban pull sequence and replenishment time requirements.

This monitoring process will be slow. The objective on the first day should be to monitor very carefully the start-up activity and resolve problems as they are discovered. This start-up process gives operators confidence and support from the implementation teams. This slow production of products will also serve to "wet" the line for subsequent days' production. To encourage feedback and initiate kaizen improvement suggestions from the operators during the start-up process, place flip charts within easy reach for operators to record any problems as they find them throughout each day. Take the time at the end of each shift to run through these issues with the operators each day during the first week. These meetings should last no longer than 20 minutes. Provide feedback on solutions as they are reached. Flip charts should stay on the Lean line during the first month.

Week One

Continue to monitor the line as products are produced with greater confidence each day. Continue to encourage flexing and make sure that not more than one product is ever placed in any individual IPK location. Watch carefully for any situation where imbalance seems to occur between operations. Study the work to identify the cause. If there appears to be a genuine imbalance caused by work content differences, apply the balancing techniques beginning with the elimination of nonvalue-added work followed by the relocation of work. If neither solution resolves the imbalance, additional IPKs can be added.

Check that the material kanban system is working well. It is normal to find that a small percentage of the parts replenish faster than expected, just as a small percentage of parts replenish too slowly. For fast-moving parts, increase the kanban size to slow the replenishment cycle down. For those parts with a slower than expected replenishment time, ask the material handlers to identify these items and decrease the kanban quantity. Keep in mind that replenishment time and inventory investment offset one another. Kanban = inventory = \$. Another factor to look for is the presentation of common materials. Work that consumes the same components in the same process should not be placed at different operations or locations.

First Three Months

After the first week of Lean production, progressively introduce more complicated products to the line. Initially, these may cause imbalances because of the higher work content at some workstations. Resist the urge to add additional IPKs as a solution when this occurs. If the work content has been balanced sufficiently, over time the line will settle down because of the mix of products on the line. The long-term solution is to experiment with better sequencing rules to accommodate the mix of parent part numbers introduced to the Lean line.

As the Lean line matures and operators become more proficient, consider ways to provide an incentive to them for maximum performance of the line. Incentives for linearity performance and operation certification are recommended. If incentives are developed and offered to the Lean line operators, create the policies, procedures, and controls that govern this activity.

Exercise Operation of the Two-Bin Material Kanban System

On the first day of operation of the newly installed Lean line, the two-bin kanban system should be in place and ready for operation. If the kanban system is not ready for operation or shortages noted during the filling of containers have not been corrected, the Lean line will experience parts shortages soon after the line starts. Parts shortages from an unfinished kanban system will immediately impact the success of the Lean line.

The kanban system will require ongoing maintenance as soon as the Lean line starts up and as long as it operates. Changes to part numbers and mix and volume of products will always require daily maintenance of the kanban system. Before the Lean line produces its first unit, the materials team should conduct the first audit of the kanban system to prepare for the Lean line start-up.

The sizing of the kanban containers for all the parts in the system should be completed with all containers filled with parts and labeled to display part number, description, refill quantity, points of consumption and replenishment, along with any other desired optional information such as bar coding, borders, or logos. The cubic volume of the containers selected should match the quantities calculated for each part. Confirm that two equally sized bins are used for each component on the Lean line and RIP locations. The preferred placement of containers is one behind the other. Sloped or roller gravity feed racks are best. If containers are placed side by side, be sure to indicate to the operator which container to pull from.

On day one, determine if the strategy is functioning, with replenishment taking place in the delivery frequency time frame planned and management backup available to handle unexpected situations. Frequent feedback on how the system is running should be directed to the kanban manager. For example, material handlers should advise the kanban manager if containers are turning too quickly or too slowly.

Training of material handlers and operators in the methodologies of kanban should be completed by line start-up but will culminate with hands-on experiences once the Lean line actually starts. Observe that all material handlers are trained and ready for line operation. Performing a pull chain audit is an important part of validating the kanban system. Test parts pull chains looking for any missing or incorrect pull sequences. Test to make sure the kanban signaling methodology is working and operators and material handlers know and correctly respond to the signal.

MILESTONE #6
Internalize

Objective: Review line performance and assess compliance to Lean methodologies. Identify variations and develop correction strategies. Review organizational responsibilities and modify policies and procedures to facilitate Lean operation. Assure all systems to operate the Lean line and kanban system are in place.

Manufacturing Management Tasks

1. Observe line for balance to Takt and operator flexing ☐
2. Validate new line performance measurements ☐
3. Document and compare lean line improvements to strategic business analysis baseline ☐
4. Review and finalize master plan ☐
5. Finalize operator training program ☐
6. Develop new employee orientation training program ☐
7. Validate daily resource planning and sequencing plans ☐
8. Validate employee qualification matrix ☐
9. Audit kanban system ☐
10. Validate adherence to 5S principles ☐
11. Validate continuous improvement program ☐
12. Demand planner identified and procedures documented ☐
13. Kanban manager identified and procedures documented ☐

Objective

Audit the Lean line performance to assess compliance with the Lean line methodologies and implement changes to improve the performance. Review functional organizations and make recommendations to support the Lean manufacturing initiatives. Assure that organizational changes reflect the requirements of the Lean line operations through the development of policies, procedures, and job descriptions.

Milestone #6 is more about managing change within the entire organization than the change that has occurred in manufacturing. The most important changes that occur in manufacturing will always be the result of observations made during daily management by walking around (MBWA) and continuous process improvement activities. While MBWA is the first best method for maintaining and improving the Lean line, it is still important to periodically audit the manufacturing activity. It is the responsibility of every manufacturing manager in the company to participate in this activity.

One of the worst things that can happen to a Lean manufacturing line is allowing it to slowly slip back into old habits and methods of producing products. Like nearsightedness, these old habits can slowly creep up on a manufacturer until the benefits of Lean manufacturing are no longer enjoyed. Introducing the methodologies throughout the entire organization is the best way to perpetuate the Lean methodologies in manufacturing.

After the Lean line has been operating successfully for one to two months and many of the issues causing imbalance to occur have been remedied and the kanban system is operating efficiently, energy should be redirected to incorporate the Lean methodologies throughout the organization so they become a way of life within the company. Every function in the company is ultimately impacted by the Lean manufacturing methods in manufacturing. If Lean methodologies are not introduced throughout the organization, they will be challenged whenever they conflict with departmental goals.

ORGANIZATIONAL IMPACTS OF LEAN MANUFACTURING

Inventory Control

All production inventories should be established in an RIP location and maintained as an aggregate quantity in the Lean line area. This inventory is nettable to all Lean line production requirements, making material allocations on shop orders unnecessary.

Accurate inventory records must still be maintained in the RIP area. All transactions must be reported into the production area from suppliers or from the stockroom. Backflush transactions are used to relieve inventory from the RIP production area. Bill-of-material accuracy must approach the 100% level to assure accurate inventory levels are maintained in the RIP location. Except for scrap or material review board, no other material transactions are required in the production Lean area.

Until suppliers can be certified for reliable and dependable deliveries, a stockroom must still be maintained, with quantity counts maintained by location. This requires transactions to be recorded when inventory is moved from one location to another. Inventory audit procedures must be formally defined and reported.

Production Planning

While the Lean line does not require the launching of production orders into the Lean manufacturing area, daily demand must still be established and transmitted to the Lean line. Production planning or scheduling must establish total demand by smoothing the combination of actual customer orders and forecasted demand. Sequencing is based on total demand as determined each day and communicated to production as a sequence of models to be produced at a daily rate. The sequenced demand is released to the Lean line each day and is visibly identified to the Lean line. Sequenced demand matching the main assembly points is required for feeder processes where unique work or one-time-use component parts are used. This may result in multiple sequencing points throughout the different processes of the Lean line. Daily reports or sequence cards are typically used at the designated sequencing points.

Parameters to define Lean line demand violations, such as exceeding material availability, past-due demand, and finished goods inventory policy, should be identified. Resolution procedures for the violations should be formally defined. Order backlog policies should be established for each product based on material availability, production response capabilities, and market position.

Production Control

Each Lean line operates as a manufacturing team. There are no more departments. Working as a team assures that success of the entire line depends on all operators being successful. Success of the line rises and falls as a team. The team structure, including team leaders and individual members, must be defined for all areas of Lean production.

It is production control's responsibility to champion continuous process improvement initiatives, making certain the improvement opportunities are recorded and followed up with employees on a regular basis as part of ongoing employee training programs. Operator improvement recommendations should be frequently reviewed and implemented with the assistance of the operator making the suggestion. Operators should interface with support organizations whenever seeking actions to realize recommended improvements. The time required for operators to leave the Lean line and implement improvements should be built into the Takt time calculation.

Engineering

New product introductions require a formal design review process that enforces proper product and part design definition. A checklist and sign-off document should be established to ensure that items are completed through each stage of the design introduction, from machined prototype through initial tooling samples and finally production runs. Checklists would include critical design attributes to be defined, such as assembly and fabrication process validation, dimensioning and tolerance requirements, product functionality, and final specification requirements.

New product design can be managed with a designated group of design engineers, while mature products can be managed with a different design engineering group. Rotation of design engineers from the new product group to the mature product group can occur as new products are brought into full production so that design expertise stays with the products in manufacturing. A focused effort to bring the Lean PFDs and SOEs into the design engineering documentation and development will contribute to improving manufacturability of new product design introductions.

Process change order routines need to be established to control all Lean documentation created during the implementation process. The corresponding SOEs, PFDs, and process maps also need to be updated if affected by process changes being made. Changes to any graphic work instructions are required when a process change order is generated. The controlling entity for the graphic work instruction is an ID number assigned to the work instruction. Component parts used at the operation and listed on the method sheets would also be referenced to this ID.

Financial Management

Current standard costing routines apply overhead cost to labor costs. This information often skews the true costs of products and drives performance measures toward the production of more inventory to absorb the overhead cost. While a longer term solution, Lean manufacturing would prefer to allocate overhead expenses to an appropriate resource activity based on the Lean process definitions. Activities that relate to product cost would use the SOE as the primary driver for all time-related resource–activity relationships.

Most manufacturing companies understand this activity-based costing concept, but the Generally Accepted Accounting Practices are not receptive to this shift in accounting methodology. The primary reason given is that changing accounting methodology erases past financial performance history, eliminating the ability to compare current-year results with past results.

While this shift in accounting methodology may or may not happen, and absorption costing may continue to be required for reporting to the outside financial community, the Lean methodologies suggest that performance measures other than absorption be used to measure the success of the Lean line. Direct labor performance reporting would not be a primary measurement. It is the smallest component of product cost. Operating income is also not a primary business performance measurement.

However, working capital as a percent of revenue should be a primary business performance measurement. Also, the inventory turn rate measured as a trend for each period should be a fundamental measurement of how well the Lean line is operating. Although measured quarterly, the average inventory turns measured monthly is the primary reported data. Measurements such as response time, actual inventory levels, and customer-quoted lead time are better indicators of the success of the Lean line and should be reported. Return on equity, economic value added, and revenue growth to average selling price are other primary measurements of overall business management performance.

Sales and Marketing

The classic relationship between manufacturing and sales and marketing in most companies has been at arm's length. In many cases, this relationship is adversarial. When the Lean line becomes operational and the response time has been reduced to the work content time, with the kanban capability to produce any model on any day, manufacturing has just become a competitive weapon in the sales and marketing arsenal, allowing the strategic capture of market share.

Sales can now satisfy customers whose primary supplier selection criterion is short manufacturing lead time. If the new lead time is shorter than that of your competitors and all other criteria are the same, there is no reason why a large part if not all of that business should not be yours. If the lead time is significantly shorter than the competitors', marketing may even choose to implement a multipricing strategy based on shorter delivery times versus the current quantity-based discounts.

Now is the time for sales and marketing and manufacturing to work together as partners that share a common goal — to increase their market share at the expense of their competitors.

9

MANAGING THE LEAN MANUFACTURING LINE

After all the hard work of designing and installing the Lean manufacturing line, getting the two-bin kanban system in place, and starting up operation, a manufacturer will begin to realize certain benefits immediately. One of the first benefits is shortened response time to the customer. With the new Lean line, response time to customers is faster because much, if not all, of the nonvalue-added work normally associated with the launch of batched quantities of shop orders and their subsequent routing through manufacturing has been eliminated.

For some manufacturers, this benefit alone is worth the time and effort to complete the implementation. A customer-quoted lead time promised faster than the competition's almost guarantees increased business from those customers that consider lead time to be the number one product differentiator among their suppliers. In addition, the Lean manufacturer also has confidence that its manufacturing facility can deliver on its faster lead time promises. This confidence coupled with the proven improvement in lead time response often leads to new sales and marketing strategies designed to take advantage of this important new differentiator.

Another benefit first-time Lean manufacturers enjoy is a reduction in work-in-process (WIP) inventories. The Lean manufacturing methodologies balance and link manufacturing processes together so that all work at the same rate to produce the next unit in sequence one piece at a time. Linking processes together and signaling the next unit of production with an in-process kanban (IPK) effectively balances the available capacities in the manufacturing processes only to the extent necessary to meet the Takt time target.

Linking processes and signaling production at the same rate regulates the output of any process with excess capacity. Prior to the implementation of the Lean manufacturing methodologies, the only way a department with excess capacity could meet its absorption or productivity goals was maximum utilization of its resources. This excess output always manifests itself in piles of WIP inventory. This is easy to confirm in the non-Lean facility by taking a walk through manufacturing and the WIP warehouse. While WIP is never zero on a Lean line, it is always limited to the total number of workstations.

Because of the rapid return on investment, it's no wonder manufacturers are excited to implement the Lean manufacturing methodologies. These first benefits become available to the Lean manufacturer almost immediately after start-up of the Lean line. Usually, the first Lean line implementation is completed in three to six months, but because a core group of seasoned team members are now available to the manufacturer, subsequent implementations can be completed at a much faster rate. Unfortunately, many manufacturers are so pleased with these first results that they become complacent about pursuing the optimization of their Lean manufacturing lines.

With ongoing dedication to continuous process improvement, the Lean line can continue to return significant benefits and competitive advantages to the Lean manufacturer.

MANAGING LINE OUTPUT TO MATCH CUSTOMER DEMAND

The goal of a Lean line is to produce only what is needed to meet customer demand. The Lean line is essentially a "pull" line, creating a signal upstream to replace units one at a time at the same rate they are being consumed by customers. On the Lean line, the signal generated by customer withdrawal of one unit continues upstream through each balanced workstation until it reaches the raw material supplier. So the key to how much a Lean line produces each day is dependent on how many units customers buy.

Many of the modern planning systems used today have a very difficult time regulating the output of their manufacturing processes to match the consumption rate of their customers. Traditional batch-based order-launched systems are not nimble or flexible enough to slow down or speed up fast enough to respond to customers' fickle ordering habits. Manufacturers overcome the lethargic response of their planning systems by placing planners on the shop floor to expedite and de-expedite released shop orders to match actual customer demand. When the day is done, the planning system relies on the feedback of the planner to assure that actual shop floor conditions are reported and recorded in the system.

Reliance on planners to guarantee the reflection of real-time activity in the planning system is not realistic. Over time, the disintegration of the critical database information in the planning system will cause its failure. However, the failure of the planning system should not lie at the feet of the planners. Planners are human and are subject to all human frailties. While planners can manage the major and most obvious variation to plan, there is no way they can keep up with all the ever-changing activities on the shop floor along with the changes in demand in the marketplace. So many sales and shop floor activities are intertwined and dependent on one another.

Customers are not aware of reactions on the shop floor to their changing demands. They don't care and they shouldn't care. They certainly don't care about the ordering patterns of other customers. They are focused on the price, delivery, and quality of your products to them. Planning system manufacturers devote a great deal of time and energy to reconciling their planning systems with actual customer demand and manufacturing output.

A common approach used by many planners is to develop level production schedules that either lower output to offset the lower demand from a previous period or increase output to replenish higher demand. There is nothing wrong with the concept of raising and lowering output to match the fluctuating demand of the customer, but it must be done on a daily basis to be most effective. Planning systems that operate with leveled schedules over longer periods of time just cannot respond that fast. Changing schedules daily would cause wild swings in start and due dates throughout the entire manufacturing facility, not to mention the impact on communication to suppliers. Imagine the life of a planner in that environment!

Along with schedules leveled over longer periods of time, and to help buffer the swings in customer demand, non-Lean manufacturers tend to keep larger levels of finished goods inventories. Finished goods inventories are the most expensive level of inventory to maintain. To predict what a customer might want in the way of finished product, a forecast of future customer demand must be made (Figure 9.1).

In addition to the reduced WIP inventory and faster customer-quoted lead times available to the Lean manufacturer, the Lean line also provides the powerful capability to change the output rate of the line every day to match customer demand that day! Because the Lean line has balanced and linked the manufacturing processes together, the only production scheduling necessary is the receipt of an IPK signal. There is no need to change due dates and quantities for a whole series of launched shop orders. There is no way large pools of WIP being pushed through manufacturing can accumulate without violating the IPK signal.

With the capability to match production output to actual customer demand, the need to maintain large amounts of finished goods inventory to buffer swings

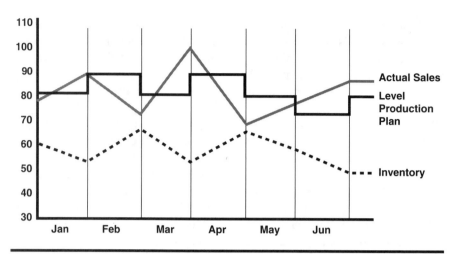

Figure 9.1 Leveling Schedule in Response to Changing Demand

in customer demand is reduced or possibly eliminated. This ability of the Lean line to build products closer to actual demand rather than tie up working capital in nonworking buffer inventory investments is a huge monetary benefit too often underappreciated by the Lean manufacturer. The product cycle time and manufacturing response time have been defined for each product (Figure 9.2).

Manufacturing response time is an important component for establishing finished goods inventory policy. Finished goods are usually required only if manufacturing response time is greater than customer-quoted lead time. Finished goods inventory may be also necessary if there are seasonal or sales patterns that exceed the designed line manufacturing capacity (V_c) or if there are quick-turn spares or other short-response order requirements. With few exceptions, a manufacturer that can take advantage of the Lean line feature of adjusting output with demand can realize significant finished goods inventory and working capital reduction.

ESTABLISHING CUSTOMER RESPONSE POLICY

If the output of the Lean line is to be managed every day, the planning team must evaluate the customer requirements on a daily basis. Customer requirements must first be validated against material availability. If the customer requirement is a parent item whose parts are used to populate the kanban system, all parts are available at the workstations on the Lean line and can be scheduled for production at the planner's discretion. If the parent part number is configured

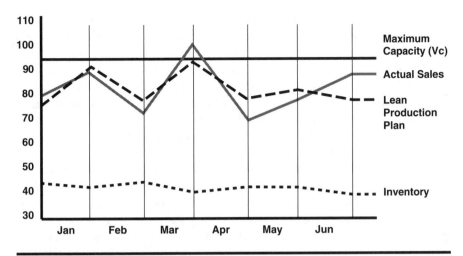

Figure 9.2   Matching Output to Changing Demand

and requires component parts other than the ones in the two-bin kanban system, the bill of material must be exploded to define component and subassembly requirements. These requirements are then tested against current material availability. If component materials are not available, or will not be available when needed to meet the original customer due date, that requirement should be resequenced to a date when the component materials will be available to manufacturing. The customer must also be advised of the new delivery date.

The desire to satisfy customer demand on the first requested date should be a matter of company order policy. The parts chosen for the two-bin kanban system will meet 80% of the first-request customer due dates; however, a company order policy must be established for responding to the remaining 20%. That is too much business to ignore, and there are other avenues a manufacturer can consider when establishing policy for this remaining business. The first is to increase the number of parts in the two-bin kanban system to meet an increased percentage of customer demand. This is an economic decision: how much additional inventory must be invested balanced against the additional sales revenue that demand represents. To justify the extra investment in inventory, the sales dollars or customer goodwill generated by this additional business must be greater than the cost to the manufacturer of holding the slow-moving inventory.

Another alternative is to establish a multitiered customer response policy. Without parts available to manufacture all possible product permutations in the sales catalogue, it is impossible to promise customers highly configured products delivered in the same time period as standard configuration products. Not only is this a recipe for chaos in the manufacturing facility, as planners turn the plant upside down scrambling to find the necessary parts, it is also unfair to customers to promise what cannot be delivered.

A better methodology is to publish a listing of standard configurations supported by the parts residing in the two-bin kanban system. The inventory represented by these configurations will meet 80% of first-request due dates of all customers. For customers that require configurations other than those on the published list, the quoted lead time must include the lead time to receive the purchased component parts in addition to the manufacturing lead time.

With a multitiered policy, customers will also have options. They can either accept the lead time policy or be motivated to switch their demand to a product listed in the standard configuration catalogue. Their other option is to take their business elsewhere. Of course, this is a scary proposition for the manufacturer and presents some business issues to consider. Is the potential revenue loss greater than the cost of satisfying the demand? Does the potentially lost business represent a target market? Is the market one the company is interested in attracting or maintaining? What is the cost of continuing to participate in that market and is the manufacturer willing to live with it?

Regardless of the ultimate decision, it must be the best financial decision for the company. The kanban system can assist in making that decision by evaluating the cost of carrying any additional inventory levels chosen to meet any company order policy developed. Once a policy is articulated, the Lean manufacturing methodologies can help to embed those policies into everyday practice.

SUBOPTIMIZING THE LEAN LINE TO MEET DAILY RATE OF DEMAND

At the factory design milestone, mixed-product Lean lines were established. The Lean line was designed to produce a future volume. The designed volume (V_c) is a statement of the capacity of the line. The Lean line is not expected to produce the planned capacity until some future point in time. The typical Lean line time frame is designed to meet a projected volume 12 to 24 or 36 months in the future. When the Lean line first begins operation, the volume of product to be produced is at today's current level and slowly grows over time until the designed volume is reached. By definition, then, the Lean line at start-up has excess capacity. If product were to be produced at the volume capacity available to the Lean line, where the output rate is greater than today's rate of sales, all of the resulting unsold units would simply become excess finished goods inventory.

If the resources of the Lean line have been designed into an integrated manufacturing line with static workstations and feeder processes linked together, and where component parts have been prepositioned to match a specified mix and volume, how can the output rate be adjusted to match actual customer demand?

A Lean line operates like a light switch. It is either on or off. One process cannot sit idle while another runs at capacity. The only way to alter the output of the Lean line is to intentionally suboptimize its resources. Since redesigning and rearranging the resources of the Lean line or changing the Takt time each day is cost prohibitive, the only other alternative available to a manufacturer is to modify the staffing of the line. Reducing the number of people on the line will reduce the output of the line. Therefore, the number of people required for each process must be calculated each day to match the mix and volume of actual customer demand. As staffing requirements are calculated for each process, the results are then summed for all processes across the entire facility and only then rounded to the next person.

After materials are validated, demand requirements are sequenced into a "daily resource plan." Using the daily customer product and demand volumes and the labor and machine times from the sequence of events (SOE), the daily resource plan calculates the impact of the daily mix and volume compared to the available resources designed for the Lean line. SOE times and volumes are multiplied and their products summed to determine the number of labor and machine resources needed to meet daily demand. When resources required to meet daily customer demand are compared to available resources, a percent of utilization can be defined:

$$\text{Staffing by Process} = \frac{\Sigma \ (\text{Daily Rate} \times \text{SOE Labor Time})}{\text{Available Minutes per Shift}}$$

If utilization exceeds 100% of the designed line capacity: (1) change the mix and volumes of products and recalculate requirements, (2) determine if manufacturing can increase available minutes over the short term (e.g., cover breaks and lunch), or (3) plan for overtime to achieve the required output. This daily resource-planning activity should be completed at least one day in advance of the manufacturing lead time horizon prior to presenting the plan to manufacturing. Because the planning horizon is continuingly rolling toward today, all planning must be completed at least one day beyond the Lean line manufacturing lead time. No changes are allowed within the Lean line manufacturing lead time. Also, if any special sequencing rules were developed for the Lean manufacturing line, the daily resource plan must be tested against those specifications.

The Lean line can continue to be operated up to its designed capacity. It may take 12 to 24 or 36 months to reach this volume. Demand in excess of the designed capacity may require the line to be operated extra hours or shifts for short durations. If daily demand begins to exceed the designed capacity on a routine basis, redesign and rebalance of the line may be called for. The line should never run at 50% or less than its designed capacity, as doing so may adversely impact quality.

Suboptimizing the Lean line to match actual daily sales can have a significant impact on the amount of finished goods inventory, but doing so can also have a negative impact on traditional productivity or absorption measurements. For the majority of manufacturers, the cost of labor in products is less than the cost of materials. Yet manufacturers continue to use the absorption of overhead into labor as a primary measure of manufacturing performance. Before taking advantage of the benefits of decreased material costs by the intentional suboptimization of the Lean line, a strategy for changing the performance measurement paradigms must be developed.

FLEXIBLE OPERATORS

Intentional suboptimization of the Lean line means that some manufacturing operators may not be assigned to work at their workstations based on the variation of actual customer demand for that day. Unless operators can be "hired or fired" on a daily basis, operators not assigned to work on the Lean line must have other work assignments made available to them within manufacturing for those days they are not needed on the Lean line. Most manufacturing facilities find it easy to identify work options other than working on the Lean line.

There are usually plenty of things to do in a manufacturing facility other than building unnecessary inventory. Temporary assignments include working on continuous improvement projects, training activities, inventory control and cycle counting, kanban material replenishment and sequencing, and other general maintenance and housekeeping chores. The reassignment of manufacturing operators to perform work other than the production of inventory may require rethinking what constitutes "productive" work versus "nonproductive" work and how each type is applied to the absorption measurement.

In order to produce completed units off the Lean line that has been suboptimized to match the daily rate of demand, the remaining operators assigned to the line that day must be able to perform the work at the workstations vacated by operators not assigned to the Lean line. In order to produce other work in addition to the SOE assigned work tasks at their primary workstations, operators must also be able to perform the SOE work tasks on either side of their primary workstations. Therefore, the capability to perform work at a primary workstation and at one workstation upstream and downstream of the primary workstation is requisite for being an operator on a Lean line. This ability of an

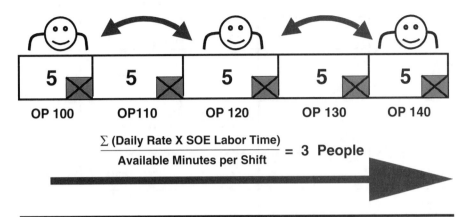

Figure 9.3 Operator Flexing to Match Customer Demand

operator to move upstream and downstream in response to an IPK signal is called *flexing* (Figure 9.3).

The Lean line requires its operators to be as flexible as possible, willing to relocate to wherever they are needed to complete work that day. Working on the Lean line is still a day's pay for a day's work. Most operators are comfortable with the idea of doing work other than that done on the Lean line and welcome the opportunity to do various other types of work. Some may even find other types of work more interesting or more rewarding and seek to be assigned to that work or workstation.

Prior to being assigned to work on the Lean line, all operators are required to be "certified" to perform the work at their three-workstation group. Being certified does limit the operator to just those three workstations. Operators may become certified in as many workstations as they can if they are able to meet the certification requirements of the workstation. The Lean manufacturing methodologies define certification at a workstation as an operator demonstrating that he or she can complete the work at a workstation within the Takt time, while meeting the quality criteria identified for that workstation.

While a simple definition of certification, the criterion is fairly exclusive of certain types of work. For example, a downstream workstation may be a skilled job that requires outside certification, like welding. Becoming certified internally may require attending a class to become certified as a welder. This is true for many skilled positions. In addition, there must be a recertification requirement so operators do not spend their time becoming certified and never perform work at their workstations. Recertification at every workstation is suggested every two weeks.

To keep track of the status of each operator's certification, the installation

Team Member	Op 100	Op 110	Op 120	Op 130	Op 140	Op 150
Mary				C	C	M
Harold	M	C	C			
Suzanne	C	C	C	M		
Tony	M	M	C	C	C	C
Paul Team Leader		C	C	C	M	T
Helen				T	C	C
Barbara	C	C	T			
Stretch			C	C	C	C
Murphy, Jr.	T					

Figure 9.4   The Operator Certification Board

of an operator certification board is recommended. By posting it adjacent to the Lean line in manufacturing, operators can maintain the status of their individual certification. An operator can be in training (T), fully certified (C), or a master (M) at a workstation. A master rating means the operator can observe other operators and certify that they have met the requirements for certification. Posting the operator certification board in manufacturing allows the team leader to easily see and track the certifications for each operator. Should reassignment be necessary to compensate for absenteeism, the team leader can readily see which operators are qualified to replace absentee operators.

REWARDING FOR FLEXIBILITY

While the ability to perform work at a minimum of three workstations is a basic requirement for working on a Lean line, operators are encouraged to learn more than their three required workstations. Flexible operators who are certified at multiple workstations are more valuable to the company as they can be assigned wherever needed on any given day. The Lean manufacturing environment should be structured to promote flexibility to include multiple certifications at multiple operations throughout the Lean facility. Some operators may be comfortable being certified and doing only the work at their minimum three-workstation assignments. These operators may need additional motivation to become more flexible in order to perform other assigned work. The more flexible the operators, the more flexible the Lean line becomes.

Because flexibility is a strength more valuable to a company than specialization, Lean manufacturing suggests rewarding operators for it. A common practice of Lean manufacturers to promote flexibility is to create an incentive program that rewards operators for becoming certified in more than three workstations. Any program designed should provide the incentive for all operators to seek certification at additional operations. These incentives can be pay based by assigning point values to workstations based on the skill level required to do the work. Thresholds of pay levels can then be established when the predetermined point levels have been achieved. Operators still intent on being certified in only three workstations, even at a master level, will not accumulate enough points to cross the threshold of a higher pay level. Although less than ideal, it will be the operators' call to disqualify themselves for a pay raise in return for the comfort of working at their three-workstation minimum.

Before the Lean line begins operation, two types of training are necessary. The first is training to be flexible and move up and down the Lean line in response to an IPK signal. While simple in concept, most operators new to Lean discover that flexing is not intuitive and does not happen naturally. All operators assigned to the Lean line for the first time must be trained how to flex and be able to operate their primary and one upstream and one downstream workstations before line start-up can be accomplished. After start-up, ongoing coaching is required to instill and reinforce the required discipline.

To assure that new employees are ready to work on the Lean line as they are hired, the Lean manufacturing methodologies recommend an academy be established to train new employees prior to working on the line. It is common to incorporate this training into any new employee orientation program a company currently has. Each new employee should graduate from the Lean academy before being assigned to the Lean line. The SOE can be used to support the training.

The second type of training that may be required is the ability to produce different models of products based on the mixed-product configuration used to design the Lean line. Previous to the installation of the Lean line, operators may have produced only specific products or products with a single-station build concept. Operators must be capable of producing any product that arrives in their workstation on any day. When not assigned to the line, operators can be paired with master operators to learn to build new models.

For the Lean line to achieve basic flexibility, it is critical that operators have the ability to flex from their primary and one upstream and one downstream operations. The three-operation flex pattern is a minimum fundamental basic to facilitate the flow of products down the Lean line. Maximum effort must be made during the design of the Lean line to locate processes and operators as close together as ergonomically possible. This will facilitate the movement required for operators to flex up and down the line in response to the IPKs. The placement of workstations close to one another not only encourages operator flexing but also results in a smaller shop floor footprint. Producing more products in a smaller space increases the utilization of the existing square footage of the manufacturing facility.

REWARDING FOR LINEAR PERFORMANCE

It is not a stated goal or the explicit purpose of the Lean line implementation to develop operational teams. However, teams are a result of that effort. Flexible operators assigned to the Lean line ultimately work as a team to achieve the best results from the Lean line. The daily success of the entire line relies on the capability of individual operators to flex within a three-operation work pattern. The success of the Lean line also depends on every individual operator's ability to produce any product presented to him or her in the three-workstation pattern. If one operator along the line fails to achieve Takt time or produces a defective unit because he or she has not been trained, the entire line suffers by failing to produce the daily rate of customer demand.

Working together as a team on a Lean line has hidden benefits that are difficult to quantify but are extremely beneficial nonetheless. Just as the "weakest link" theory, because success of the Lean line is dependent on the success of all operators working together, each individual is responsible for the success of the team. Teams that must work together for the success of all generally become self-managing teams. As a self-managing team, individual team members assume responsibility to ensure the total team's success. This is usually done with little outside management support.

Working together, self-managed teams can usually resolve most manufacturing problems with the resources available to them every day with little help from supervisors or managers. Independently, teams can use the balancing or continuous process improvement techniques to resolve balance and quality issues on the line. Disciplinary problems with individual team members can also be resolved within the team framework without intervention from human resources or manufacturing management. Team resolution of discipline and manufacturing problems fosters a sense of ownership and encourages a friendlier work environment. A friendlier workplace can soften adversarial employee/management relationships.

To encourage the evolution and formation of self-managed teams, Lean manufacturing recommends implementation of a proactive incentive program that promotes team cooperation. The team incentive initiative program requires the implementation of a new performance measurement in addition to on-time delivery, response time, working capital as a percent of revenue, inventory turn rate, actual inventory levels, and customer-quoted lead time. The linearity of manufacturing output is the recommended performance measurement.

A daily linearity performance measurement reflects every action taken on a daily basis on the Lean line and measures its impact on a day-to-day basis over a specified period of time (e.g., monthly). Every action on the Lean line has a direct and measurable impact on the overall measurement, and team members must understand the cause-and-effect relationship of their actions on the measurement.

Linearity is a volume measurement. It compares the number of units expected to be produced with the number actually produced. If the actual output of the Lean line deviates from the plan on any given day, whether greater or less than plan, the deviation is recorded at the absolute value (ignore plus or minus). Deviations are monitored and posted daily, weekly, and for the month. Reasons for any deviations, whether greater or less than the planned daily rate, are also recorded. The goal is to produce product at a linear rate, achieving the planned daily rate each day.

If the actual output rate consistently exceeds the daily rate, it may be a sign of an unbalanced Lean line. Among other reasons, line imbalance may be caused by improper workstation definition, inaccurate SOE times, or overstaffing of the line based on the required mix and volume for that day or an atypically favorable mix of low-work-content products.

Lower output against the daily rate can indicate quality issues, improper alignment of parts, understaffing of the line based on mix and volume, an inordinate amount of high-work-content products, and untrained operators. Causes of over or under daily performance must be tracked and quantified for resolution using the kaizen or continuous improvement processes.

Linearity is calculated by subtracting the actual output from the planned output. The difference is absolute (neither positive nor negative):

Actual = 44	Plan = 40	Difference = 4
Actual = 44	Plan = 48	Difference = 4

For the measuring period, sum both the absolute deviations and the planned daily rate quantities. Subtract the sum of the absolute deviations from one and divide the difference by the sum of the planned quantities. Multiply the results by 100 to define the percent of linearity.

Day	Daily Rate Sequenced	Actual Units	Absolute Deviation	Σ Absolute Deviations	Daily Linearity %	MTD Linearity

Figure 9.5 Monthly Linearity Report

$$\text{Linearity} = \left[\frac{1 - (\Sigma \text{ Absolute Deviation})}{(\Sigma \text{ Planned Daily Rate})} \right] \times 100$$

Linearity is recorded each day and totaled for a predetermined period of time. A month is a common period of time for performance measurement. A week is usually too short, as it may not be possible to resolve the cause of deviations in the span of a week without unfairly skewing the performance of the line. A quarter is too long, as the source of deviations may be obscured by the greater number of daily entries recorded (Figure 9.5).

The linearity incentive plan establishes self-managed team bonus levels, paid monthly, based on attaining predetermined levels of linearity. The minimum required goal for linearity during a period is 80%. As the minimum, no team bonus would be paid for an 80% linearity performance level. As the linearity performance increases, the self-managed team receives a team bonus to be shared among all members. A shared bonus incentive based on Lean line performance assures all team members work together to accomplish the Lean line goals.

RESISTANCE TO CHANGE

The Lean manufacturing methodologies are not difficult to understand. Frequently, manufacturers comment on their simplicity and innate common sense.

Other manufacturers claim, "We used to do it this way." The methodologies have been around for 100 years and have gained and lost popularity during that time. There is a popular resurgence now as more and more manufacturers look for ways to become more flexible in order to satisfy their customers' increasing demand for more product variety, lower prices, and faster deliveries with faster response and smaller working capital investment.

To recent generations of manufacturing professionals who used modern MRP systems throughout their careers, the Lean methodologies may seem almost mystical. In the beginning, it can be very difficult to reconcile the complex MRP batch-based, order-launched planning system with the simplicity of the resources and parts only Lean manufacturer. The two methodologies simply approach manufacturing from two different standpoints.

While there is no empirical information to substantiate the reasons for the curiosity of planning system practitioners about the Lean methodologies, it may be that they have perfected the operation of their MRP systems as much as they can but still remain unsatisfied with the benefits received. By looking at the Lean methodologies, manufacturers may be "kicking the tires" in case there is something they can squeeze from Lean methodologies that will take them to the next level in seeking perfection of their operating systems.

For those manufacturers who have decided that they like what they see in the Lean manufacturing methodologies and are ready to begin implementation, there are caveats to consider. There will be resistance to change with the Lean methodologies! As the Lean champion in your company, you must be prepared to deal with the resistance.

Resistance will not be obvious at first. The Pareto model (80/20 rule), used liberally throughout the Lean methodologies, can be applied to the levels of resistance encountered: 50% of the people affected will go along with the changes and be good soldiers and good employees, while another 30% will be skeptical and challenge you and the methodologies. This 30% represents employees who have the best interest of the company in mind and are truly concerned whether the changes will be beneficial to their future and the future of the company. They can be quite vocal with their opinions. Do not discount them because, in the long run, they can become your best allies for Lean. As the Lean champion, you need to spend the time necessary to make this group your ally.

Between the good soldiers and the skeptical, 80% of the employees will ultimately support you. How the final 20% is managed will be the barometer of success for your transformation to Lean. Unlike the skeptical group, these employees will quietly make it unknown to you whether they are in the good soldier group or the skeptical group. They may even publicly support the Lean initiatives while subverting them in private. This group is the most difficult to recognize and to convert to Lean. In most cases, they are not bad people and will not actively sabotage efforts in order to cause failure. They simply have no motivation or incentive to make any change occur, Lean or otherwise. During implementation, they often work passively behind the scenes to avoid making any change. The Lean champion must be aware and be prepared to deal with this passive-aggressive group at all times.

Implementation of the Lean methodologies leaves much room for compromise. This is a blessing and a curse for the Lean champion. During implementation, the methodologies present a series of trade-offs. There will always be some people who find reasons why elements of the Lean methodology cannot be implemented. It is up to the steering committee, the Lean/steering committee coordinator, and the implementation teams to avoid compromises to the Lean methodologies. Compromise reduces the benefits of Lean manufacturing.

To sufficiently battle resistance to change from all levels in the organization, implementation of the Lean manufacturing methodologies must be sponsored by higher levels of management in the company. Grass-roots sponsorship is frustrating and cannot be expected to persuade higher management levels if they do not want to participate in the change.

While managing people issues and the resistance to change consumes a significant amount of the Lean champion's time, there are institutional issues that must also be managed. In some cases, these issues can be the most difficult. If your company is just one manufacturing facility and the boardroom is located in the corner of the building, managing these issues might be simpler from the standpoint that all key decision makers are located in one place where frequent interface can take place. If your Lean facility is one division of a large conglomerate, tackling institutional issues can be a more daunting challenge. Regardless of your situation, strategies to overcome these institutional issues must be developed to ensure the success of your Lean manufacturing implementation.

An example of a corporate institutional issue that must always be addressed is productivity performance measurement. This measurement is stated as either efficiency and utilization or absorption. Lean performance measurement is more interested in on-time delivery and inventory turns, whereas order-based systems are focused on utilization of resources. These goals are conflicting objectives. Often, their reconciliation must be elevated beyond the plant level to assure the Lean methodologies are a success. Resolution of the absorption/inventory debate is a key action item for the Lean champion.

INDEX